Praise for Gwen Cooper's Books

Homer's Odyssey

"Touching...one not to miss."
—USA Today

"This memoir about adopting a special-needs kitten teaches that sometimes in life, you have to take a blind leap."
—People

"Cooper is a genial writer with a gift for conveying the inner essence of an animal."
—The Christian Science Monitor

"Delightful...This lovely human-feline memoir, following in the footsteps of Vicki Myron's bestselling *Dewey: The Small-Town Library Cat Who Touched the World*, is sure to warm the hearts of all pet lovers."
—Library Journal

"A poignant story, well written with...tenderness and realism...Your life will be richer for having taken this journey with [Gwen and Homer]."

—*I Love Cats* **magazine**

My Life in a Cat House

"This book perfectly encapsulates the unique and amazing experience of being owned by cats and the joy they bring into our lives. That alone is reason enough to read it."
—**James Bowen, international bestselling author of** *A Street Cat Named Bob*

Cooper's witty, breezy writing, her unabashed love of felines, and her admission that her spoiled cats have trained her will delight and resonate with cat people."
—*Library Journal*

"Fans of *Homer's Odyssey* will rejoice upon hearing that Homer's owner, Cooper, has returned with more true cat stories...both hilarious and deeply moving. Readers...will delight in these anecdotes of cats who seemingly have something to say about everything. Fans of Vicky Myron and Brett Witter's *Dewey* and James Bowen's *A Street Cat Named Bob* will be highly satisfied."
—*Booklist*

"If you've ever lived with a cat, then this book is for you... In *My Life in a Cat House,* Cooper lovingly and humorously depicts the ups and downs of a life with cats and the ways in

which they mimic human behavior and feelings. A fun read for all animal lovers."
—*New York Journal of Books*

"A literary fur fix for Homer fans!"
—*Catster* **magazine**

"As Gwen shares the joys, sorrows, laughter and tears of sharing her life with her cats, both past and present, you will find yourself nodding in recognition and perhaps remember the antics of a cat long gone. You may even gain a deeper understanding of your own feline companions."
—**The Conscious Cat**

"Gwen has the uncanny ability to touch our hearts with her gift of conveying thought-provoking and heart-stirring emotions...Gwen's writing is unpretentious, it's authentic, it's REAL. Whether like me you have nearly all of Gwen's books, or if this one is your first, you will delight in her descriptive, often hilarious and loving stories about her cats."
—**Cat Chat with Caren and Cody**

"There's something about Gwen Cooper's cat books that touch my heart like few others, and *My Life in a Cat House* is no exception. Whether you've enjoyed every one of Gwen's cat books or this is your first, snuggle up with a cat or two while you're reading. I guarantee with each turn of the page you'll pull them just a little bit closer as you realize just how empty your life would be without their unconditional love."
—**Melissa's Mochas, Mysteries and Meows**

"Gwen Cooper is the Queen of Cat Love—and in these fun and frisky stories, she perfectly captures all the reasons felines rule our hearts and our homes. No cat lover should be without this book, but more important, give it to the folks who haven't yet seen the light. At least they'll understand us better!"
—**Sy Montgomery, bestselling author of** *How to Be a Good Creature: A Memoir in Thirteen Animals*

"What a pleasure to read [Gwen Cooper's] beautiful stories, brimming with her cat-love and even more important her ability to get you to actually see her cats . . . You will want to see more and more. She can become your next obsession, as she has become mine!"
—**Jeffrey Moussaieff Masson, international bestselling author of** *The Nine Emotional Lives of Cats*

Love Saves the Day

"Prudence is a sassy but sensitive feline heroine."
—**Time**

"Once again Gwen Cooper shines her light on the territory that defines the human/animal bond. That, in itself, is a reason to stand up and cheer."
—**Jackson Galaxy, star of** *My Cat From Hell*

The HOMER Collection!
GWEN COOPER

HOMER'S ODYSSEY: A Fearless Feline Tale, or How I Learned About Love and Life with a Blind Wonder Cat
and
HOMER: The Ninth Life of a Blind Wonder Cat

Copyright © 2009 by Gwen Cooper

All rights reserved.

No portion of this book may be reproduced in any form without written permission from the publisher or author, except as permitted by U.S. copyright law.

Originally published in hardcover in the United States by Delacorte Press, an imprint of The Random House Publishing Group, a division of Penguin Random House, Inc., in 2009.

Originally published in paperback in the United States by Bantam Books, an imprint of The Random House Publishing Group, a division of Penguin Random House, Inc., in 2010.

Cooper, Gwen.
Homer's odyssey: a fearless feline tale, or how I learned about love and life with a blind wonder cat/Gwen Cooper.
ISBN: 979-8-9895401-2-9
Nonfiction; memoir; pets

Photos copyright Gwen Cooper

Also by Gwen Cooper

Homer: The Ninth Life of a Blind Wonder Cat

Homer and the Holiday Miracle

Spray Anything: More True Tales of Homer & the Gang

My Life in a Cat House: True Tales of Love, Laughter, and Living with Five Felines

The 10th Anniversary Homer's Odyssey *Scrapbook*

PAWSOME! Head Bonks, Raspy Tongues & 101 Reasons Why Cats Make Us So, So Happy

YOU are PAWSOME! 75 Reasons Why Your Cats Love You, and Why Loving Them Back Makes You a Better Human

Homer's Odyssey

GWEN COOPER

A Fearless Feline Tale,
or
How I Learned About Love and
Life with a Blind Wonder Cat

For Laurence, always

Contents

FOREWORD		11
Prologue: The Cat Who Lived		15
1.	Socket to Me	25
2.	What Do You See in an Eyeless Cat?	37
3.	The First Day of the Rest of His Life	44
4.	The Itty Bitty Kitty Committee	57
5.	The New Kid	69
6.	Don't Be Happy. Worry.	81
7.	Gwen Doesn't Live Here Anymore	91
8.	The Ballad of El Mocho	98
9.	"Dogs and Cats, Living Together…"	106
10.	Running on Faith	119
11.	A One-Bedroom of One's Own	128
12.	Pet Sounds	134
13.	Lord of the Flies	144

14.	Mucho Gato	150
15.	My Homer/My Self	158
16.	Cats and the Single Girl	164
17.	"The Pussy Galore Tour"	177
18.	Cool for Cats	194
19.	A Hole in the Sky	203
20.	September 12, 2001	220
21.	None So Blind	243
22.	A Canticle for Vashowitz	264
23.	Intimations of Immortality	286
24.	Reader, I Married Him	301

FOREWORD
DR. PATRICIA KHULY, VMD

When I first saw the kitten, he was a minuscule bit of black fuzz cupped in a young woman's outstretched hands. No different from any other kitten, it would seem—that is, until he raised his head and emitted an impressive yowl for a creature only four inches in length, tip-to-tail.

Tiny though he was, he turned to the sound of my voice. That's when I saw his eyes. This two-week-old foundling was clearly suffering from a severe infection that would surely take his sight, if not his life.

The well-meaning couple who'd found him practically begged me to euthanize him immediately. Despite their entreaties, I performed a careful physical examination as the kitten struggled, legs flailing, and mewled vigorously on the stainless-steel exam table. Finally, I announced that the kitten seemed perfectly healthy—if you discounted his ocular condition. Would they consider adopting him if I was able to treat his infection?

For a long list of reasons, the couple could not provide a home for such a young kitten. They worked. They had a dog. They didn't have the money. And what were the chances that he would ever be able to see again, anyway?

Oh...none. No chance. I explained that I intended to surgically remove his eyes to save his life.

I'm pretty sure that's when I lost them. Shaking their heads in disbelief, they elected to sign him over to my care. His pitiable cries probably pushed their decision along the path of rejection—they were convinced he was suffering terrible pain.

After his rescuers agreed to give him up, he was mine to treat as seemed in his best interests. I still had my doubts, but they were laid to rest once the source of his immediate discomfort was revealed: hunger. A small bowl of cat food mashed with milk replacer stifled his cries. He was peacefully asleep within minutes, sealing my decision to treat his eyes, never mind the blindness to come.

After all, I thought, this kitten had never had the benefit of sight. Unlike human babies, cats are born with their eyes sealed to the world for ten to thirteen days. This two-weeker's relatively long-standing infection had almost certainly prevented any emerging vision. Once treated, he'd be blind without ever missing the sensory capacity for sight. Like many animals, kittens are capable of rerouting their neurologic faculties for successful survival through a process called individual environmental adaptation—my fancy term for "I refuse to put him to sleep." How could I renege on my duty to alleviate suffering if I could maintain a life worth living?

Ask any young, idealistic vets, and they'll likely confess to the same kind of sin I committed the day this blind kitten came my way. If the animal is afflicted yet healable—and even remotely adoptable—*It's meant to be*, we reason. They're the ones who always strum our heartstrings with their astonishing survival skills and irresistible ugly-duckling potential.

I knew there was no way I could keep a blind kitten in my toddler-, allergy-, and big-dog-inhabited household. Yet I certainly couldn't let a vigorous kitten die over a pesky little issue like homelessness. *Someone in my circle of friends and family will doubtless find him as appealing as I do*, I rationalized. He'd find a home if I could just find someone with the requisite mix of eccentricity and empathy to take on a "special-needs" case.

What followed was a couple of weeks of rejection after rejection. I enlisted my family, an animal-loving clan who dutifully spread the word of the blind kitten in need of a safe home. I placed ads and sought out vet school friends with a penchant for the pitiful. None of it yielded any potential takers.

By this time I'd dispensed with all my rationalizing and self-flagellation. The kitten had bounded back to life after surgery—so much so that my staff and I were irretrievably in love with him. There were days when I really couldn't bear the thought of parting with him.

How could I help but be smitten with his scraggly little blackness, his tiny sunken sockets, his insatiable appetite for feedings, pettings, cuddlings, and play sessions? Yes, he even romped like a normal kitten, despite his eyelessness. In short, he was eminently lovable...at least, by all standards except the one with which most humans preoccupied themselves: his appearance.

Finally, one young woman with two cats of her own who were treated at my practice promised to have a look. But when I finally handed my dark furball over to this prospective owner, I felt a twinge of trepidation. Would she look at him with disgust the way others had? Demur due to an inability to take on such a strange and disabled thing?

Instead, she whispered gently to him. She picked him up and held him. The kitten purred in her arms. To my surprise and utter relief, she earned my eternal gratitude when she said, "I'm taking him home."

Homer was the first "hopeless" case I'd taken on in my then-short career. Though I've had many more since, his was the seminal experience, one that ultimately paved the way for so many others.

Homer's "odyssey" will doubtless mean different things to different people. But for me, Homer will always be an intensely personal reminder of what veterinary medicine can pull of when it's infused with the idealism of youth. He'll always remind me that there's nothing a partnership between a veterinarian, a loving owner, and one fighting patient can't achieve.

Homer's story is one for all of us to live by.

PROLOGUE • The Cat Who Lived

Sing to me, O Muse, of that ingenious hero who traveled far and wide...

- HOMER, *The Odyssey*

THE ROUTINE WHEN I get home at the end of the day is always the same.

The *ding!* of the elevator is the first cue to sensitive ears that my appearance is imminent, and by the time my key hits the lock I hear the soft press of paws on the other side of the door. I've found that I tend to open all doors—even those in other people's homes—with enough caution to prevent any furry miscreants from tumbling outside. Rather than seeking the floor, however, it's only a matter of seconds before those paws have found their way from the door to the front of my legs and a tiny black cat makes his best effort to shimmy his way up my body as if I were a tree trunk.

To prevent injury to either my clothes or the skin beneath—his claws are small, but highly effective—I squat down with a cheerful, "Hi, Homer-Bear!" (A nickname given when he was a kitten on account of his glossy ebony fur, like a black bear's coat.) Homer takes this as his cue to jump onto my knees, placing his front paws on my shoulders and rubbing his nose against mine with much loud purring and a series of short, clipped *mews* that sound uncannily like the yips of a puppy. "Hey, little guy," I say, scratching him behind his ears. This sends Homer into veritable convulsions of delight, and—no longer content with mere nose-to-nose contact—he presses his entire face to my forehead, sliding it down to my cheek and back up again.

Squatting in the high heels I typically wear (I'm only five foot one, but I refuse to live life as a short person) is even more painful than it sounds, so I pick Homer up and deposit him back on the ground, rising to my feet and finally entering the apartment I share with my husband, Laurence. Keys, coat, and bags are quickly stowed away. When you live with three cats, you learn that the best way to prevent fur accumulation on the clothes you wear publicly is to change into knock-around-the-house garb immediately upon arrival. So from there I head to the bedroom and make a quick change.

A fuzzy shadow trails my steps through the apartment, leaping to the tops of any and all furniture along the way. Homer jumps effortlessly from floor to chair, from chair to dining room table, then back to the floor again, like Q*bert on speed. As I make my way from the living/dining area to the hallway, Homer's up on top of a side table, then hurls himself recklessly to the third shelf of the bookcase diagonally across the hall, perching for a precarious moment until I've passed. Then he's down on the ground once more, zipping along ahead of me and occasionally, in his enthusiasm, running smack into one of my other two cats until he reaches the doorway to the bedroom. Stopping at precisely the same point each time, he pauses for an infinitesimal moment, then cuts a hard left through the bedroom door, as if he were drawing a large capital *L*. He jumps to the top of the bed, where he knows I'll sit to remove my shoes, and crawls into my lap for another round of purring and face rubbing.

This routine is the same from day to day. What changes is the closer survey of the apartment I take once I've changed clothes. Homer is a creature of many and varied hobbies, and it's hard to know from one week to the next what new projects he's decided to immerse himself in.

For a while, his goal seemed to be setting the world record for number of items pushed from the top of a coffee table in a single day. Laurence and I are both writers, so we have the usual writers' effluvia—pens, pads, and scraps of paper with notes we've taken—scattered among the magazines, paperbacks, tissue boxes, ticket stubs, sunglasses, matchbooks, breath mints, remote controls, and takeout menus. One day we came home to find our coffee table swept entirely clean—books, pens, remote controls, and all, spattered across the floor like a Jackson Pollock canvas. We restored the items to their rightful place (not without a certain amount of shamefaced tidying up), but this pattern continued for several weeks. We weren't sure which of the cats was our phantom housekeeper until the night I came home and caught Homer in the very act, quivering with pride at his accomplishment and wholly unrepentant.

"Maybe he's objecting to the clutter," I suggested to Laurence. "It's probably disconcerting for him to have everything in a different place whenever he jumps onto the table."

Laurence isn't as prone as I am to examining the hidden motivations of our pets. "I think the cat just likes pushing things off the coffee table," was his reply.

We've also learned to tie closed the sliding closet doors in our home. It's apparently easier than one would think for a small cat to hoist the full weight of his body up a hanging pair of jeans (denim being a nice, sturdy material that's well suited to climbing), then propel himself onto a top shelf where boxes of old photos, wrapped birthday and holiday gifts (which make a delightful crinkling-paper sound when they're clawed open), and comfy piles of soft clothes make their homes. Garbage cans—no matter how tall—can be leapt into and toppled onto their sides. Scratching posts made of coiled rope can be completely unraveled, given enough persistence. Bookcases can be scaled and novels hurled from their highest shelves. The same goes for records, CDs, and DVDs stacked in an entertainment center. With enough imagination, the acts of mischief and minor destruction that one small cat can discover over the course of an average workday are endless. If there's one valuable life lesson I've learned from Homer, in fact, it's the importance of finding worthwhile projects to occupy one's time.

Most recently, Homer has trained himself to use the toilet. Why, at twelve years of age, he suddenly chose to add this feat to his bag of tricks, I couldn't tell you. I've heard of cats being trained by their owners to use the bathroom instead of a litter box, but I've never heard of a cat taking the mastery of this particular task upon himself.

The first time I discovered his latest achievement was by accident. I awoke early one morning and stumbled into the bathroom. Flipping on the light, I found that it was...already occupied, Homer balancing on the edge of the toilet seat.

"Oh, I'm sorry," I said automatically, still half asleep. It was only after I'd left, considerately closing the door behind me, that I thought, *Wait a minute...*

"Our cat's a genius!" I gushed to Laurence later that day.

"When he teaches himself to flush, he'll be a genius," Laurence replied.

It's true: The art of the flush is still beyond Homer's grasp. So checking toilets is another item I've added to the mental checklist I go through when I get home at night, while I survey the apartment for overturned picture frames, pried-open cabinets, and knocked-over knickknacks.

Because I never know exactly what to expect when I walk in the door—and because seeing Homer can be a startling sight all on its own for the uninitiated—I try to prepare guests when they visit for the first time. In the years since I met Laurence and stopped dating, and as I reach an age where the number of new friends I make becomes fewer, this is something I've had to do with less frequency.

Still, I remember one occasion when I failed to give a new boyfriend the rundown before a first-time visit. At the outset of the evening, I hadn't expected to invite my date back to my apartment. By the time the decision was made, talking about my cats seemed like the sort of thing that might kill a romantic mood.

Homer, in those days, was particularly enamored of playing with tampons. Having encountered one by chance, he was fascinated by the way they'd roll around, and by the string at the end. He liked them so much, he figured out where I kept them stored in the cabinet below the bathroom sink and—with unerring patience and accuracy—mastered the task of forcing open the cabinet door and raiding the tampon box.

When I walked in with my date, Homer ran to greet me at the door. And there, hanging from his mouth, was a tampon. The whiteness of it stood out against his black fur in vivid, mortifying relief. He scampered around in gleeful triumph for a moment, then promptly ran over and sat expectantly on his haunches in front of me, tampon clutched firmly between his jaws like a dog with a rawhide bone.

My date looked taken aback, to say the least. "What the...is that a..." He stammered for a moment, before finally managing, "Did something happen to your cat?"

I hunkered down on my heels, and Homer happily climbed into my lap, dropping the purloined tampon at my feet. "He's fine," I answered. "He doesn't have any eyes, is all."

My date appeared staggered by this piece of information. *"No eyes?"*

"Well, he was born with eyes," I explained. "But they had to be removed when he was a kitten."

THERE ARE SOME NINETY million cats residing in roughly thirty-eight million U.S. households, according to Humane Society estimates—and so, in a sense, Homer is entirely typical. He eats, sleeps, bats around crumpled-up balls of paper, and gets into more trouble than I can keep him out of half the time. And, just like any other cat, he has very fixed opinions when it comes to what he likes and what he doesn't. Happiness, in Homer's world, is tuna fresh out of the can, climbing anything that can support his weight, pouncing with mock ferocity on his two unsuspecting (and much, *much* larger) sisters, and napping in the patch of sunlight that falls into the living room just before sunset. Unhappiness is being the last of my cats to score a prime spot next to Mommy on the couch, a litter box that isn't immaculately clean, permanent denial of access to our apartment's balcony (blind cat, high ledge—it's easy math), and the word *no*.

But Homer looms larger than life in my imagination, and I often think his story can only be thought of in epic terms.

He's the Cat Who Lived—an orphaned, half-starved stray who survived an illness grave enough to take his eyes at two weeks of age, and who nobody wanted to give a home to once it was clear he would pull through. He's Daredevil, the famed Marvel Comics superhero who lost his sight in an accident while saving a blind man, but who gained superhuman use of all his other senses. Like Daredevil, Homer's senses of hearing and smell, his ability to map and negotiate all obstacles in an unfamiliar room simply by walking through it once, border on the preternatural. He's a cat who can smell a single flake of tuna fish from three rooms away, who can spring straight up, five feet into the air, and catch a buzzing fly in midflight. Every leap from a chair back or tabletop is taken on faith, a potential leap into the abyss. Every ball chased down a hallway is an act of implicit bravery. Every curtain or countertop climbed, every overture of friendship to a new person, every step forward taken without guidance into the dark void of the world around him is a miracle of courage. He has no guide dog, no cane, no language in which he can be reassured or made to understand the shape and nature of the hurdles he encounters. My other cats can see out of the windows of our home, and so they know the boundaries of the world they inhabit. But Homer's world is boundless and ultimately unknowable; whatever room he's in contains all there is to contain, and is therefore infinite. Having only the most glancing of relationships with time and space, he transcends them both.

Homer initially came into my home because nobody else wanted to take him. So it never fails to amaze me how fascinated people are—even people who aren't particularly interested in cats—when they meet him, or even when they just hear about him. He's the ultimate conversation starter, something I hadn't anticipated when I first adopted him. Ninety million cats out there means there are at least ninety million cat stories, but—at the risk of sounding unbearably prejudiced—I've yet to encounter a cat as remarkable as mine. At least once a week, every week for the past twelve years, he's done something that has amused me, infuriated me, or flat-out astonished me—and he's never more astonishing than when I see him for the first time all over again through somebody else's eyes.

Oh, how sad! is often the first thing people say when they hear that Homer's eyes had to be removed at two weeks of age. I usually respond that if you can show me a happier, more rambunctious cat anywhere in the world, I'll give you a hundred bucks just to get a look at him. *How does he get around?* they'll ask. On his legs, I answer, just like any other healthy cat. On occasion, when he's especially enthusiastic in his play, I'll hear the *bonk!* of his little head bumping into a wall or table leg he'd forgotten was there. It's something that always draws a laugh from me, even while my heart cracks down familiar lines. I laugh because anybody who's witnessed a cat in a playful frenzy, falling backward off a sofa or charging headfirst at a closed glass door, can't help but chuckle. And my heart breaks because, in the best of all possible worlds, Homer would have been found a week earlier, when the eye infection he'd had might have been diagnosed as "serious" rather than "incurable."

Of course, in that world, Homer almost certainly wouldn't have entered my life in the first place.

My favorite moment in the celebration of Passover—the holiday commemorating God's leading Moses and the Israelites out of Egyptian slavery and into the Promised Land—is always the Dayenu, a joyous song sung loudly and accompanied by much clapping of hands and stomping of feet. Hebrew for *it would have been enough*, the Dayenu recounts the miracles God performed on behalf of the Israelites, insisting after each one that it, all on its own, would have been enough: If He had brought us out from Egypt and not carried out judgments against them, *dayenu!* If He had carried out judgments against them and not parted the sea for us, *dayenu!* If He had parted the sea for us and not supplied our needs in the desert for forty years, *dayenu!*

And so on.

Living with Homer, over the past twelve years, I've composed a Dayenu of my own. If Homer had simply managed to live beyond two weeks of age, it would have been enough. I he had simply learned to find his food bowl and his litter box all on his own, it would have been enough. If he had simply taught himself how to get from room to room in our home without any guidance, it would have been enough. If he had simply learned to run, jump, play, and fearlessly do all the things they told me he might never do, it would have been enough. If he had simply made me laugh out loud every single day for over a decade, it would have been enough.

And if he had done nothing more than become one of the most loyal, affectionate, and courageous sources of joy and inspiration I've ever known…well, that would have been more than enough.

In a seemingly hopeless situation, when no rational person could expect *anything* good, yet somehow ends up receiving *everything* good—these are things we call miracles and wonders. A few of us are lucky enough to see such wonders in our everyday lives.

So this book is for the others like me, but also for the ones who've given up on believing in everyday miracles and heroes; for people who love cats and for people who consider themselves firmly anti-cat; for those who think *normal* and *ideal* mean the same thing, and for those who know that, sometimes, stepping slightly to the left of what's normal can enrich your whole life.

To all of you I introduce Homer, the Wondercat.

Dayenu!

1 • Socket to Me

Yesterday made the twentieth day that I have been tossing about upon the sea. The winds and waves have taken me all the way from the Ogyian island, and now fate has flung me upon this coast.

– HOMER, *The Odyssey*

Years ago, back when I still had only two cats, I was fond of saying that if I ever adopted a third I would name him Meow Tsetung and call him "The Chairman" for short.

"Don't look at me like that, it'll be *cute*," I would insist when my friends regarded me as if I were a loon. "Little Chairman Meow."

The joke was twofold: the name itself, and also the idea that I would adopt a third cat. I might never have taken the monumental step (so it had seemed to me at twenty-four) of adopting two except that I'd been living for three years with Jorge, the man I was sure I'd marry. We'd split up recently, and I had gained custody of our feline offspring—a sweet-tempered, fluffy white beauty named Vashti and a regal, moody gray tabby named Scarlett. I was grateful for my two girls every day, but also painfully aware of the potential complications they would create in my newly single life, complications I had never contemplated back in the days when I'd thought Jorge and I would be together forever.

I was staying in a friend's spare bedroom while I tried to save up for an affordable place to live, for example, but I would never be able to move into a more reasonably priced pet-free building. There was no point in even considering a relationship with a man who had cat allergies. I worked in nonprofit, running volunteer programs for the United Way of Miami-Dade, and I never had more than fifty dollars in the bank at the end of the month. Nevertheless, routine vaccinations, injuries, and illnesses would have to be paid for by me alone, no matter what their impact on my finances.

"Not to mention the social implications," my best friend, Andrea, would say. "I mean, there are only so many cats you can have when you're twenty-four and single. The neighborhood kids will start calling you Old Widow Cooper and throw rocks at your windows and say things like, *that's where Old Widow Cooper, the cat lady lives. She's craaaaazy...*"

I knew she was right; I wasn't completely out of touch with reality. In my present circumstances, talking about a third cat was an absurd hypothetical, like daydreaming about what I might buy if I won the lottery.

Then one afternoon, a couple of months after Jorge and I broke up, I got a call from Patty, a young veterinarian only three years older than I was, who was the newest member at the practice that treated Scarlett and Vashti. Patty told me a long, sad story that would have been perfect for a cable movie, if only there were a station called *Lifetime for Cats*.

An orphaned, four-week-old stray kitten had been abandoned in her office, she said, after a virulent eye infection had required surgical removal of both his eyes. The couple who had originally brought him in didn't want him. Nor did any of the people on her adoption list, not even the ones who had expressed a specific interest in adopting a handicapped cat. Nobody, it seemed, wanted to face this particular handicap. I was her last call, the last possibility she could think of before...

She didn't finish her sentence, and she didn't have to. I knew there was almost no chance that an eyeless kitten would be adopted from a shelter before his time ran out.

Don't, warned the Greek chorus that lives inside my head. *Yes, it's sad, but you're in no position to do anything about it.*

I'd always been an obsessive reader, a passionate lover of books, and I knew the kind of power words had over me. Pitting me against words like *blind, abandoned, unwanted,* and *orphan* was like sending someone armed with a toy rifle into trench warfare.

Still, I recognized the wisdom of my inner Greek chorus, even if I couldn't be as coolly analytical as it was. So I said, "I'll come in and meet him." I paused. "I'm not promising anything, though."

I should note that, prior to this, I had never taken an *I'll meet him and we'll see* attitude when it came to pet adoption. It never occurred to me to meet the pet in question first, to see if he was "special" or whether there was some sort of unique bond between us. My philosophy when it came to pets was much like that of having children: You got what you got, and you loved them unconditionally regardless of whatever their personalities or flaws turned out to be. While I was growing up, my family adopted or fostered numerous dogs, almost all of whom were strays or had been abused in their previous homes. We'd had dogs who couldn't be housebroken, dogs who chewed up carpeting and wallpaper, dogs who dug compulsively under fences or who even occasionally snapped when they were startled. My cats, Scarlett and Vashti, had been adopted a year apart from acquaintances who'd found them as six-week-old kittens—mange-ridden, half starved, and covered in fleas and sores—wandering the streets of Miami. I had committed to them sight unseen; the first time I'd met them had been the day they'd come to live with me.

So I felt more than a little dishonest, driving down to my vet's office the following afternoon. Patty might not know it, but I knew myself well enough to understand that when I'd said, "I'll come in and meet him," what I'd meant was, *I really don't want a third cat right now, but I'd feel like a bad person if I gave you a straightforward* no *after hearing this cat's story. So I'm leaving myself room to wriggle off the hook.*

"We have to take him. We have to let him live here," had been the immediate response of my roommate, Melissa, when I'd told her about the blind kitten the night before—"here" being Melissa's one-story, two-bedroom, waterfront South Beach home, where I split the cost of utilities, groceries, and other household expenses while I tried to save up for my own place. But Melissa was beautiful, and an heiress, and the everyday obstacles that appeared insurmountable to me at this juncture in my life weren't even blips on her radar screen. Melissa didn't have to agonize over things like higher vet bills, or being unable to eventually find a home for herself and her brood of three (*three!*), or the prospect of being undateable. (I could already hear imaginary conversations among these mythical men I hadn't even met yet, let alone started dating. *Dude, she's smart, she's cute, she's a lot of fun—but she's got* three *cats! That's just messed up, dude.*)

I couldn't decide if I was even the right person for a kitten like this, a kitten who would undoubtedly have special needs I couldn't begin to anticipate. What if he never learned to get around on his own? What if my other two cats hated him on sight and made his life miserable? What if I simply wasn't up to the challenge of taking care of him? I could barely take care of myself. Arguably, given that I was living in somebody else's home at the moment, I *couldn't* take care of myself.

I'd been encouraged, briefly, by Melissa's use of the word *we*. I wouldn't be in this alone. In some small, crafty corner of my brain, it occurred to me that I could bring the kitten home and, if I proved unequipped to handle him, Melissa could always…

"Of course, you're the one who has to make the final decision," Melissa had added a moment later, "because he'll go with you when you move out."

THE THING THAT WAS speeding me toward my vet's office as surely as the wheels and motor of the car I was driving, the thing that had gotten me to agree to meet this kitten in the first place, was guilt. If I didn't take him, no one would. I had always been an easy mark when it came to animals, and everybody knew it. I was a veteran weekend volunteer at Miami's various animal shelters, and—back when Jorge and I were still living together—I'd always come home in tears, pleading with him against all reason to consider adopting one of the dogs or cats who stood to be euthanized if nobody stepped forward. My only run-in with the law thus far had been the time in college when I'd been arrested at a protest outside of my university's primate research center. I'd been the kid who neighborhood dogs and cats followed to school because I would give them all the food out of my lunchbox, without considering how I planned to feed myself at lunchtime.

And it was exactly that kind of hazy, immature thinking, I told myself somewhat viciously as I slid into the parking lot outside my vet's office, this heedless disregard for future consequences, that had landed me exactly where I currently was in life—broke and alone after years of carefully constructing what I'd thought was an unshakeable future.

I realize now that I was trying to manufacture a sense of anger. It was far easier to convince myself I was angry and put-upon than it was to admit I was terrified.

It was a ferociously muggy, late-August day. Silvery waves of heat shimmered and rose like evil genies from the pavement fronting the strip mall where my vet had her office. The receptionist greeted me warmly as I entered, summoning Patty, who popped her head out from a door behind the reception desk with a cheerful, "Come on back!"

I followed her past rows of cages holding cats and dogs, which I'd noticed before but never paid much attention to. I'd always assumed they'd been left in the temporary care of my vet by owners who would eventually come to retrieve them. For the first time, I wondered how many of them were actually homeless, waiting to be looked over by people like me who might or might not end up adopting them.

We reached the last examination room at the end of a narrow, wood-paneled corridor, and Patty opened the door for me. On the exam table was a lidless plastic box ("So you can interact with him," she explained). I walked over and peered in.

He's so tiny was my first thought. Both of my cats had been almost this young when I'd taken them in, but I'd forgotten how absolutely tiny a four-week-old kitten is. He couldn't have weighed more than a few ounces. He had curled himself up in a miniature sphere in the farthest corner of the box, a fuzzy softball that would have fit easily into the palm of my hand. His fur was all black, and it had that static-electricity fluffiness that very small kittens have, as if their fur has actively rebelled against the notion of lying flat. Where his eyes had been were two tiny stitches, and around his neck was one of those plastic cones they put on pets to keep them from scratching stitches out.

"I sutured the lids shut," Patty said. "So it won't look like he has sockets or anything—it'll kind of look like he has his eyes closed all the time." She was right. Looking at the X-shaped stitches where his eyes would have been, I was reminded of childhood cartoons where the drunkenness or demise of a character was indicated by X's drawn over his eyes.

"Hey there," I said softly. I scrunched down a bit, so my voice would come from the kitten's level and not sound too booming or scary. "Hey, little guy."

The black fuzzball in the corner of the box uncurled itself and stood up hesitantly. I tentatively reached a hand—a hand that suddenly seemed monstrous in size—into the box and lightly scratched the bottom of it. The kitten walked slowly toward the sound, his head bobbing uncertainly under the weight of the plastic cone. His nose bumped against one of my fingers, and he sniffed it curiously.

I glanced up at Patty, who said, "You can pick him up if you want to."

I lifted him carefully, cradling him just below my chest with one hand supporting his bottom and the other around his chest and front legs. "Hi, little boy," I whispered.

At the sound of my voice, he turned himself around and reached up to my left shoulder with his front paws; they were so small, they sank between the cables of the light cotton sweater I was wearing. He struggled a bit, and I could tell he was trying to hoist his full weight onto my shoulder. But his claws, such as they were, were too tiny to get a good grip. Giving up, he twisted again and brought his face as close to where my jaw met my neck as the plastic cone would allow. He tried to rub his face against mine, although all I felt was plastic against my cheek. Then he started to purr. The cone funneled the sound until it was so loud, he sounded like an improbably small motor.

I had expected that, having no eyes, he would be incapable of conveying much expression—and it occurred to me that this, perhaps, was the secret fear of the people who'd refused to adopt him. A pet whose face couldn't register love, couldn't reflect emotion, might always feel like a stranger in your home.

As I held him, though, I realized that it isn't the eyes that tell you how someone is feeling or what they're thinking. It's the muscles around the eyes, which pull the corners up or push them down, crinkle them at the edges to convey amusement or narrow them into slits indicating anger.

This kitten didn't have his eyes anymore, but the muscles around them had been left intact. And I could tell, from the shape the muscles were taking, that if he'd had eyelids they would have been half closed in an expression eminently familiar to me from my other two cats. It was an expression of utter contentment. The ease with which he slipped into it suggested that, despite everything he'd already been through—despite every reason he'd had to expect the opposite—in the depths of his kitten-y little soul, he'd always known there would be a place where he could feel completely warm and secure.

And now, at last, he'd found it.

"Oh, for God's sake." I put him gently back into his box, then rooted around in my purse for a tissue. "Wrap him up, I'm taking him home."

Patty was insistent that the kitten remain with her a little while longer. She wanted to keep an eye on his stitches, concerned about possible infections. And she also hoped he might gain some weight before being subjected to the tender mercies of solid food and two full-grown cats. "You can take him home in a few days," she promised.

I was finally getting my Chairman Meow, but somehow a prefab name didn't seem right anymore. "You should call him Socket," Melissa suggested.

"That's awful!" I exclaimed. "His name is *not* Socket!"

She shrugged good-naturedly. "He'll always be Socket to me."

I hadn't had much difficulty in naming Scarlett or Vashti. Scarlett had come to me named already; she'd been one of a litter of stray kittens found by my mechanic, who'd named her Scarlett because she'd been so dehydrated those first few days that she kept fainting. I named Vashti for the biblical Persian queen who'd refused to dance naked at a feast for her husband—the king of Persia—and a group of his drunken buddies. She was banished from the kingdom as a penalty for her refusal, an early feminist martyr as far as I was concerned. That *my* Vashti had grown from a sad, half-bald bag of kitten bones into an exotic longhaired stunner, who looked a bit like a Persian cat, had been a happy coincidence.

I didn't want to stick this new kitten with something cutesy or obvious ("Ray" and "Stevie" had already been suggested by well-meaning friends as exactly the right name for a blind black cat), but I also didn't want to hang anything too solemn or portentous on him. He would always be blind, it would always be an inescapable part of his life, but I knew—even way back in the beginning—that I didn't want his whole life to be defined by his blindness alone.

I visited the kitten at the vet's office often over the next few days. His short life had already been more bewildering than anybody could imagine—I wanted there to be something familiar and reassuring when he finally came home with me, even if it was only my smell and the sound of my voice.

But I was also still nervous in more ways than I cared to admit. He was mine now—there was no going back from it—but I wanted to see for myself how he got around, how he encountered the world around him and learned to make his way through it.

So every afternoon, when I'd finished work for the day, I would stop by Patty's office. She would take the kitten from his kennel and set us up in one of the exam rooms, allowing him to roam freely while I sat mostly silent in a corner of the room and watched him.

I could tell already that he was a tireless explorer. The weight of that plastic cone around his neck, which went before him like the shield of a knight-errant crossing enemy terrain, made it difficult for him to hold his head fully erect. But he almost always kept his nose to the ground, anyway. The exam room was minuscule, but not an inch of it went unsniffed. When he encountered a wall or table, his tiny paws would cautiously make their way up its side, an engineer testing dimensions and thickness. The only thing he attempted to climb was the chair that stood in one corner of the room, although a large potted plant that stood in the opposite corner was also fascinating. This was my first instance of using the word *no* with him; I didn't want him to end up with a coatful of dirt, or to inadvertently tear the plant to shreds.

Finally it was the day before the kitten was supposed to come home, and still he was nameless. It seemed as if Socket was in danger of becoming his name by default.

He needed a name, and it needed to be the right one. So I tried to think of him as if he were a character in a story. His life had already begun as so many of the best stories do—with trials and suffering, miraculous reversals and innumerable obstacles still to be overcome.

But it occurred to me that he wasn't just the subject of a story; he was also a creator of stories. Lacking even a concept of vision, I was sure he made things up to account for the world around him. How else to understand a chair that mysteriously appeared to block his path in a spot where only yesterday there had been no chair? What *was* a chair? Why and how did chairs come to be? And how to explain the omniscience of an adoptive mother who could instantly tell—no matter how silently he crept—the precise moment he was contemplating something forbidden? The fourth time he attempted to climb into the large, dirt-filled pot of the plant in the corner, I issued my fourth firm and unexpected, "No!" The kitten's face crinkled into perplexity. He was, of course, unable to distinguish between "soundless" and "invisible." *I was walking so quietly! How can she always know?*

You think, when you adopt a pet, that he will become a supporting character in the story of your life. But I was beginning to think I was now a character in this kitten's story. From a struggling single girl, racked with self-doubt and saddled with three cats, I had become an all-knowing and implacable deity, a being of great benevolence and mystery.

I watched him tentatively traverse that exam room—a landscape so small and, by now, familiar to me, so vast and unknowable to him. He navigated between the Scylla and Charybdis of a table leg and a small bowl of water that had been left out for him. Once he tumbled, face-first, into that bowl of water. I snatched him up protectively, murmuring *Good kitty, good boy*, and he purred, content that the heavens favored him once again. No matter how many times he encountered the wrath of the water bowl, or leapt and misjudged the height of a chair, or ran into a table leg he'd forgotten was there, he persevered.

There's a place on the other side of this, he seemed to tell himself, *and things I must do there.*

He was a hero on a quest. But he was more than that; he was also the one who created heroes and myths about the gods—for the same reason myths have always been created: to explain the inexplicable. He was Odysseus and he was also the blind storyteller who'd imagined Odysseus, who'd seen life on an epic scale even when he couldn't see anything at all.

And then I knew what my kitten's name was.

"Homer," I said aloud.

He responded with a lusty *mew*.

"Good, then." I was pleased we agreed. "Homer it is."

2 • What Do You See in an Eyeless Cat?

You ought not to practice childish ways, since you are no longer that age.

– HOMER, *The Odyssey*

DURING THAT WEEK WHEN Homer and I were first getting to know each other within the sanctuary of Patty's office, Melissa was busily spreading the news of Homer's imminent arrival among our circle of friends. The offhand question, "Did you hear we're adopting an eyeless kitten?" was the kind of thing that was sure to dramatically shift the flow of general conversation, inviting a flurry of additional questions in its wake. "Eyeless? *Eyeless?* You mean, like, he has no eyes *at all?*" So it was that, even before he came to live with me, the story of Homer was repeated so often and so identically that it came to feel like an official part of the family legends and formative anecdotes that made up the ongoing narrative of my life—the way, for example, my parents have spent more than thirty-five years relating in the exact same way the tale of how my mother went into labor with me at a rock concert, two weeks ahead of schedule, because "Gwen couldn't wait to hear all that music."

(Had I gone on to become a rock star instead of a writer, by the way, that story would carry far more dramatic resonance today.)

It's true that I still slip into precisely the same language and cadence when telling the story about Homer's adoption as I did back then. But that's only because the questions I'm asked haven't changed at all. I've gotten questions about Homer from hundreds of people over the years, and they're always—*always*—some variation on the same three: *How did he lose his eyes? How does he get around? Can he find his litter box/food/water?*

And yet, I never get tired of answering. Not because I'm so fond of talking about my cats in general, but because even though I've long since gotten used to Homer's blindness, I've never taken for granted, or stopped being inordinately proud of, how brave, smart, and happy my little boy has turned out to be.

I was having dinner with a new work-related acquaintance recently, and the subject of Homer came up. She had been telling me about her kitten, adopted less than a month earlier, and I regaled her with anecdotes of Homer's kittenhood adventures and misadventures. I had never discussed Homer with her before, but she found him as interesting as most people do when they hear about him for the first time. Then, out of nowhere, she hit me with a question that stopped me cold:

"Why did you adopt him?"

It was a question that might have sounded aggressive or hostile coming from somebody else, as if to say, *What could you possibly see in an eyeless cat?* Yet the woman's face was kind as she asked it, her tone gentle and sympathetic. It was a question posed in a straightforward way, with an apparently straightforward interest in hearing my answer.

And I wanted to give her an answer—one as simple and straightforward as the query had been. But it was a question that I literally had never been asked before; for the first time in twelve years I had no simple, automatic response at my disposal.

Because I'd never been asked this question, it had never occurred to me to wonder why nobody else ever asked it. Thinking about it now for the first time, it made perfect sense that nobody would ask why I had adopted Homer, because the answer, on the face of it, seems obvious. Either I'd been so affected by his hard-luck story that I would have been miserable and guilt-ridden if I hadn't rescued him from almost-certain death in a shelter—or we'd so immediately bonded, falling instantly in love with each other from the moment I first picked him up, that I couldn't have borne to leave him there. I realized that everybody, even the people who knew me best, my family or the friends I'd had for decades, probably thought that those were the reasons I'd adopted Homer.

And everybody was wrong.

What I remember most from those first few months after breaking up with Jorge was the overwhelming sense that I'd failed the first important test of my adult life. Everyone, including me, had assumed that Jorge and I would get married. What was the point of spending three years with someone if it didn't lead to marriage? But one sunny Sunday morning Jorge had informed me, in an entirely respectful and matter-of-fact way, that he wasn't in love with me anymore.

If I was honest with myself, I'd have to admit that I wasn't in love with him anymore, either. I had been twenty-one when we'd first met, and at twenty-four I hardly recognized the girl who'd fallen in love with Jorge. She was a scrapbook filled with old photos of someone who looked much like me, with my nose and my eyes, but whose clothes and hairstyle looked more like the girls' I'd gone to college with than the way I looked now. I'd been vaguely aware—on some not-quite-conscious level—that I was gradually changing, that the things I'd been sure I wanted only three years earlier might not reflect this newer me, whoever she was. But hearing the words *I'm not in love with you anymore* had struck me like a body blow. What if, I couldn't help wondering, the person I was becoming wasn't lovable?

I was also beginning to have doubts about my career path. Back when Jorge and I had been together, the typically low nonprofit salary I earned had been almost a luxury I'd indulged in, justified by the fact that I was combining it with Jorge's much larger salary. It was increasingly clear that it wasn't a salary that could carry me safely into this new phase of my life. On the other hand, I wasn't sure what else, exactly, I was qualified to do.

It would be an overstatement to say that I had lost all faith in myself. But I was considerably less confident and optimistic than I had been only a year earlier.

I'd found it impossible to say no when Patty called and I heard Homer's story for the first time. But that doesn't mean I wouldn't have been able to say no eventually—in fact, I'd deliberately left myself the option of turning him down, believing that I probably would. Heartbreaking as Homer's story was, even I knew that I couldn't save every animal who deserved saving—I would have told myself that I'd already rescued two cats and was doing the best I could for them. I might have hated making that decision, I might have cried for days the way I used to cry when I came home from volunteering at an animal shelter, but, ultimately, I could have lived with it.

It's also true that, when I did meet him, Homer crawled into my arms with a seemingly immediate willingness to love and be loved by me. Even when I was holding him in that moment, though, I'd known that it wasn't really about *me* specifically—that if somebody other than me had shown up at my vet's office, and whispered to him softly, and picked him up gently, Homer would have been equally willing to love that person.

Sensing that he could have loved anybody as easily as he could love me was actually the first thing that grabbed my heart. Whatever else he might or might not turn out to be, this kitten was a creature with a tremendous capacity for love. The idea of someone having nothing but love to give, yet being unable to find anybody who wanted that love, struck me as unbearably tragic.

The other thing I realized was that, while he seemed loving, he wasn't scared or desperate to be loved, the way you would expect a kitten—or even a person—who'd experienced nothing but pain, hunger, and fear to be. Nor was he hostile or defensive, a kitten who'd let a hard life stomp all the love right out of him. He was merely curious and affectionate. It was as if there was some innate source of courage within him, some inborn willingness to engage the world openly and joyfully, that even all the suffering and hardship he'd been through hadn't taken away from him.

It was a staggering concept for me at the time. I had been dumped, forced to move out of my home, and was having financial problems—and I'd consequently developed an unfortunate tendency to approach life as if it were a grim struggle, to allow self-pity to consume me whenever I lost some of those struggles.

But here was this cat, whose ordeals made my own worst days seem like a week at Disney World, and his attitude upon meeting me appeared to be, *Hi! You seem goodhearted and fun! Don't you find that people generally are goodhearted and fun?*

It probably sounds like I'm about to contradict what I said earlier, that I ended up adopting Homer because I thought there was something special about him. It wasn't that, though. Not exactly.

What happened was that I caught a glimpse of something I desperately needed to believe at that point in my life. I wanted to believe there could be something within you that was so essential and so courageous that nothing—no boyfriend, no employer, no trauma—could tarnish or rob you of it. And if you had that kind of unbreakable core, not only would it always be yours, but even in your darkest moments others would see it in you, and help you out before the worse came to the absolute worst.

Or, as my grandmother used to put it, "God helps those who help themselves." If I recognized all that within this kitten now, and took him home because of it, then I would be proving my own theory right.

So I didn't adopt Homer because he was cute and little and sweet, or because he was helpless and he needed me. I adopted him because when you think you see something so fundamentally worthwhile in someone else, you don't look for the reasons—like bad timing or a negative bank balance—that might keep it out of your life. You commit to being strong enough to build your life around it, no matter what.

In doing so, you begin to become the thing you admire.

What I'm trying to say is that, when I decided to bring this eyeless kitten home with me, I made my first truly adult decision about a relationship. And, without realizing it, I established the standard by which I would judge all my relationships in the years to come.

3 • The First Day of the Rest of His Life

> A good woman, Eurrycleia, daughter of Ops,
> guided [him] to his room, and she loved him
> better than any other woman in the house did, for
> she had nursed him when he was a baby.
>
> - HOMER, *The Odyssey*

SCARLETT HAS ALWAYS ENJOYED sleeping on soft, cloth-y piles of things, like pillows or towels or piled-up blankets. Vashti prefers dozing on hard surfaces. As I left for work on the morning of the day when I brought Homer home for the first time, Scarlett was napping on a pile of laundry in the back of my closet, while Vashti rested (comfortably?) on top of a wooden desk, her cheek pressed against the sharp corner of a large dictionary.

They looked so peaceful as they regarded me with their heavy-lidded, half-sleeping eyes that I felt a momentary twinge at the havoc I was about to wreak in their lives. "I'll see you guys later," I said quietly on my way out the door. "With a big surprise…"

Vashti responded with a gentle cooing sound, while Scarlett merely blinked at me once and rolled over to sprawl on her back, all four paws in the air.

I left work at exactly five thirty that afternoon and headed straight for Patty's office. Homer had already been loaded into a small purple cat carrier with *HOMER COOPER* scrawled on a strip of masking tape across the top. I peeked inside, but Homer was all-black and eyeless, and the only thing I could make out clearly was the white of the plastic cone around his neck. Everybody, including Patty, was almost tearful as they waved the two of us off.

Homer was completely silent during the car ride home. In the first instance of what would prove to be a decade of constant and frequently irrational worries, this concerned me. I hadn't spent much time around cats growing up, so what I knew of them came primarily from things Patty had told me and my hands-on experience with Scarlett and Vashti. And Scarlett and Vashti *hated* their carriers, screeching like howler monkeys the second I loaded them in—particularly Vashti, who was so unassertive under normal circumstances that she never raised her voice above the level of a squeak.

It seemed unnatural that Homer was so quiet. It might be that he was simply sleepy, or wearily used to being removed from one place and brought to another for reasons that were, to him, inexplicable. Perhaps he even enjoyed the seclusion of the carrier (Vashti and Scarlett loved to make small caves themselves in boxes and shopping bags) and found the motion of the car soothing.

Or, a dark corner of my mind pondered, maybe he was so terrified at this bewildering turn of events that he was afraid to make a sound. I tried to speak to him reassuringly as I drove. *We're almost there, Homer. We'll be home soon, little boy.*

I had thought a great deal about the best way to introduce Homer to his new home. My first resolution was that he should be confined to a relatively small area for a day or so. I felt he was more likely to grow comfortable and familiar with his surroundings if he wasn't intimidated by too much space all at once. While this would be true of any cat—Scarlett and Vashti had been introduced to their new home one room at a time over a period of days—I reasoned that a blind kitten in particular was likely to be overwhelmed by more than a single new room at first. And, I was sure, he would be far more likely to get lost or tripped up, unable as he was to create a visual memory of how one room led into another. Truth be told, I wasn't entirely sure he would ever be able to do this—and I was more anxious on this score than I cared to admit—but I had gained a certain amount of confidence after watching Homer seamlessly navigate the exam room in Patty's office after one or two passes, and I had decided to worry about these eventualities if and when they came up.

I also planned to keep him completely separated from Scarlett and Vashti until his stitches came out. Vashti was very social and extraordinarily patient, but she hadn't encountered a new cat since I'd first adopted her and introduced her to Scarlett—and I suspected that, sweet-tempered though she was, she'd also grown accustomed to being the "baby," and to receiving all the attention Scarlett never seemed to want anyway.

Scarlett had been far from overjoyed when I'd first brought Vashti home. Although, in fairness to Scarlett, it should be noted that Vashti, who had been infected with a horrific case of mange (fur loss and itchiness caused by tiny mites on her skin), had come home with me fresh from a sulfur dip at the vet's office. The sulfur had not only turned what was left of her long white fur a startling and unnatural shade of yellow, but also left her reeking with the stench of rotten eggs.

Vashti had been beside herself when she realized that added to the ecstasies of being well fed and itch-free for the first time in her six weeks of life was another cat for her to play with. Scarlett had spent the next few days alternately hissing at and fleeing from this tiny, smelly, bright yellow puffball that followed her everywhere and cavorted in joyous circles around her whenever she put so much as a paw out from under the bed, where she'd taken up a resolute temporary residence.

Scarlett had grudgingly gotten used to Vashti, however, and had even come to enjoy having another cat to scamper around with. So I was hopeful that, with time, Homer would integrate just as seamlessly into our family.

I entered the front door of Melissa's house carrying Homer in his purple kitten carrier, and Scarlett and Vashti ambled over to sniff at it curiously. Homer persisted in not making any sound, but I felt his weight shift as he balled himself up in the far corner of the carrier. Vashti peered with interest at the carrier's contents, but Scarlett took one whiff and immediately backed up several feet, a deeply disgusted expression on her face. *Oh, God...not* another *one...*

"You guys can meet your new brother later," I told them and headed into my bedroom, closing the door behind me. *"Later" can be "never" as far as I'm concerned,* Scarlett's retreating backside and haughty tail flick clearly indicated. But Vashti wasn't used to being shut out of a room that I was in and gave a few half-swallowed squeaks of protest (*ngeow! ngeow!*) from the other side of the door.

The spare bedroom I was utilizing at Melissa's house was connected to a small bathroom, which was where I had set up Homer's litter box. I set the carrier down beside it and unlatched it, lifting Homer out and placing him in the litter box. There were three things I wanted to be certain Homer would know how to find: his litter box, his food dish, and his water bowl. I knew that blind people learned how to find things in their homes by counting the steps from, say, a kitchen stove to the dining room door. While I didn't expect Homer to actually count his steps, I thought that if he got to know the rest of our home in relation to where those three things were, he'd be more likely to find them on his own.

I'll admit that I was apprehensive, both that Homer might be unable to find his litter and that he might not know what it was for. Scarlett and Vashti had immediately grasped the concept of a litter box and hadn't required any additional training. I was therefore unsure how to litter-train a kitten, and hoped I wouldn't have to.

When I set him in the litter box, Homer immediately squatted and peed, then dug around furiously to bury it. "*Good* boy," I told him. "*Good* boy!"

From there I walked slowly, and with deliberately loud footsteps, through the door that led to my bedroom, where I had set up his food and water in the exact center of the room—easier to stumble upon by accident, I guessed, even if Homer couldn't learn or remember on his own where they were, I crouched next to the two tiny bowls containing dry food and moist food (I wasn't sure if Homer would be able to smell dry food, so I'd put down both), tapping the tile floor next to them with my fingernail and making a *pss-pss-pss* sound that I'd found always served to summon Scarlett and Vashti.

Homer, when he had finished tidying up in the litter box, obligingly hopped out and made his way over to where I crouched. His neck bobbed from side to side beneath the plastic cone he still wore. He walked in that bandy-legged way of very young kittens, and he wove unsteadily, as if he were slightly drunk. Although I was usually haphazard when it came to storing shoes and clothes in the closet, I had been careful to clean all extraneous items from the floor of the room, to minimize any chance that Homer would bump into something. Even the shoes I'd worn that day and removed upon my arrival at home had been placed on top of my desk, and there was nothing to impede his progress from the doorway of the bathroom to where I was stationed ten feed away with his food.

Still, Homer seemed confused at first by all the empty space around him. The bedroom was relatively small, probably no more than 150 square feet, but it clearly struck Homer as cavernous. He hesitated for a few seconds, his head and his little comma of a nose crinkling as if he were attempting to discern a clear path by smell. But the repeated tapping of my fingernail on the floor seemed to reassure him. Once he realized there was a purpose to the sound, and that the sound came from me, he made a fast-trot beeline toward it and the food bowl. His nose bumped into the small mound of moist food, and he took a few eager bites.

I had no idea if water had a smell that was discernible to a kitten and didn't want to leave it to chance that he would find it on his own. I had placed the water bowl next to the dish that held the dry food, and I wiggled a few fingers in the water. "Are you thirsty, kitty?"

At the light splashing sound my fingers made in the water, Homer raised his head from the moist food and cocked it slightly to one side. Then, as if he'd intended to do it all along and had simply been awaiting a cue, he buried one minuscule paw in the bowl of dry food and immediately began to fling it into the water bowl. The sound it made as it hit the water was nearly identical to the sound my fingers had made splashing around in the bowl, and Homer turned a proud, expectant face in my direction.

I burst out laughing. "Not exactly what I had in mind," I told him. "Let's try this again."

I walked back over to the litter box and called Homer over. As he had before, he headed straight for the sound of my voice. When he reached me, I once again picked him up and placed him in the litter box. This time Homer appeared confused. *Didn't we do this already?* Then I repeated the walk over to the food bowl, and Homer once again ate eagerly from the moist food. I waggled my fingers in the water bowl, and Homer once again flung the dry food into it.

I wasn't sure if Homer found this entertaining or if he was doing what he thought I wanted him to do. Either way, I decided it was best for all concerned if I moved the water bowl out of range of the dry-food dish. This time, when I splashed my fingers around in it, Homer walked over and drank. Scarlett and Vashti, when drinking rom their water bowl, would center their heads over the bowl and drink from the middle. I noticed that Homer, however, carefully pressed his tongue against the inside of the ceramic bowl, forcing a few drops at a time into his mouth. I remembered when he'd fallen face-first into the water bowl at the vet's office, and it occurred to me that he was afraid it might happen again.

By now, the square of sunshine in the bedroom window had purpled into twilight. I heard Melissa's car pull into the driveway. The front door opened and closed, and then there was a light knock at my bedroom door. "Is he here?" Melissa's voice said softly through the door. "Can I see him?"

"Come on in," I replied in an equally restrained voice.

Melissa opened the bedroom door a crack, poking her face in and peering around before she quickly opened the door just wide enough to slide her slender frame through, closing it soundlessly behind her.

Homer was sniffing around the edge of the bed, but he came to an abrupt halt when he heard the door open. He turned his face up in Melissa's direction. The blackness of it, in the middle of that plastic cone and unbroken by any color of any kind, looked like the velvety black heart of a sunflower.

"Ohhhhhh," Melissa whispered. Her hands flew to cover her mouth. "He's so tiny!" She took a step toward him, and Homer uncertainly backed away. Melissa looked at me. "Can I pet him?"

I patted a spot next to me on the bed. "Let's see what he does," I told her.

I was curious to see what would happen. Many cats are shy of newcomers—it's one of their most common traits. And Homer had more reasons to be leery of new people than most cats. But I had also sensed, when I'd first adopted him, that he was friendlier than the average cat.

Now we would see.

Melissa settled next to me on the bed, and both of us held our breath. Homer walked slowly in our direction. "It's okay, Homer," I said. He appeared unsure how to get from the floor, where he was, up onto the bed, where the sound of my voice was coming from. He reached out a paw tentatively and sank his claws into the bed's comforter, which hung all the way down to the floor, tugging it slightly as if testing its weight. Finding it to be strong enough for climbing, he hauled himself up onto the foot of the bed.

"Hey, Homer," Melissa said. She lightly patted a spot on the bed in front of her. "Come here and say hi."

Homer trotted across the bed with his wide-legged, neck-rolling gait, his fur even fluffier after his climb. Purring loudly, he placed his two front paws on Melisssa's leg and stretched his head up again, sniffing the air around her. Melissa gently rubbed behind his ears and under his chin, and he fervently pressed the entire front of his face against her hand. It was as if, because there were no eyes to become irritated by such a gesture, there was nothing to keep Homer from rubbing as much of his head as he could against someone else.

It wouldn't be a stretch that say that I'd always been somewhere intimidated by Melissa. She had been a good friend to me—after all, she'd taken me in with my two cats after Jorge and I had broken up—but it had always seemed to me that there was something flinty and unyielding in her. That she was compassionate was something I knew; Melissa clocked even more hours than I did with nonprofit causes. But on a strictly personal level, she could be tough. She had little patience with my everyday fears and foibles, and this made sense—because when you were as beautiful and wealthy as Melissa was, what could you possibly know of ordinary human failings?

But, holding Homer, something in her seemed to unbend. Her face lit up in a way I'd never seen. We flipped on the TV to catch part of an old movie and chatted idly for a while about nothing in particular—her day at work, a party we were supposed to attend later in the week—but she was almost wholly focused on Homer, who purred and nestled happily into her lap.

Eventually, Homer climbed out of Melissa's lap and walked carefully toward the side of the bed. When he reached the edge and his outstretched paw encountered empty space he paused, obviously flummoxed. My first impulse was simply to pick him up and place him on the floor. *It would be so easy for me to do it for him,* I thought.

Homer, however, gave no indication that he was waiting for assistance—from me or from anybody. He backed up into a slight crouch, then took a wild leap. He landed with enough force that his front legs splayed out a bit, and the bottom of his cone hit the floor and bounced back up. "Oh!" I exclaimed, one hand rising involuntarily to my face. But Homer was fine. He collected himself for a moment, then took off in a loopy half run toward his food dish. I was somewhat surprised, yet enormously pleased, to note that he seemed to remember exactly where it was—either that or the smell of the moist food was detectable enough to guide him in its direction.

"Are you concerned about how unsteadily he's walking?" Melissa asked.

I *had* been concerned about it, to the point that I'd been mulling over whether I should call Patty in the morning. But I heard myself saying, "No. I think...I think it's just because of the cone he's wearing."

I'd started out wanting to deny that I was worried, in that irrational way that makes *saying* you're unworried seem like the same thing as *being* unworried. As I said it, though, I knew it was probably true. At first I'd thought the cone was too heavy for Homer and was tempted to remove it, even if it meant jeopardizing his stitches. But then I realized that it wasn't the heaviness of the cone—it was the fact that it was interfering with Homers ability to use his whiskers.

Cats have two sets of "eyes"—their actual eyes and their whiskers. Cats' whiskers are three times thicker than the rest of their fur, and the roots go far deeper than other hair roots, connecting all the way to their nerves. Whiskers are a constant source of sensory feedback for a cat: They detect air currents that alert cats to movement around them, and they sense the presence of furniture, walls, and other solid objects, acting as a sort of extended peripheral vision that helps a cat maintain balance and a sense of orientation in space. They're part of the reason why cats are so famously able to see in the dark.

But Homer's whiskers were trapped inside that cone, unable to do him any good. Deprived of both regular vision and sensory input from his whiskers, he was truly and completely blind. It was the reason why he staggered about the room like someone who'd been blindfolded and spun in circles. Any cat would be thrown off balance if deprived of his whiskers. Homer was doubly so.

Removing the cone, however, would mean the possibility of scratched-out stitches. Much as it pained me, there was no question that Homer's cone would have to remain where it was for the time being.

Melissa and I finished watching the movie, and when she left I decided to turn in early. Homer followed me—either by smell or sound (or both)—into the bathroom and sat next to the sink while I brushed my teeth and washed my face. He used his litter box one more time, finding it with no trouble whatsoever, then trotted back into the bedroom after me. I turned out the lights and settled into bed, planning to pull Homer up, but he was already climbing after me on his own. The street outside was quiet as I lay down and settled onto the pillows, and the silence in the room was broken only by the faint sounds of Melissa chatting on the phone in the other room, and of Vashti squeaking in mild indignation (because Vashti had, heretofore, *always* slept with Mommy) on the other side of the bedroom door.

Homer crawled up the length of my body, climbing onto my chest and turning around in a circle a few times before settling down on the spot just above my heart. I was drifting off when

I heard an odd, squelching sound and felt something tickling my ear.

I opened my eyes but couldn't make out much in the dark. Then I realized that Homer was nursing on my earlobe. The cool outer edge of his cone pressed against my cheek. His front paws kneaded the patch of pillow directly behind my ear, and his purr was a low thrum, steadier and more subdued than it had been earlier while Melissa was petting him.

I held my breath, sensing that if I moved at all, Homer would stop what he was doing—although he probably *should* stop, shouldn't he? I felt a little silly. It was the kind of thing where, had somebody burst unexpectedly into the room, my impulse would have been to shove Homer away from my ear and insist, *It's not what it looks like!*

This was an entirely new experience for me, something that neither Scarlett nor Vashti had ever done. It was obvious that Homer had missed having a mother, that—whatever Patty or I wanted to tell ourselves about how Homer would forget, may have already forgotten, the trauma of his early life—on some deeply fundamental level, Homer remembered that he'd been deprived of something he was supposed to have. He was supposed to have a life that included a mother's care, that was comprised of affection and adequate nourishment and comforting rituals in the dark.

My hand rose to stroke his back, and his purring grew louder.

I realized something else. It meant something to be trusted by this cat. There was a difference between being trusted by cats or even animals in general and being trusted by this kitten in particular. I was too sleepy to pursue the thought, or articulate it in any logical way, but I understood in that moment that this was something I'd felt without being aware of it from the first moment I'd picked Homer up in the vet's office.

My last conscious thought was that Melissa had known this, too, and that it was why she had appeared so much softer when she was holding him.

4 • The Itty Bitty Kitty Committee

"Alas," said he to himself, "what kind of people have I come amongst? Are they cruel, savage, and uncivilized, or hospitable and humane?
— HOMER, *The Odyssey*

HOMER'D HAD A GOOD first day. Nevertheless, my apprehensions remained. Homer had seemed anxious simply walking from the bathroom to the bedroom. The sound of my hand and my voice had drawn him forward—would that always be what it took to make him feel at ease in his new life? Would his life be the constant struggle against fear and limitations that everybody appeared to think likely? Most people who heard about Homer seemed to take it for granted that his life would be circumscribed by trepidation and disability.

But one of the first things I learned about Homer the following morning was how ecstatic he was merely to wake up. I was surprised to see that he had slept the whole night through curled up on my chest, barely moving at all. I soon found that Homer was eager to sync his schedule with mine—sleeping when I slept, eating when I ate, and playing whenever I was in motion. Whether by nature or necessity, he was the quintessential copycat.

I would also learn that Homer was a remarkably happy little kitten. Just about everything contributed to the surfeit of joy he found in his new world—even things I would have normally classified as "cat-adverse." The whirring of the garbage disposal, for example, or the apocalyptically loud whine of the vacuum cleaner (sounds that terrified not just Scarlett and Vashti, but every dog or cat I'd ever seen) brought him straight over at a fast waddle. His ears would be fully pricked up, his neck and cone turning from side to side as he ran. *Yay! A new sound! What is that new sound? Can I play with or climb onto it?*

But nothing thrilled him as much as waking up at the beginning of each day. As soon as I sat up that first morning, he began to purr in a humming, distinctive way. There was a melodic, trilling undercurrent to it, like birdsong. He rubbed his face so urgently against my hands that he lost his balance and flipped over onto his back, struggling against the weight of his cone and looking for all the world like an incapacitated beetle. Undeterred, he righted himself with a mighty heave and climbed into my lap to prop his front paws on my chest, rubbing his whole face vehemently against mine. I felt the softness of his kitten fuzz and the prickliness of his stitches on my skin.

This is so great! I'm still here and you're *still here!* He was so tiny that a single stroke of my hand sufficed to cover his entire body. When I touched him, he dug miniscule claws into my shoulder and attempted to pull himself up, latching onto my earlobe and suckling at it once again.

"I'm going to assume that means you're hungry," I said. "Let's see if you remember where your food bowl is."

I sat up and deposited him on the floor next to the bed. He was unprepared for this, apparently, because he tripped over his first step, his cone-encased chin once again hitting the floor. But he bounded up quickly enough and toddled straight for his food bowl, after which he scurried to the litter box.

The discovery that food and litter were exactly where he had left them the night before was another moment of bliss. His singsong purring continued unabated, audible even from where I sat clear across the room.

HOMER'S HAPPINESS, ASTONISHINGLY, SEEMED to because of, and not despite, the fact that his world had grown so much larger. Lacking vision, Homer's universe was only as big as whatever space he was in. It's true that it had once been far larger than it now was—when he was a stray, it had encompassed all of Miami and the world beyond that—but that universe had been lonely, painful, and incomprehensibly dangerous. The relief from pain and danger had come at a price, and his world had shrunk to the size of his kennel at the vet's office. But Melissa's house was an eternity of possibility, an infinity of space and smell and sound.

Homer proved to be so incredibly reluctant to be left alone—and so eager to explore—that by his first afternoon in Melissa's house, we released him from the confines of my bedroom, although I was careful to ensure that Scarlett and Vashti were never in the same room that he was in at the same time.

The miracle was that, within all this space and possibility, Homer was safe. There were things he could count on here, despite how big everything was. Food and water were available in abundance, and could be found predictably in the same spot every day. In this new world, an unusually loud noise meant opportunity, not danger. He could fall asleep at night knowing that no predator would harm him while he slept, and wake up each morning in the arms of someone who loved him.

To say that he must have regarded these things as miraculous would be assuming too much similarity between a kitten's mind and a human's. If anything, I was the one who thought in terms of miracles whenever I contemplated what his life had been—and what it would be still, if not for the quirk of fate that had brought us together. But Homer's happiness was there, and it was indisputable. I had moments of sheer, unreasoning joy in witnessing it, but at the same time it impressed upon me a sense of responsibility, accompanied as it was by the knowledge that it fell to me to ensure the safety that enabled his joy.

"I will always keep you safe, little boy," I would murmur, caressing his fur while he slept.

Upon hearing about Homer for the first time, Melissa's father had asked us whether we planned to get a Seeing Eye dog for our blind cat. He'd meant it as a joke, of course, but the question remained as to how I would teach Homer to get around, giving him as free a rein as possible in this new, bigger world while minimizing any of the perils that world might hold for him.

I had spent the days before bringing Homer to live with us trying to think through what it would take to blind-kitten-proof the house. I bought soft felt caps for the sharp edges of tables and bed frames, invested in childproof locks for cabinets where cleansers and other hazardous materials resided, bought childproof latches for the toilet lids (a small, eyeless kitten who accidentally fell in and couldn't see his way out might drown, I thought), and plugged crevices around the entertainment center where a blind kitten might wedge himself in or hopelessly entangle himself in wires and extension cords.

It was impossible to anticipate everything, but I ended up being glad I had spent so much time thinking about things beforehand—because Homer was impatient to discover and claim every nook and cranny. Homer solved the Seeing Eye dog problem by utilizing me as his Seeing Eye human—following my footsteps so closely everywhere I walked that, if I happened to stop short, his little nose ran straight into my ankle.

"I feel like Mary," I said to Melissa. When she looked at me quizzically, I added, "You know...*and everywhere that Mary went, the lamb was sure to go.*"

At first, I thought Homer trailed me with so much determination because he was afraid to investigate on his own. Patty had warned that Homer was likely to be more timid and less independent than other cats. "But he won't know that he's blind," she'd added. "It's not like the other cats are going to tell him, *Hey, you're blind!*"

It was soon apparent, though, that Homer didn't follow me so doggedly because he was nervous about exploring on his own. It was simply the most efficient way of learning his way around, of discovering where the nemeses of table legs and umbrella stands were lurking to trip him up. Leaving a pair of discarded shoes or a wet umbrella lying in the middle of the floor went from being an act of carelessness to bordering on animal abuse. I stepped over small things that changed place from day to day—but Homer, who walked in a persistent straight line wherever I had just been, would trip and halt in the confusion of an obstructed path that, only the day before, had been clear. *Was this here yesterday? I don't remember this being here yesterday.* I'll admit I had always tended toward the sloppier side of the neatness spectrum. But living with Homer required the discipline of order, and I soon learned habits of tidiness that would come to define my adult life.

In addition to not knowing he was blind, Homer had also clearly never been informed of his "underachiever" status. He got into absolutely everything—anything I was doing, he had to be a part of. If I was cleaning out a closet, Homer was next to me, digging away at stacks of old clothes or boxes. If I was making a sandwich, Homer would scuttle up the side of my denim-clad leg (to this day, there's nothing he loves climbing so much as a pair of jeans) and propel himself onto the kitchen counter. If I was sitting on the couch, he would scale the side of my body until he reached the top of my head, resting there for as long as I could maintain my posture and hold my head level. Catching sight of our reflection in a darkened window one night, with the cone-wearing Homer curled up atop me, I thought we looked like some sort of futuristic half-human/half-satellite cyborg. Homer frequently fell asleep right in the middle of whatever he was doing, as kittens are wont to do, one paw clutching a pilfered scrap of paper or wrapped around his food bowl, like the lesser characters in *Sleeping Beauty* who, enchanted along with her, slumbered in the act of threading a needle or salting their soup.

By following and exploring so relentlessly, Homer got to know our home astonishingly quickly. Melissa and I were astounded at how, within only a couple of days, the only time Homer bumped into anything—*in the whole house*—was when he got into one of what we called his "whirling dervish" modes, where he would hyperactively spin around like the Tasmanian Devil until he'd lost his sense of where he was in space. At such times, the *clomp!* of the front of his cone connecting with a wall or table leg could be heard echoing through the house.

There was only one limitation placed on Homer's freedom and happiness in those early days, and that was when it came to his eating habits. Melissa and I learned that some official discipline was in order the first time we prepared a meal for ourselves in Homer's presence. We had just settled ourselves onto opposite ends of the couch with dishes of food when Homer leapt onto the couch and unceremoniously climbed directly onto my plate, hungrily grabbing whatever tidbits were closest to his mouth.

I was reminded of an early scene in *The Miracle Worker* when, before Annie Sullivan's arrival, Helen Keller would walk around the family dinner table and put her hands into everybody's plates, helping herself to whatever she wanted. This, clearly, was unacceptable behavior, and I decided to nip it in the bud.

I lifted Homer up and placed him on the floor. "No, Homer," I said in a tone that left no room for argument.

Homer cocked his head back and forth in a way I would soon become familiar with—it meant that he was trying to figure out from my tone of voice what I wanted from him. He did it a few times before responding with the plaintive, cheeping *Eeeeuu* that kittens make—the kind that seems to require the entire force of their body to produce. Reaching up the side of the couch with his two front paws, he repeated, indignantly this time, *Eeeeuu!*

Melissa and I couldn't help laughing, but we refused to give in on this one. "I said *no!*" I told him.

Homer sat for a moment with his face turned up toward us, as if waiting for a sign of leniency. Then, with a small sigh, he prowled away toward his own food in the other room.

There was a certain amount of defiance in his step, as if he were consciously keeping his kittenish waddling down to a minimum. *Fine, then. I have my own perfectly good food right here...*

IT WAS HOMER'S FIRST lesson in discipline, and it was made tougher to reinforce by the indulgence of our inner circle of friends, who came over eagerly to meet him. If there was one thing Homer dearly loved, it was meeting new people. And if there was one thing the people who met Homer loved, it was letting him do whatever he wanted. Suddenly Homer was part of an extended family, what Melissa and I referred to as the "itty bitty kitty committee," which included innumerable indulgent godparents who were perfectly happy to sneak him bits of tuna or turkey or meatballs from their plates. They also showered him with the toys they'd brought over for him: toys from their own childhoods and toys purchased specifically for cats; toys that hummed, buzzed, rang with attached bells, or were otherwise made enticing by their ability to produce sound. Everybody, myself included, assumed that playthings with bells and whistles—and not the visual stimuli of feathers and doodads—would hold the most appeal for a blind kitten.

Homer had to be introduced to new people in just the right way or else he was apt to be hesitant. With his whiskers trapped in that cone he still wore, it was nearly impossible for him to sense any movement in his close vicinity—so it always took him by surprise when a hand other than my own came to rest on his head or back, seemingly out of nowhere.

We developed an introduction ritual, wherein I would hold the new person's hand in my own and bring the two of them together under Homer's nose, so that he could smell my familiar scent mingled with the new one. Once Homer had been properly introduced and knew that the new person was Mom-approved, he was eager to make friends. Any kind of physical contact was a source of profound joy to Homer, who was so much more tactile than sighted kittens and who loved to burrow, nuzzle, cuddle, rub, and bring as much of his small body into contact with others as he could.

What visitors found most astonishing was Homer's ability to distinguish among people he knew, and to remember the difference between someone he'd already met and guests who were strangers. "I met him once for five minutes," a friend remarked when, upon a second visit, Homer headed directly for him and climbed into his lap. "How can he recognize me when he can't even see me?"

"Well, he can *smell* you," I replied. Cats actually tend to recognize each other more by smell than by sight anyway—this ability was simply fine-tuned in Homer.

As fascinating as Homer's super-keen sense of smell was his ability to hear things that nobody else—not even other cats, or so it seemed—could hear. I remember one of our friends, eager to test the widely held theory that deprivation of one sense let to super-enhancement of the others, waving her hand back and forth silently in the air, about twenty feet from where Homer lay sleeping in my lap. As soon as her hand began to move, Homer's head was up, his ears, nose, and neck turning and twitching. This in itself wasn't so unusual—Homer's ears and nose were always at work when he was awake, giving him a constantly kinetic air. But the sound of the air currents shifting around the hand that moved silently up and down all the way across the room had reached his ears—with enough force to wake him up. He jumped from my lap immediately, standing on the floor as his head bobbed up and down in perfect time with our friend's waving hand. He toddled across the living room straight for her, his front paws stretching imploringly up her legs as he arched his head and neck into the air. *What's making that sound? Bring it down here!* Laughing, she lowered her hand for Homer to sniff before scratching him affectionately under his chin while he purred in loud contentment.

People were instinctively gentle with Homer. The sense I'd had that first night with him, that it meant something different to be trusted by Homer, was clearly a sense that others had as well.

South Beach at that time was populated by people who had, for the most part, moved there from other places, and who had grown used to being called "misfits" or "freaks" back in their original hometowns. They were artists and writers, costume-loving club kids or cross-dressing performers at the local drag bars. There was a reason why, in our more sardonic moments, we referred to South Beach as "the Island of Misfit Toys."

Melissa loved collecting strays and misfits, creating a constant salon of sorts in her home. Perhaps it was because Homer was also a "freak" who had been shunned remorselessly by so many others that everybody took to him so quickly.

But I don't think so.

A friend once asked me why it was that stories about animals and their heroism—a cat that pulls her kittens from a burning building, say, or a dog that walks across fifty miles of Iraqi desert to reunite with the soldier who fed him—are so compelling.

I didn't have an immediate answer, beyond observing that I also loved those stories. A few days later, though, it occurred to me that we love them because they're the closest thing we have to material evidence of an objective moral order—or, to put it another way, they're the closest thing we have to proof of the existence of God. They seem to prove that the things that matter to and move us the most—things like love, courage, loyalty, altruism—aren't just ideas we made up from nothing. To see them demonstrated in other animals proves they're real things, that they exist in the world independently of what humans invent and tell each other in the form of myth or fable.

Homer's blindness didn't imbue him with mystical qualities. It didn't make him more perceptive or a better judge of character than other animals. But he did bring out the best in those around him. Our friends knew that the couple who had originally brought Homer to my vet had insisted he be put to sleep, and that a score of others had refused out of hand to adopt him. This created unequivocal "us" versus "them" camps. To be one of "us," to understand how remarkable Homer was, to show him greater kindness and accept him despite his differences, was to be a better person than the "them" who'd rejected him.

Homer, for his part, was grateful for every bit of the attention he got from the people around him.

Cats are what's known as solitary hunters, which is science's way of expressing what most of us can observe—the extent to which cats are more independent than dogs, the way they can fend for themselves and crave "alone time" in ways dogs typically don't. Dogs in the wild form packs, but cats hunt on their own or form loose social groups that are more about respecting one another's individual territory than tracking down food cooperatively.

But Homer was always a pack animal—realizing, instinctively, more than any other cat, that his safety depended on numbers. Humans became his pack. I was the pack leader, and anybody I introduced to him was accepted without question. This was a kitten who everyone thought would have been *more* leery and reluctant to accept others than a typical kitten, but it was Homer's nature to be accepting of the people he met, to climb into their laps and purr and rub affectionately against them at the first overture of friendship.

I remember somebody remarking once, as I extracted an alarmed Homer from an afghan he'd become tangled under, how patient I was with him. It struck me because it was the first time anybody had called me patient—probably because I wasn't a particularly patient person. It wasn't that I couldn't *be* patient. But it was certainly the case that, whenever I was, it was because I was consciously instructing myself to do so. (*All right...be patient now...*), the way that you have to remind yourself to do the things that don't come naturally.

But with Homer, it did come naturally. I didn't have to give it any thought at all.

For his own part, Homer wasn't much of a philosopher. All he knew was that he was happy, and he was loved. And he would go on, over the course of years, to do all kinds of things that dazzled and amazed me.

But some of the most amazing were things he didn't do at all. They were things that happened around him, merely because he was there.

5 • The New Kid

Anyone with even a moderate amount of right feeling knows that [you] ought to treat a suppliant as though he were [your] own brother.

- HOMER, *The Odyssey*

FOR AS LONG AS Homer had his stitches in and his cone on, he had to be kept separated from Scarlett and Vashti. The logistics involved in keeping them apart—while giving Homer plenty of time and space to acquaint himself with his new home; while also giving Scarlett and Vashti a fair amount of freedom and reassuring them they weren't suddenly unloved just because there was a new kitten in the house—were even more complicated in practice than they sounded in theory. When Melissa was home, I would sometimes give Scarlett and Vashti free range while Homer stayed locked up with Melissa in her bedroom. When Homer, or Melissa, or both of them, lost patience with their confinement, I would hustle Scarlett and Vashti into my bedroom and allow Homer his run of the house. If Scarlett and Vashti were still in my bedroom come bedtime, I shepherded them back out so Homer could sleep with me.

As the days went by, I began to feel like the philandering husband in a French romantic farce, with the constant opening and closing of bedroom doors and doing everything in my power to ensure that the wife and the girlfriend never ran into each other. It got to the point where the creak of the bedroom door drew baleful looks from Scarlett and Vashti. *We know, we know…other room…*

The situation was far harder on Vashti, who was just over a year old, than it was on Scarlett. Vashti was an outgoing cat who loved to be around people, especially me. She had never tracked my footsteps as closely as Homer did, but before Homer's arrival she'd always followed me from room to room and had slept every night curled around my head on the pillow. After more than a week being separated from me so much of the time, she was becoming noticeably morose.

Scarlett had traditionally been more of a loner. At two years of age, Scarlett was the cat that people who didn't like cats thought of—aloof, independent to a degree that bordered on anti-social, and stiff as piecrust if anybody besides me attempted to touch, pet, or otherwise approach her. Poor Scarlett suffered from a serious PR problem on this account. Even my best friend from college, Andrea, who now lived in California with two cats of her own, was apt to refer to Scarlett as "that wretched cat."

To my own ears, I sounded like a girl with an abusive boyfriend when I defended our relationship: *You don't know what she's really like! You don't know how sweet she is when we're alone together!* This was true; Scarlett was capable of a great deal of affectionate cuddling and purring, as well as spirited games of chase-the-paper-ball or hide-and-seek, when she and

I were one-on-one. And it's also true that Scarlett had grown to enjoy playing with Vashti—on a selective basis, and at moments of her own choosing. For the most part, though, she was content to be left to her own devices. Constantly being locked up when Homer was around didn't sadden her so much as it offended her sense of personal dignity. *As if I* wanted *to mingle with the riffraff out there.*

The hardest part of all this enforced separation was that I'd been forced to confine Homer to my bathroom when I left for work in the morning, concerned that unmonitored time alone with the other two cats would imperil his stitches. When I put him in there he would howl—not the loud, complaining meow of a cat who's being confined against his will, but the gut-wrenching, awful screams of an animal experiencing stark terror. Brave though he was, the one thing that terrified Homer nearly beyond endurance was being alone. This made sense, actually, because even though Homer technically didn't know he was blind, instinct told him his greatest vulnerability was that something, or someone, could sneak up on him unawares. That same instinct undoubtedly knew it would be far more difficult to sneak up on a kitten surrounded by people or other cats than on one kitten by himself. Alone, therefore, was an unnatural state of affairs from Homer's perspective. Even making a nest for him out of some of my old clothes, so he would have something that smelled like me, and placing a small radio in the bathroom turned to NPR—of all the "constant human voice" stations, this one struck me as the most soothing—didn't ease his anxiety.

Listening to his cries from the bathroom, it took every ounce of willpower I possessed not to let him out. My first impulse was to open the door, fly into the room, scoop him up into my arms, and assure him that nothing bad would ever, *ever* happen to him as long as I was there. Thinking about what might have gone into producing his terror, what he'd been through blind and defenseless on the streets before he'd been found and handed over to my vet, was the kind of thing that kept me awake many a night as I pressed him closer to my chest and buried my face in the warmth of his fur.

At last, after a week in his new home, the great day arrived when Homer's stitches came out. This meant that his cone, too, was a thing of the past. He would be able to start grooming himself, and I would no longer have to wipe his bottom for him after he used the litter box. And he would never have to be alone again.

"Although you might wish you were," I told him as we drove to the vet's office, imagining Scarlett's probable reception of him.

Eeeeuu! Homer replied from the confines of his carrier in the backseat of my car.

LIBERATION FROM THAT PLASTIC cone was a pure draught of sweet ecstasy. Upon being released from his carrier after arriving home from Patty's office, Homer went straight for the living room rug, where he lay on his back and flipped from side to side, rapturous that he could now do so without any limitation on his range of motion.

Scarlett and Vashti entered the room cautiously—half expecting to be locked up again, or simply suspicious of the newcomer. Homer was still rolling around on his back on the living room rug, but he jumped up immediately and sat at attention as Scarlett and Vashti approached him.

I'd always known he was tiny—he was still under six weeks old, after all—but he looked positively dwarfish as Vashti and Scarlett circled him. I held my breath as they took turns sniffing him inquisitively, flinching backward with slitted eyelids when Homer responded in kind. When Homer reached up an impish paw toward them, they recoiled. Scarlett's own paw came up in immediate response, batting at Homer's head in a manner that clearly indicated he was to sit still until they'd finished inspecting him. Homer lowered his paw and hunkered down his neck a bit, huddling himself up as tightly as he could while still sitting upright.

Vashti sniffed around his ears a few more times, then began to gently lick the top of his head. I was encouraged by this, and so, apparently, was Homer. He lifted his head once more to sniff around Vashti's nose and whiskers, and his paw rose again as he attempted to touch her face and fur. Startled at his touch, Vashti bolted a few feet away, continuing to regard Homer from this safe distance.

Scarlett meantime had had enough and walked slowly away in Vashti's direction. After a moment's hesitation, Homer toddled after them. When Scarlett saw this she picked up her pace and made for the bedroom door, having no intention of allowing Homer to catch up to her.

"Don't worry, you guys will get used to each other," I said, with more confidence than I felt.

Doubtful, the look on Scarlett's face indicated, and her walk quickened into a run.

People ask me all the time if Scarlett and Vashti know that Homer is blind. I think blindness is too abstract a concept for a cat to grasp, so what I usually say is that Scarlett and Vashti realized Homer was different at first—klutzy, as far as they were concerned, and somewhat rude, and not terribly good at being a cat—but that, by now, they've come to accept him as he is. I know it confused them when, for example, this bumbling little kitten would leap enthusiastically onto the couch and unwittingly land atop one of their sleeping heads, backing up hastily upon realizing the spot was occupied. Couldn't he see somebody was already sleeping there? When awakened in this fashion, Vashti and Scarlett would grimace in annoyance and cast a look at me that said, *What's with the new guy?*

Homer was also apt to play much rougher than Scarlett and Vashti were accustomed to. The two of them had a favorite game, one that was mostly of Scarlett's devising with Vashti happy to follow her lead. The game went like this: At some point when Vashti's back was turned or she was otherwise distracted, Scarlett would leap upon her and whap her in the face a few times with her front paw. Scarlett's claws were always retracted (retracted claws were an essential part of this game). Vashti would respond in kind, and the two of them would engage in a full-blown slap fight, whapping at each other's faces and paws, until Vashti landed what was—in Scarlett's opinion—one blow too many. Whereupon Scarlett would flatten her ears and arch her back slightly, a signal to Vashti that it was time for her to knock it off. Once Scarlett had decreed Game

Over, the two of them would go off, unruffled, in their separate directions.

Homer was a boy, and he didn't have much use for these kinds of subtle girly games. Homer wanted great life-and-death battles, the fierce drama of perseverance and triumph in the face of crushing odds. Homer's idea of the perfect game had nothing to do with slap-and-retreat. His favorite game was to leap onto Scarlett's and Vashti's backs and pin them down while they struggled furiously, sinking teeth and claws into whatever he could reach.

He didn't intend to hurt them by doing this, and would always back up in confused alarm if either of them squealed in pain or anger. But as far as Homer knew, anything that escaped his grasp could disappear into the black void of *gone forever*. Homer could never assume that any plaything—whether a squeak-toy or the body of another cat—would be findable again once he was no longer touching it. If I dangled a string in front of him for him to try to catch, a game that Scarlett and Vashti both loved, he could sense the string but always went for my hand instead, digging his claws into my skin to keep both string and hand from disappearing. It was this same tendency that made him grabby when it came to sharing toys with the other cats. If Scarlett and Vashti were batting around a ball of paper between them, Homer would bound over and clasp the ball of paper tightly in his claws to keep it from spinning off into infinity. This inevitably led Scarlett and Vashti to walk away—clearly, Homer was hogging all the action—while Homer was left to bounce the ball of paper around in his tight claw with a perplexed expression at finding himself so suddenly alone. *Don't you guys want to play with this anymore?*

So he tended to dig his claws into things, like the other cats' flesh, without meaning to do them any harm. I spent long hours training Homer to retract his claws when playing—mainly by encouraging him to play with me, then issuing a harsh *"No!"* and abruptly ending the game when his claws came out—but in the meantime, he wasn't winning Vashti and Scarlett over.

I think what most surprised Scarlett and Vashti, who weighed eleven and nine pounds respectively, was that Homer never got tired of stalking, or at least attempting to stalk, the two of them. Surely, had he been able to see how very much bigger they were than he was, he would never have contemplated it.

But Homer couldn't see how much bigger they were. What's more, it's entirely possible that he had no understanding of the concept of relative size. He might have been a six-week-old kitten who still had a distinct waddle to his walk, but in his mind's eye he was one of the Big Cats—a panther, maybe, or a mountain lion.

His efforts at playing the mighty hunter hardly ever produced satisfactory results. He was able to leap upon Vashti whenever he wanted, but only because Vashti—conditioned by a lifetime of bending to Scarlett's will—adopted a philosophy of passive nonresistance. Homer would jump onto her back, a minuscule black mound atop a much larger white one, nipping at Vashti's neck in a vain effort to get her to fight back or do *something*, for crying out loud.

But Vashti would just lie there patiently while Homer thrashed around, turning resigned eyes upon me that seemed to cry, *Oh, the humanity!*

Scarlett, by contrast, was nobody's patsy and always put up a fight. She was Homer's White Whale, his mortal nemesis. The unequivocal sacking of Scarlett was the pot of gold that lay at the end of all Homer's rainbows, and I think it was the dream of his life to finally—indisputably—best her.

The will was there, but his tactics were woefully inadequate. Homer had all of a cat's normal instincts to creep noiselessly and crouch down before springing. Unfortunately, he never understood that, since he wasn't crouching down *behind* anything, he wasn't any less conspicuous to his intended victim than he would have been if here were preceded by a marching band.

It was as good as a play, watching the drama unfold when Homer would take it into his head to attempt yet another assault on Scarlett. You could tell the exact moment when, with a tilt of his head, he caught the faint sounds of her stirring across the room. He would hunker down into his stalking posture, taking a few breathlessly slow, silent steps in her direction Then he would stop. Still crouched low, he would run for four or five more steps. Then he would stop again. He repeated this process—slow, then fast…slow, then fast—"sneaking" up on Scarlett directly from the front.

You could almost hear Scarlett heave a sigh and see her roll her eyes heavenward. *Again?* The look on her face was invariably one of bemused contempt, as if she were observing some new species of idiot. She'd wait for him to get close enough to spring, wriggling his backside in joyful preparation for what would assuredly be his moment of victory, and then—with a casual disdain that verged on boredom—Scarlett would swat him a few times on the head with her front paw, making it painfully obvious that she'd known exactly where he was the whole time. Homer would sit there flummoxed (*Why didn't it work* this *time?*), and Scarlett would turn and stride with cold dignity into the other room, swishing her tail as if to say, *That's quite enough of that.*

Perhaps realizing the futility of trying to take an unsuspecting Scarlett from a sitting position, Homer would sometimes attempt to catch her midflight. One afternoon, I saw a gray blur whiz past me at a breakneck speed, followed by Homer—racing as fast as his little legs would carry him—in mad pursuit. I laughed long and loud at the visual of this half-pound kitten chasing an eleven-pound, full-grown cat. Scarlett leapt to the safety of a kitchen countertop, glaring down at Homer who was making his best, if unsuccessful, efforts to scale the side of the counter to reach her.

Homer never caught her, but he did frequently come close. I would often come upon a disgruntled Scarlett, angrily settling herself onto a sofa arm or the top of a coffee table, and a few feet away would be Homer, sitting on his haunches, a tuft of gray fur in his mouth.

"Homer, were you just chasing Scarlett?" I would ask in a severe tone.

Homer would turn toward me with an innocently blank expression, unaware that *I could see* the incriminating clump of gray fur still clinging to his snout. *Who, Scarlett? I don't think she's been here recently...*

Poor Homer had no truly bad intentions; he didn't want to hurt anybody. He was a kitten and he wanted to play. He was blind and he wanted to be sure that whoever he was playing with didn't run away from him. Why didn't Scarlett and Vashti understand that? Many was the time when I found Homer, having been recently abandoned by the two of them, turning his head and ears from side to side as he tried desperately to track down the slightest sound that would indicate where they were. He would utter a sad little *mew?* as if he were playing a game of Marco Polo all by himself, waiting for a response that never came. *Hey, guys? Where'd you go?*

"You know, they'd probably play with you more if you weren't so rough with them," I would tell Homer. The pity in my voice always brought him over for a round of cuddling and head rubbing. *Why don't they like me, Mommy?* But the advice—alas!—was never heeded.

In true big-sister fashion, however, it was Scarlett who ended up being Homer's most instructive influence, who encouraged him to develop his abilities to climb and leap as he did everything in his power to keep up with her. If Scarlett could climb a six-foot cat tower to get away from Homer, then why couldn't Homer climb it, too? If Scarlett could leap to the top of a desk or dresser, then there was no reason why Homer couldn't climb up the side of it, even if he wasn't able to leap directly up the way Scarlett did.

Homer was a typical little brother in many ways, always wanting to play with the big kids, who were far more interested in playing with each other and who regarded him, at best, as a mildly annoying "baby." But like all younger siblings, he learned by imitation—trying things he might never have otherwise tried and learning more quickly than he would have on his own.

And it was usually in Scarlett's presence that Homer could be found whenever I wasn't there. When curling up for a nap with me wasn't an option, Homer always felt safest sleeping somewhere near Scarlett. I think, in his mind, Scarlett was the strongest one in the house next to me, despite the fact that she was also the "meanest"—or maybe because of it. When Homer wasn't in one of his hyperactive, jump-on-Scarlett-at-all-costs moods, it was surprising how respectful he was of her.

Safety in numbers, right? you could almost hear Homer thinking as he curled up (always curled up, because Homer never—ever—slept sprawled out on his side or back) wherever Scarlett was dozing, close enough for protection but with enough distance left to indicate courtesy.

Scarlett would open one eye and regard him indulgently for a moment before settling back into her nap. *Don't push your luck, kid.*

6 • Don't Be Happy. Worry.

He might have known that he would not prevail with her, for when the gods have made up their minds they do not change them lightly.

– HOMER, *The Odyssey*

IT MAY HAVE STARTED with the plastic bag. The excessive worrying, I mean.

Like many a new mom, I found myself growing eyes in the back of my head where Homer was concerned, as well as an extra set of ears and an almost preternatural awareness of where Homer was, what he was doing, and what his needs were at any given time.

This had become doubly true since Homer's stitches had come out and he'd taken to tearing around the house after Scarlett and Vashti. Soon he wasn't content merely to cover the ground they did, and he began discovering mischief all on his own. Sometimes I would lose track of him for a few minutes and find him in the most unbelievable places—dangling by his front paws from the middle shelf of a bookcase (how had he even gotten up there?), or wedged in the back corner of the cluttered cabinet beneath my bathroom sink, having managed to prise open the cabinet door.

His new obsession was scaling the floor-to-ceiling drapes that hung in the dining room, like one of those Spider-Man types you read about who hand-over-hand their way up the side of an office building. *"Homer!"* I would shriek when I found him hanging on the drapes by a single claw, six feet in the air. Homer would swing the slight weight of his twelve or thirteen ounces around until all four claws clung to the drapes once again, climbing as quickly as he could to put himself above my reach.

Look, Ma! I always imagined him thinking. *No eyes!*

In contemplative moments, I would reflect that there was something inspirational in the way Homer was willing to climb and climb anything at all without any idea as to how high he was going, or any plan for safely regaining the ground once he'd reached the top. There was something to be said for that level of fearlessness.

For all that it was inspirational, however, it was also terrifying.

Every parent knows those moments—the ones when you suddenly realize you haven't seen your child for at least fifteen minutes. Your curse yourself for having become so occupied with something else that you lost track of his whereabouts. *Where is he? What if something happened to him? Why wasn't I paying attention?*

It had already become a point of pride with me to insist that Homer was a perfectly normal kitten. Better than normal, even. I would have taken the head off of anybody who suggested that Homer needed "special" care because of his "special needs," angrily insisting that Homer was just as capable of taking care of himself as either of my other two cats, or as any "normal" cat out there. When people asked whether and how a blind kitten could find his litter box, I would reply that Homer could not only find his litter, he could find his way to the top of the kitchen counter and into the cabinet where the canned tuna was kept, distinguishing between a can of tuna (which he loved) and a can of tomato soup (to which he was indifferent), while both were still in their sealed cans. He'd root around in the cabinet, shoving all other canned goods out of his way, until he identified the can of tuna fish, using paws and nose to push it from the cabinet and onto the counter. *Feed me this!*

Beneath all that righteous indignation, however, and my insistence that I didn't need to worry about Homer any more than I worried about Scarlett and Vashti, was the truth: Homer *wasn't* like other cats, and I did worry about him more than I worried about my other two.

This fear was all my own, and Homer shared none of it. It had been predicted that his blindness would make him more hesitant and less independent than a typical cat. But if anything, the opposite was true. Because Homer was unable to see the hazards in the world around him, he lived in blissful unawareness of their existence. What was the difference between climbing to the top of a three-foot-high sofa and nine-foot-high drapes if you couldn't see how high you were going anyway? And what was the difference between jumping down from either one when every leap you ever took was a leap into uncertain outcomes, based on nothing but blind faith in invisible landing points?

In the Daredevil comic books, the occasional story line finds Daredevil regaining his vision. Although he retains the rest of his superpowers, he suddenly finds himself incapacitated, afraid to attempt the daring stunts he normally undertakes when blind. *Are you crazy?!* he seems to ask the reader. *I'm not jumping off that! Look how high it is!*

But there was no omnipotent writer who, with the stroke of a pen, could restore Homer's eyes to him. The only absolute fear Homer knew was that of being alone. As long as somebody was with him—whether it was me or one of his feline sisters—Homer had no notion that there were other things in the world that could harm him.

Which brings us back to the plastic bag.

It was a late-fall afternoon, and Homer was now about four months old. He had lost his kittenish bandy-legged gait, and both his walk and his coat were decidedly sleeker than they'd been when he was only a few weeks of age. Every hair on his body, down to the lush whiskers that now exceeded the width of his body by a good three inches on each side, remained a luxurious onyx black. He was growing, although not as quickly as my other two cats had grown—and this, in itself, was something I worried about. Patty assured me, however, that kittens, like children, grow at different rates. And it was also clear that Homer was destined to be a petite, fine-boned cat, one who would undoubtedly remain smaller than average into his adult life.

It was a Sunday and I had decided to enjoy my day off by immersing myself in a novel. I had been concentrating deeply when I realized, on a level that hadn't yet risen to fully conscious thought, that it had been some time since I'd last seen Homer.

Homer liked to curl up in my lap while I read, but the fact that he hadn't this time wasn't something that, in and of itself, would have alarmed me. It wasn't unusual for him to prowl around for mischief and mayhem while I was distracted with something else.

Then I heard the sound of a plastic grocery bag rustling in the kitchen. I had been shopping that morning, and I'd left a plastic bag on the kitchen counter for the small refuse items we didn't like to leave in the larger trash can that was emptied once a week. Homer—who had by now climbed up my leg to reach the counter often enough to gauge its height on his own—was clearly up there playing with the bag. Happy that I knew where Homer was and what he was doing, I settled back into my book. A few minutes, later, however, I heard a panicky and repetitive *Mew! Mew! Mew!*—the kind of cry that, previously, Homer had only uttered when he'd been locked up alone in the bathroom.

I tossed my book aside and raced into the kitchen, where I found Homer entangled in the plastic bag. He had stuck his head through one of the handles and twisted it up somehow, so that it was slowly tightening around his neck. His head was buried in the bag itself, and his back claws worked helplessly to free his head and upper body. It looked as though he'd crawled into the bag but, unable to see how to get back out, he had mistaken the opening of the handle for an exit, which was why he had snared himself so far into it.

"It's okay, Homer," I said. I tried to sound calm, for his sake as well as my own. It was difficult to tell exactly how tightly the bag's handle was pressing into his neck, but I was as terrified as he was—afraid he would suffocate or strangle himself before I was able to rescue him.

I lifted both kitten and bag from the counter, slipping a finger between the handle and Homer's neck—to keep it from tightening any further—and murmuring, *It's okay little boy, it's okay.* Homer was still struggling fiercely, but I was able to quiet him enough that I could work his neck and head free of the bag.

What kind of a moron leaves a plastic bag lying around with a blind kitten in the house? I berated myself. *What would have happened if you hadn't been home? Homer would have died and it would have been ALL YOUR FAULT!*

For all that I worried over the perils of Homer's climbing and jumping and running around recklessly and leaping wildly, headfirst, from some six-foot perch and falling off backward from God only knew what, this was what had finally felled him: a plastic bag. I had thought that maybe I worried about Homer too much—but apparently, I hadn't been worried enough. For all the foresight I tried to command in keeping his home environment safe, there were dangers lurking that neither of us had foreseen.

Homer quickly bounced back from his near-death experience. After half an hour of burrowing his face so far into my chest that it was like he was trying to find a way inside my body, he fell into a deep sleep and woke up refreshed and ready for more trouble. Vashti was in the other room nosing around a bottlecap she'd found, and Homer bounded to her side, hoping to get in on the action. The plastic bag, and its attendant moments of terror, seemed completely forgotten.

But it stuck with me for a long time. I kept a much closer eye on Homer after that, unwilling to let him do much more than walk in a straight line across the floor. Anything more daring earned him a swift and inarguable *"No, Homer!"*

EVEN AS A KITTEN Homer was far more verbal than most cats, and more sensitively attuned to the sound of my voice. If it had been too long since I'd last spoken to him, Homer would paw at my leg and mew insistently. When I did talk, he would sit in front of me with a serious expression on his face, cocking his head from side to side as if attempting to decipher the meaning of my words. Cats are notorious for being untrainable, but Homer knew his name and responded to simple commands. The sound of my *"No!"* always brought him to an immediate halt, no matter how clear it was that he wanted to continue whatever he was doing.

After weeks of my reprimanding Homer whenever he attempted anything more adventurous than playing with his favorite toy, a small stuffed worm with a bell in its tail that had first belonged to Scarlett, a new meow was added to his vocabulary. I thought of this as his "checking in" meow. If he wanted to climb a tall piece of furniture, or forage in the bottom recesses of a closet, he would check in with me first. *Mew? Can I?*

"No, Homer," was the almost invariable response.

Can I follow Scarlett and Vashti onto the screened-in porch? "No, Homer." *Can I climb up to that small empty shelf on the entertainment center?* "No, Homer." *Can I bat around these cords on the Venetian blinds?* "Good God, Homer! Do you know how quickly those cords could wrap around your neck and strangle you?"

I could tell that Homer was becoming anxious and frustrated. To act boldly, to investigate every intriguing sound or smell he came across, was in his nature. Holding himself back was not. But if an errant plastic bag could be the cause of a near household tragedy, who knew where else perils were hiding? As much a I hated myself for constantly thwarting him, I was sure I was doing the right thing.

Sure, that is, until one day when Melissa observed me forbidding Homer from climbing up a ladder-back chair. *He's so little,* I thought. *And that chair looks so high!* "You know," Melissa said, "I think you may be over-parenting him." When I didn't respond, she added, "Come on, Gwen, give him some space. You'll end up raising him all stunted and nervous."

That was easy for Melissa to say. Melissa wasn't the one who was responsible for Homer. The world was a dangerous place for a blind kitten, and I had made a promise to Patty, to Homer, and to myself—not a promise spoken aloud, but certainly there'd been an understanding—that I would make the world safe for Homer. Even if "the world" that Homer occupied was confined to the square footage of our home.

But did I want to do that at the expense of Homer's high spirits and sense of adventure?

You don't normally think about how you're going to "raise" a pet. You bring him home, train him as necessary, teach him a few tricks or commands, and then simply enjoy each other's presence.

I was twenty-five at the time, and not accustomed to thinking about how I wanted anybody's life to turn out other than my own. But now I found myself thinking about Homer's life and how I wanted to raise him—what kind of, for lack of a better way of putting it, person I wanted him to grow up to be.

When I put it to myself that way, the answer was simple. I didn't want him to be crippled by fear and self-doubt. I wanted him to be as independent and "normal" as I already made a point of telling everybody he was.

AFTER A HARD DAY at work a few nights later, I decided to relax in a warm bath. Homer followed me into the bathroom, greeting me with a high-pitched *mew?* that meant he was asking permission to jump onto the ledge of the tub so I could pet him while I bathed.

My first impulse was to refuse, afraid he might lose his balance and fall into the tub. But I found myself wondering...why shouldn't I let him? The water wasn't especially hot. It wasn't like he was going to get soap in his eyes, and he wouldn't drown as long as I was there to catch him. So I said, in a tone I knew Homer would recognize as encouraging, "Okay, Homer-Bear, you can come up if you want to."

Homer scrabbled his way onto the ledge of the tub, and it was all of about thirty seconds before he slipped on the tile and fell into the water. He flailed around for half a second, but by the time I had reached over to assist him, his front legs had found the side of the tub and he was already lifting himself out.

I climbed out also. If there's one thing that's the stuff of cats' nightmares, it's sudden and total immersion in water. I would have thought the experience would be even more nightmarish for Homer, who had probably had no idea that water existed in larger quantities than what could be found in his water bowl. I picked him up in one hand, expecting him to be scared stiff. But the rhythm of his heart was as steady and untroubled as if he were lying on my chest at night, waiting to fall asleep.

Homer's thoroughly drenched fur stuck out from his body at crazy angles that would have been comical under different circumstances. I reached for a towel to dry him off. As soon as he felt the stroke of the cloth, however, he squirmed and struggled until I put him down on the ground, where he promptly began to lick himself clean. Water-rumpled though he was, there was dignity in his posture. *I can do it myself!*

"Okay, Homer," I said quietly. I opened the bathroom door a crack so that Homer could leave if he wanted to and stepped back into the tub.

I assumed that Homer would bolt as quickly as he could from what had proven to be an aquatic chamber of horrors. But there was an overhead heat lamp in the bathroom. It was, I suppose, as good a place to dry off as any.

Homer leapt back onto the ledge of the tub, stepping carefully for a moment or two until he found a spot that was still dry. Then, with an enormous yawn, he settled down to doze peacefully while I bathed.

7 • Gwen Doesn't Live Here Anymore

Zeus does not bring all men's plans to fulfillment.
– HOMER, *The Odyssey*

HOMER WAS JUST OVER five months old when Melissa told me the time had come for me to find a place of my own.

Melissa and I hadn't been friends for very long—only a few months—when I'd broken up with Jorge and she'd invited me to move in with her. Our friendship was one that had sprung up suddenly, and we'd come to feel so extraordinarily close within such a short period of time that we hadn't actually been as comfortable with each other as we'd thought before we became roommates.

The reason on paper for my eviction was that Melissa had another friend who needed a place to stay for a while. Neither of us had expected, when I'd first moved in, that I would end up staying the nearly seven months I'd been there. Our mutual concern for Homer had smoothed over numerous small, day-to-day tensions, but undoubtedly, had it not been for Homer, I would have moved out long ago.

"Homer's welcome to stay as long as you need him to," Melissa rushed to assure me. "I'd be happy to keep him."

My nonspecific life plan, up until I adopted Homer, had been to scrape by on my current nonprofit salary, living with roommates until some hazy, undetermined future date when I would either land a big enough promotion to be entirely self-sufficient or get married. Neither a big salary boost nor wedding bells seemed to be in my immediate future, however. Nor did I have any friends who were hunting for roommates. Under different circumstances, I might have scoured the classifieds for some up-and-coming professional girl of about my own age who would have been happy to split rent and share a home with my two relatively mellow cats.

I didn't have two cats anymore, though. Now I had three.

Three cats were a lot to ask somebody else to live with—especially when one of them, Homer, was active enough for five. And I was still (and always) concerned enough about Homer's safety that the restrictions I would impose on somebody else's home life could be both unfair and unattractive. In addition to super-hearing and super-smell, Homer of late had developed super-speed. He was frantic to know what lay on the other side of the front door to Melissa's house, through which people disappeared and didn't come back for hours at a time. As soon as he heard keys jangling outside, Homer would race for the door at breathtaking speed—less cat than comet-like black blur—hurling himself through even the smallest crack between door and door frame and making it halfway down the driveway on a few occasions before Melissa or I could catch him.

The one thing that could *never* be permitted was for Homer to get lost outdoors. To thwart our little would-be Houdini, we were forced to enter the front door of the house sideways, keeping the door closed as far as possible while still allowing ourselves just enough space to squeeze through, one leg extended at Homer-level to block him from slipping past.

How could I ask a stranger to live that way? How could I ask somebody to childproof toilets or tie closed sliding closet doors (which Homer was a whiz at prying open) without sounding like a nut?

And even if I could ask somebody to do those things, and I found somebody who was willing, could I trust somebody else? Anybody I lived with would have to be someone *I knew* was 100 percent trustworthy. Where would I find such a person?

These were questions without good answers. To keep Homer would mean that I had to have a place of my own. But I could no more afford a place of my own than I could grow Homer's eyes back for him.

When I reached this point in my calculations, I started giving serious thought to Melissa's request. (And it was a request, not an offer—because Melissa loved Homer and wanted to keep him almost as much as I did.) I'd like to say that I never so much as considered her proposition, that I made some grand pronouncement along the lines of *Whither I goest, this kitten shall go, too.*

But I did consider it.

I even told myself it might be better for Homer in the long run. One of the biggest challenges for a blind cat was getting to know the space he lived in. A sudden move to a new home would be a big jolt for him. He knew Melissa's home intimately, and she was likely to stay there for a while.

It took him all of forty-eight hours to figure out his way around Melissa's house, I reminded myself. *Don't pretend you think he'd be traumatized by a new place.*

I spent the next few days hoping for some kind of epiphany, for a crystalline moment of insight and clarity that would show me what, precisely, was the right thing to do.

It was a moment that never came. Instead, I found myself more aware of small things—of the way, for example, I was the only one who could tell when Homer was deeply asleep, as opposed to half awake, by the slight tension of the muscles in his face that would have controlled his eyelids. A sudden gust of air would also cause those muscles to contract, closing eyelids that weren't there to protect the eyes he didn't have.

I noticed how Homer was never content merely to lie next to me. If he wanted to sleep beside me, he would press his face against the outside of my thigh, then turn his head slightly and slide all the way down to my knee, the rest of his body following behind so that, by the time he had settled into his sleeping position, he was wedged as tightly against me—with as many points of contact between us—as he could possibly achieve. If Homer was sleeping on his own, he would curl himself up into the tightest ball he could manage, his tail coiled around his nose and his front paws wrapped around his face. Melissa and I laughed at what looked like somebody who was determined not to allow even the slightest hint of light to disturb his slumber; Homer, of course, wouldn't have been able to detect any light on his face.

But I knew it was because, no matter how reckless he was when he played, Homer always felt vulnerable in sleep. It was only when he was sleeping on or next to me that the tension went out of his sleeping posture, that he might lie on his side with his paws still curled beneath him but not hugged defensively around his body.

I had important decisions to make, but there is no logic in some things. Watching Homer sleep with his paws clutched protectively over what should have been his eyes, my heart would break. *Too late, too late!* I would think, with a degree of pity that seemed unwarranted when he was in one of his more boisterous waking moods. He trusted me, more than he trusted anybody else. Hadn't I committed, not so long ago, to being strong enough to build my life around Homer's goodness? Things would have to be far worse than they were for me to decide that either of us would be better off without the other.

So I was once again back to my impossible situation. I needed a place of my own, but I couldn't afford it. I could afford to live with somebody else, but I couldn't live with somebody else and also live with Homer. I couldn't leave Homer because...

Because I simply couldn't leave him.

And this is where the moment of epiphany did, finally, kick in.

If I couldn't afford to support myself and Homer given my current career path, then I would simply have to find a more lucrative career. There were skills and interests I'd developed during my nonprofit stint that, surely, would prove valuable in the private sector. I wrote newsletters and press releases and coordinated networking events and volunteer projects and fundraisers, and I wrangled television and newspaper reporters to cover all of these things. I managed budgets and served as the public face of my organization on many occasions, and I was outgoing and did a pretty good job of interacting with the public in general.

This sounded a lot like the jobs of the friends I had who worked in public relations and event marketing. Even the ones who were still young enough that they earned what was considered an entry-level salary topped my own salary by a good fifty percent.

But I also knew that people hadn't simply walked into those jobs. They'd had marketing or communications majors in college (my own major had been creative writing), and they'd spent summers interning and months freelancing for the kinds of firms they eventually went to work for.

If starting over was what I needed to do, and if interning and taking freelance jobs was what it would take to make that happen, I was willing to do all those things. I was even willing to pick up side jobs bartending or waiting tables at night, so that my days would be available to work cheap-to-free until I gained experience and found something permanent.

But that put me right back where I started—because doing all of that, even if I were willing, would put me no closer to being able to afford my own apartment in the short term. This was a plan that could pay off in a year or two, that could make Homer's and my life more stable in the long run, but I needed a new home for us *now*. And that was when I had my second epiphany.

I called my parents.

"Of course you can move back in," my mother said. "And of course you can bring the cats."

I knew this had cost her something. Not only did my parents dislike cats on general principle, they also had two dogs who'd been with my family since I was in high school. Adjustments would have to be made by everybody to make this situation feasible—and by "everybody," I didn't just mean the cats and dogs.

"Are you sure this is okay?" I asked my mother. "I know you guys don't really like cats."

"We love you," my mother replied, "and you love the cats." Then she laughed and said, "Besides, if you think living with cats is the biggest sacrifice your father and I have made as parents, you don't know what being a parent means."

Maybe not. But I was starting to get an inkling.

8 • The Ballad of El Mocho

Bless my heart, how he gets honoured and makes friends whatever city or country he visits.
– HOMER, *The Odyssey*

EVEN WITHOUT THE CATS, moving back in with my parents would have been an enormous adjustment. Would they treat me like I was still in high school, questioning me every time I went out and inquiring who I was meeting and when I'd be back? Would they attempt to exercise parental authority over things like the tidiness of my bedroom?

Adding the cats to the mix would make things even more complicated. I wanted to figure out practical ways to keep the cats out of my parents' way, and to keep the cats and dogs separated from each other, while still allowing everybody as much liberty as possible. Throw in all the standard confusion involved in a move—boxes to be unpacked, closets and shelves to be stocked, items to be sorted through and placed in storage—and it was clear that, ideally, there would be a time buffer of a couple of weeks between the day I arrived back on my parents' doorstep and the day the cats joined me.

So I decided to make my second difficult phone call in as many weeks. I called Jorge.

Jorge still lived in the home we'd shared when Scarlett and Vashti were adopted. The two of them knew the house, and they also knew Jorge. Homer didn't know either, but Jorge was part of a large extended family that was, collectively, even crazier about animals than I was. He'd grown up with more cats, dogs, birds, gerbils, hamsters, and goldfish than anybody I'd met.

We had communicated a few times since the breakup, in that strained and awkward way you end up talking to your ex during the early weeks after you're no longer together—when your rationalization is, *Hey, we can still be friends*. Such conversations had decreased as the months went by. I never ended one without a strong sense of remembering why it was we'd broken up in the first place. I was positive Jorge felt the same way.

Nevertheless, if somebody had asked me to name the one person I would have trusted with my cats if I were unable to take care of them, I would have named Jorge without hesitation.

Jorge was more than accommodating when I pitched the idea of having the three cats stay with him for two weeks while I got things set up at my parents' house. "I'd love to see Scarlett and Vashti again," he said. "And I'll take good care of Homer."

I gave Jorge the basic rundown of Homer dos and don'ts ("My advice to you: Don't keep tuna in your house while he's there.") and some new issues that had cropped up in the past few months. It turned out that moist cat food gave Homer tremendous gas—it was astounding that one small kitten could produce such huge, horrible smells—but Vashti had been through a recent bout of colitis and was temporarily off dry food, making feedings more complicated than they used to be. I promised to stock Jorge with everything he'd need to care for the cats, as well as some written instructions.

My only concern was how Homer would bear the separation. He hadn't been apart from me for so much as twenty-four hours in the six months since I'd brought him home. The day I dropped the cats with Jorge, I pretended to leave something behind half a dozen times so I could run back and peek in on him before driving off. The last time I tried it, mumbling something about a lipstick I was *positive* had tumbled out of my purse, Jorge said in exasperation, "*Go!* I've been taking care of cats longer than you have. We'll be fine."

I waited two days before going over again to check on everybody, although I called Jorge nightly to ask how the cats were doing, particularly Homer. "He's fine," Jorge told me. "He's having a great time here, actually."

I soon discovered why. When I arrived at Jorge's house for my first visit, the first thing I saw was one of Jorge's friends with a palm high in the air, upon which Homer rested on his belly, all four legs dangling down. Jorge's friend was spinning Homer around and around rapidly, making airplane noises as he spun.

"Are you *crazy?!*" I exclaimed. "*Put him down now!*"

Jorge's friend, looking both startled and shamefaced, hastily complied. Homer staggered, punch drunk, for a moment (as well he should be), but after recovering his balance he stretched his front paws beseechingly up the side of Jorge's friend's leg. *Again! Again!*

"You see? He loves it!" Jorge's friend insisted proudly. Then, affecting the mock-deep intonations of a wrestling announcer, he added, "For he is *El Mocho*, the cat without fear!"

I raised an eyebrow at Jorge. "*El Mocho*? Is that what we're calling him now?"

Jorge grinned and shrugged. "Well, you know how these things take on a life of their own."

Mocho was a Spanish word that meant *maimed* or referred to something that had been lopped off like a stump. To call Homer *el mocho* was, essentially, to call him "Stumpy" or "the maimed one."

It doesn't sound particularly flattering, but among Spanish speakers the giving of nicknames is tantamount to a declaration of love. Things that would sound insulting outright in English were tokens of deep affection when said in Spanish.

"He likes his new name," Jorge's friend chimed in. "Watch this. *Ven aca, Mochito.*" Homer's ears pricked up and he trotted right over to Jorge's friend, sitting on his haunches at full attention.

"Oh, Homer," I said mournfully. "Have a little dignity."

"He has nothing but dignity," Jorge's friend protested, his eyes alight with humor. "He is *El Mocho*. It is the code of *El Mocho* to meet all opponents with dignity and honor on the field of battle."

Even I had to laugh at that one.

Homer adjusted to Jorge's home with an enthusiasm I found almost unsettling. Jorge reported that, after the first day or so, Homer was able to find his way around without bumping into anything. And he absolutely adored Jorge's friends, all of whom insisted on calling him *El Mocho*.

Homer had been used to living with a bunch of girls, none of whom—as it turned out—were willing to play as rough-and-tumble with him as he would have liked. Jorge and his friends were more than happy to chase Homer around the furniture in elaborate games of tag, which ended when

Homer sprang out from under a bed or behind a table leg to attack their ankles. They tossed and spun him a good six feet in the air (I learned of this later, because after that first incident they were careful not to do it when I was around), or flipped him onto his back and wrestled him around. During one visit, I noticed that Homer, as soon as a couple of Jorge's friends walked in, rolled immediately onto his back and pawed frantically at the air with one leg, in a posture that practically begged, *C'mon, rough me up!*

"He walks around the house at night crying," Jorge told me after the first week. "He won't sleep with me. He'll only sleep near Scarlett. I think he misses you."

I felt a twinge of guilt—although, I'm ashamed to admit, it was reassuring to receive some small sign that Homer missed me, at least a little.

"And where's Scarlett sleeping?" I asked.

"Anywhere I'm not." Jorge gave a rueful laugh. "You're the only one she was ever friendly to."

"One more week," I said. "I promise."

But the cats wouldn't end up staying at Jorge's house another week. On day nine, I got a call from him. "Somebody's been peeing all over the house."

"Hey, I've told you for years that you shouldn't let your friends drink all that light beer."

"I'm serious, Gwen."

I sighed. "All right, I'm sorry. Which one and where?"

"I haven't caught anybody in the act, but whoever it is peed on the sofa, my laundry bag with all my clothes in it, and my new leather jacket." He paused. "I think it's Scarlett."

"It's not Scarlett," I responded immediately. "It's Vashti."

"Has she done this before?" He sounded annoyed, and I could tell he was wondering why, with all the minutiae I'd prepped him with beforehand, I hadn't bothered to mention this small problem.

"No, she hasn't. But I'm sure it's her."

"If she hasn't done it before, how can you be sure?"

"A mother knows," I said wryly.

It was a simple process of elimination, really. I knew why Jorge thought it was Scarlett—because Scarlett, as I mentioned earlier, had a definite perception problem on account of her unfriendliness. Scarlett was so "mean" that, presumably, she was exactly the kind of cat who would pee with abandon all over somebody's house out of pure malice.

But Scarlett, mean though she was (to other people), was fastidious about her litter box. There were minimum acceptable standards of cleanliness, specific brands of litter that had to be provided, and a modicum of privacy that she absolutely insisted upon. I couldn't imagine her doing anything as *plebian* as urinating out in the open like some common street cat.

As for Homer, this was clearly a spite peeing—Homer didn't even have a concept of spite.

That left Vashti. And it made sense, when I thought about it. Vashti had been the worst off of any of them when I'd taken her in. Homer and Scarlett had come to my home after spending days at the vet's office, where they'd been treated and fed before being sent to their new home. Vashti had been found by a coworker of my mother's at the elementary school where she taught. They'd locked her in a toolshed to keep her from wandering off while my mother did the only thing she could think of to do for a kitten. She called me.

I'd gone down to my mother's school on my lunch break, stopping at the pet store for a small carrier and some Similac, and brought Vashti back to my office. I'd honestly thought, that first day, that Vashti's pink nose was black, so encrusted was it with dirt. Through the bald patches on her skin that the mange had left, I could feel her bones poking through, and her ears were bloody and swollen from ear mites. I'd kept Vashti warm on my lap throughout the afternoon, feeding her the Similac through a dropper, until I was able to get her to the vet's office that evening. She'd come home to live with us the following morning.

In a way that was different from Scarlett and Homer, who'd come to me through other hands, I think Vashti truly believed I'd saved her life. It was Vashti who always gazed at me with undiluted hero-worship in her eyes. I hadn't considered the difficulties she might face in being left at Jorge's house, which was the first home she'd ever known. Insofar as I was her "mother," Jorge was her "father." We had adopted her together, and I knew he loved her.

Vashti loved him, too. But after one too many visits to Jorge's house, when I'd ended up leaving without her, something must have clicked in Vashti's mind. She must have thought she'd been taken back to Jorge's and left there forever, that I was never going to live with her again.

My guess was that Vashti was sending a message. And the message was: *I'm not living anywhere without Mom.*

My suspicions were confirmed the next day when Jorge called to tell me he'd caught Vashti in the act of peeing on his stove. Since she had failed to communicate her point the first few times—as evidenced by the fact that she was still with Jorge and not with me—she'd obviously decided to escalate matters. I marveled at the idea of Vashti jumping all the way up to the countertop stove—Vashti who, to my knowledge, had never once jumped half that height in her entire life.

"I'm sorry," Jorge told me, "but she has to go."

"I'll come get them tonight," I replied.

Loading the cats into their carriers was never an easy task, but for once Vashti climbed in as eagerly as if she were crawling into my lap. I put Homer in last; since he couldn't see the carriers, he didn't run and hide the second they were brought out. He spent his last few minutes in Jorge's house playing with Jorge's friends, charter members of the *El Mocho* fan club, who'd come to see him off. They held small bits of the tuna Jorge hadn't been able to resist buying high in the air, encouraging Homer to leap straight up and grab the tuna from their fingers. "*Salta, Mochito!*" (*Salta* being Spanish for *jump*.) As I deposited Homer into his carrier, Jorge's friends cried, "No, no! The other two, they can go, but *El Mocho* can stay!"

"You know, he *is* welcome to stay if that would make things easier for you," Jorge said.

For a kitten nobody had wanted, the offers to take Homer off my hands certainly seemed to be piling up.

"Sorry, guys," I said. "They're a package deal."

The one profitable outcome of this episode in Homer's life (I use the word *profitable* loosely, because I practically bankrupted myself repaying Jorge for the damage Vashti had caused) was that I was decidedly less anxious about Homer's ability to adjust to life in my parents' house. With all the concerns I had for Homer over the years, I never again worried about his ability to adapt to new spaces and new people. Even my parents' dogs no longer felt like the impassable barrier to Homer's happiness that I had been agonizing over.

For he was *El Mocho*, The Cat Without Fear.

Viva El Mocho!

9 • "Dogs and Cats, Living Together..."

There is nothing dearer to a man than his own country and his own parents, and however splendid a home he may have elsewhere, if it be far from his father or mother, he does not care about it.

– HOMER, *The Odyssey*

PERHAPS SAYING EARLIER THAT my parents didn't like cats was an unfair characterization. It would be more accurate to say that my father, who owned his own medical auditing business, wasn't so much anti-cat as he was staunchly pro-dog. But he was also more sensitive when it came to animals generally than just about anybody else I knew. He was one of those people with an ability to understand and respond to an animal's emotional state that went beyond simple compassion and seemed almost to be direct communion. Of all the stray, abused, and abandoned dogs that had come through our home over the years, there had never been one—no matter how traumatized or skittish—who had failed to melt into warm affection in my father's presence, even if that warmth was reserved for my father alone. It was my father I'd always thought of when I'd volunteered at animal shelters, hoping to capture at least some of whatever mysterious ability he had.

My mother, on the other hand, when she was a small child had seen a cat kill a bird. She, too, was capable of deep compassion where just about any animal was concerned, but the trauma of this single act of feline avicide had left her, as she put it, incapable of emotionally investing in cats the way she could in dogs.

"Cats aren't loving and loyal the way dogs are," she'd say. Upon hearing my own cats indirectly maligned in this fashion, I was tempted to ask her what, exactly, in her zero years of cat companionship, qualified her to make such an assessment.

Remembering the fruitless dinner-table political arguments of my adolescence, however, I forbore. I considered this forbearance a mark of the maturity I'd attained since I'd last lived with my parents.

That my parents were willing to take the four of us in, despite their antipathy toward cats, was a testament to how much they were willing to do for me—even though we weren't as close at that time as, perhaps, we could have been. It wasn't so much that there was any overt hostility between my parents and me; but where some of my friends had drifted with seeming effortlessness into adult relationships with their parents, my own parents and I were still figuring it out. I often thought I heard a distinct grownup-talking-to-a-child tone when they spoke to me—and, as it was uncomfortably close to some of my own darker insecurities about myself, I resented it accordingly.

More than anything else, I wanted to make them proud of me. But it didn't seem as if I'd done much in my post-college life thus far to inspire pride, unless you counted one major failed relationship and being broke enough to require my moving back in with them.

But my parents were willing to take the four of us in, and they were even willing to divide their house into "cat zones" and "dog zones." Casey, a yellow Lab mix, and Brandi, a miniature cocker spaniel, had been with my family since I was a teenager. They were always giddily thrilled whenever I turned up at my parents' for a visit, following me closely and looking doleful if I so much as walked past the front door, anticipating the moment when I would leave and not return for days or weeks. If I spent the night, the two of them would pile into bed with me, as they'd done when I was still in high school.

Once I'd been living in my parents' house again for a week and change, the novelty of having me around wore off a bit and they weren't so apt to follow me *everywhere*. This was something I'd counted on; conflicting demands on my time and attention from the dog and cat camps wouldn't engender the kind of mutual goodwill I was hoping for.

But I realized there was only so far diplomacy would go. Cat/dog animosity was at least as old as history itself, and neither my cats nor my parents' dogs had ever been called upon to share quarters with members of the opposing faction. Remembering the dictum that "good fences make good neighbors," my parents and I retrieved the folding wooden childproof gates from the storage spot they'd occupied since my younger sister and I were toddlers. "I knew we'd end up using them again," my mother said, although not without tossing me a glance that added, *Of course, I thought we'd be using them for our grandchildren.*

The gates attached to the walls with suction cups and reached about waist-high on the average adult. We put them up where a hallway split off to my bedroom and another bedroom, connected by an adjoining bathroom—effectively creating a three-room apartment that the dogs would be unable to access. I conducted a rigorous cleaning—trying to eliminate as much anxiety-inducing dog smell as I could—then installed cat beds, scratching posts, litter box, and food and water bowls. The cats' new home was complete.

"What do you guys think?" I asked the cats when I brought them in for the first time.

Scarlett and Vashti crept forward cautiously from the safety of their carriers, noses to the ground and ears at full attention. Casey barked in the other room, and they immediately scrambled under the bed. It was two hours before I could get them to do more than peek their whiskers out through the bed's eyeleted dust ruffle, a relic of my preteen years.

Homer was unfazed, however. His ears flicked momentarily at Casey's barking, but he was more interested in exploring what was in front of him. Homer had never encountered anything with the texture of the '70s-style shag carpeting in my childhood bedroom. He spent a few minutes stalking carefully through the carpet strands that reached halfway to his chin—a black panther in perfect miniature prowling an electric-blue savanna. Once he realized the superior traction carpet afforded, far better than the hardwood or tile floors he was used to, Homer took off at a run, racing in blurred circles around the room and bouncing off walls and furniture like a rubber ball fired from a slingshot. *Yippee! Look how fast I can go in here!*

"He's a little nut, isn't he?" my mother, who hadn't been able to resist a quick peek, observed.

"You have no idea," I replied.

Despite some of the concerns I'd had before moving in, my parents didn't unduly interfere with my day-to-day activities. I did tend to let them know, as I was walking out the door, where I was going and approximately when I'd be back, but it was a level of basic courtesy that I would have extended to friendly roommates. The majority of my friends still lived on South Beach, and there were inevitable late nights, but my parents refrained from asking intrusive questions.

What I hadn't counted on ahead of time was being on the receiving end of their parenting advice when it came to the cats.

"I don't think you're giving them fresh water often enough," my mother announced one afternoon, a few weeks after we'd moved in. "I checked on them while you were out, and poor Vashti was standing next to her water bowl making such sad eyes at me. I refilled it for her and the poor thing acted like she hadn't seen clean water in days."

I *always* changed the cats' water twice daily—once in the morning and once in the evening. And "poor Vashti" was something of a con artist when it came to her water bowl. Vashti was a cat who, oddly enough, was obsessed with water. She loved to hold her paws under running faucets, immerse them up to her shoulder joint in full drinking glasses, and roll around in recently used showers while the tile was still wet. The refilling of her water bowl was one of the high points of her day; the beguiling roll of water caused by setting a full bowl on the ground mesmerized her, and she gave me no peace most mornings until I'd recreated this daily miracle for her.

I was about to explain this to my mother when a new thought occurred to me. "Wait a second—what were you doing with them in the first place?"

"Well, I wanted to say hello to Vashti," my mother replied. She emphasized Vashti's name in a way that meant there was a difference between *cats*, which she didn't care for, and *Vashti*, who merited a degree of interest. "I *am* the one who found her when she was a kitten."

"Yes, you did." I smiled. "And you sent her to a good home, one where she gets all the fresh water she needs."

A few days later, my father piped up with a suggestion of his own. "I don't think the cats have enough toys," he said. My father was the kind of indulgent dad who brought home new toys for the dogs every few days, to the point that my parents' otherwise immaculate house looked like a chew toy graveyard. "You should buy more toys for them."

"They're not like the dogs, Dad," I explained. "They're not into store-bought toys." This was true, with the exception of that stuffed worm Homer still loved dearly. The bag that new toys came in was always an adventure—a large paper bag made an excellent cat fort. The receipt for the toys could be crumpled up into a ball that a cat could bat around and chase. The plastic wrapping around the toys was a bonanza for Scarlett, who loved nothing more than licking plastic wrap. (If a genie were to grant me the wish of the cats' being able to talk for a single day, the first question I would ask is, *What's so great about licking plastic bags?!*) But the toys themselves held little interest for my brood.

"You should really do something about Scarlett," my mother said once. This was after she had found me reading a book with a purring Scarlett curled in my lap. She'd held out her hand and Scarlett sniffed it. Taking this as encouragement, my other had attempted to pet Scarlett, who had hissed and recoiled from my mother's touch so forcefully that her head nearly bruised my breastbone. "Brandi used to be afraid of new people, and look how well she does now."

"Scarlett isn't afraid of people, Mom," I told her. "Scarlett *doesn't like* people."

The problem could be summed up in a nutshell: My parents were trying to dog my cats. Having never spent much time around cats, they tried to take the accumulated knowledge of more than three decades of dog ownership and apply it to these strange new creatures who now inhabited their home. To the extent that the cats' reactions differed from a dog's, it was most likely because I didn't yet have enough experience being responsible for pets.

I tried to weather their input with good grace, but it was hard. I was my parents' child, reflexively defensive at any perceived parental criticism. I was also my "children's" parent, bristling instantly at the slightest implication that I wasn't caring for them properly, or that they were anything other than exactly what they should be.

But the one thing I could plainly see—that touched me, even though I was never very good at articulating it—was that my parents were trying. They were trying to care about the cats, to interest themselves in their happiness and wellbeing.

I had worried that my parents would treat me like a child. Maybe, in talking to me about being a parent, they were trying the best way they know how to treat me like an adult.

It was only when it came to Homer that my parents were abashed to offer advice or constructive criticism. This was understandable. The idea of a pet who was blind—and not just blind, but eyeless—was far enough beyond their experience to feel exotic and mysterious. They often observed that, "you *do* seem to understand him," and left it at that.

Homer initially inspired more pity in my parents than anything else. The most frustrating fact of life for Homer in my parents' home was that he was confined to only a few rooms—rooms I wasn't necessarily in when I was in the house. Homer would sit at the childproof gate and wail piteously if he heard me talking in the kitchen or down the hall.

"Poor baby," my mother would say, real empathy in her voice. "Life must be so hard for him."

It wasn't life that Homer found hard to bear, of course. It was his enforced separation from me and from the other human voices he could hear but never meet. Homer didn't understand a world in which I was present but not with him, in which there were other people who didn't exist solely to befriend and play with him.

It wasn't long into our stay before Homer made his first daring escape from behind the childproof gate. I customarily slid it open just far enough to allow myself entry to or exit from the cat-designated portion of the house. One day, as I was entering, Homer sort of flattened himself sideways and pressed through the mere inches of space between my leg and the wall, like toothpaste being squeezed from a tube. He didn't get very far that time; being unfamiliar with the layout of my parents' house, he stopped to get his bearings after only a few feet.

That was the first time.

Homer was impossible to contain after that. I tried to prevent him from squeezing past me by climbing over the gate rather than opening it, but that just gave Homer the idea of jumping over it himself. Vashti and Scarlett could have jumped over the gate all along, but the two of them didn't especially like to jump—nor were they anxious to encounter the dogs who dwelled on the other side of the gate. Homer had no such compunctions. The only thing holding him back had been his belief that, unable to see the gate's true dimensions, it must have stretched all the way up to infinity. Once he realized its actual height was more like three feet, there was no stopping him.

My parents, as so many before them, were astounded at how quickly Homer learned his way around their home. A sharp right turn out of (or over) the gate brought him into the main hallway. An equally sharp left turn, precisely fifteen full-tilt gallops down, brought him into the living room. A couch to the left of the living room's entry was flush against the wall and a cinch to climb. Four or five steps along the top of it and he could clamber down behind an end table—wedged in a corner between the couch and the love seat—and hunker down into a spot where it was impossible for humans to follow and catch him. Although, while I was reaching for him over and around the couch, it was easy enough to dart through the legs of the end table, up the side of the love seat, back down onto the ground behind me, and off to farther points unknown.

"That cat's a *meshugana!*" my mother always said in a kind of wonder upon witnessing Homer's feats of speed, dexterity, and *chutzpah*.

"It shouldn't be this hard to catch a blind kitten," my father, gasping slightly, insisted after a chase that had taken him all the way down the other main hall, into my parents' bedroom, under and over their bed, and had finally culminated atop my mother's vanity.

In this way, it became inevitable that Homer's daring would bring him face-to-face with Cassey and Brandi. Like Odysseus encountering Cyclopes and Sirens, Homer one day came upon these foreign and heretofore undreamed-of beasts for the very first time.

Case was a fairly large and tightly muscled dog, although also extraordinarily gentle. Upon running into her (literally) for the first time, Homer didn't hiss and flee the way Scarlett and Vashti did whenever they thought Casey had strayed too close to the gate separating them. Homer puffed himself up as far as his hair follicles would allow and crouched down defensively, his nostrils going wild as he inhaled and processed Casey's dog smell. *What the heck* is *this thing?* His attempt to make himself appear bigger to Casey, who weighed more than eighty pounds, would have been comical if I didn't realize how scared he must be.

Homer reached out one tiny, tentative paw to touch Casey's nose and face. I hovered a few inches away, ready to snatch Homer up at the first sign of growls or aggression. Casey sniffed him with great interest as Homer stood stock-still, almost holding his breath. Then Casey's enormous pink tongue, bigger than Homer's whole head, descended onto his face. Homer's facial muscles contracted, and I knew that if he'd had eyelids they would have been screwed shut to protect sensitive areas from this sudden assault of rough wetness. Undeterred by his obvious reluctance, Casey began to lick and groom him methodically.

I don't think Homer cared very much for being groomed by Casey, but he didn't have much choice in the matter if he was unfortunate enough to wind up trapped beneath one of her large paws, which Casey employed to keep a squirming Homer in place while she licked him "clean" from top to bottom. If I wasn't there to separate them, a thoroughly rumpled Homer would end up drenched in dog saliva and spend the next half hour indignantly licking himself free of its odor.

No matter how well you think you understand a pet, there's always a level on which the workings of their mind remains a mystery. I couldn't tell you how Casey, who was intensely loyal to our entire family, understood that Homer—a *cat* –was one of us. But she did. When Homer reached seven months of age and was brought to the vet to be neutered, Casey, according to my parents, sat at the front door and howled for twenty minutes after Homer was taken off in his carrier. When Homer returned, it was Casey who spent two full days guarding the gate that separated her from a groggy, stitched-up Homer. If a car outside backfired or the mailman rang the doorbell, Casey—who had never been anything but affectionate with everybody she'd ever met—raised her hackles and issued a low growl of warning. Whenever Homer turned or whimpered in his sleep during this recovery phase, Casey would yelp an alert, a signal that meant I really ought to check on him.

It took Brandi a bit longer to warm up to Homer. Brandi had a favorite habit of hiding the dog treats my parents gave her in various corners throughout the house. It was infuriating to her that Homer unfailingly sniffed out each and every one of them with the tenacity of a bloodhound. But Brandi was a playful little thing, as was Homer, and she soon discovered the joys of having a playmate who didn't tower over her the way Casey did.

The two of them killed many an hour chasing each other throughout the house, and soon Brandi was even sharing some of her treats with Homer. Her favorite food was baby carrots, and she'd bring them to Homer by the dozen, dropping them at his feet and wagging her tail. She could never understand why Homer's only interest in the carrots was to bat them around and chase after them. Who didn't love eating baby carrots? When Homer would fling them down the hall with his paw, Brandi retrieved them with great patience, depositing them in front of Homer once again and even taking a small bite as if to show him what he was missing. *See? They're for eating, not playing.*

Homer's frequent escapes also brought him into closer contact with my parents. Soon enough, it wasn't unusual for me to come home in the evening to find Homer purring on the couch next to my mother while she stroked his back and worked on a crossword puzzle or watched an old movie. "He looks so comfortable," she would say, almost apologetically. "I didn't want to disturb him."

And I would catch my father awkwardly petting Homer—realizing that the way cats like to be petted is different from dogs, and doing his best to smooth Homer's fur in an even, soothing fashion. "Who's a good boy? Who's such a good boy?"

Homer often brought his stuffed worm along with him when he engineered one of his breakouts, the Bonnie to his Clyde. It became a featured player in his interactions with my father. Homer would toss the stuffed worm up into the air, his head tilted at a slight angle as he listened for the bell in its tail to hit the ground and jingle its precise location. Then he'd pounce on it ferociously, turning onto his back with the worm clutched between his front paws while he kicked at frantically with his hind legs, as if to indicate the worm was putting up a fierce struggle. Having finally "subdued" the bedraggled thing, he would carry it over to my father and drop it at his feet—sitting eagerly in a posture that suggested he was waiting for my father to throw the worm across the room so Homer could wrestle it into submission and bring it over to him once again.

"He wants to play fetch with me!" my father would say, as if this dog-like behavior was a revelatory code understood only between the two of them.

It was during one of these games of fetch, a couple of months after Homer was neutered, that my father turned to me and said, "You did a good thing, you know." He threw the worm for Homer to catch and, as he watched Homer tear across the room, he said it again. "You did a good thing for this cat."

My eyes, quite unexpectedly, filled with tears.

"Thanks, Dad," I said.

10 • Running on Faith

I saw Sisyphus at his endless task, raising h is prodigious stone with both his hands. Staining with hands and feet, he tried to roll it up to the top of the hill, but always, just before he could roll it over onto the other side, the pitiless stone would come thundering down. Then he would begin trying to push it uphill again.

– HOMER, *The Odyssey*

I WORKED HARD OVER the next year and a half, starting over again at the entry level career-wise. I worked internships, freelance jobs, low-paying jobs, no-paying jobs, and anything else that had the slightest chance of adding another line of experience to my résumé. To augment my alarmingly slim earnings, I took additional work tending bar at some of South Beach's more upscale hotels and restaurants—the kinds of places that were likely to close at two a.m. rather than five a.m., granting me a decent shot of at least a few hours' sleep before once again pounding the pavement the next morning.

There were moments of great optimism—a three-month freelance gig with one of the most prestigious PR firms in Miami, which I hoped would eventually lead to a fulltime position; a job assisting in marketing and publicity for a cabaret series of legendary Broadway stars that ran on Miami Beach. I even helped out with fundraising events and press opportunities on behalf of some of the nonprofit organizations I'd cultivated relationships with over the years, this time working in a PR capacity rather than an administrative one.

But there were also days when I felt profoundly discouraged. Full-time PR positions in Miami weren't as plentiful as I'd hoped, and my short-term jobs tended to end as soon as the project I was working on did. Sometimes I told myself that the whole idea of a career change had been a foolish one, that it was obviously impossible for me to start over and actually be successful, even in the very narrow terms by which I would have defined success (i.e. being able to pay rent on a smallish, reasonably well-located apartment). I seemed to have nothing but friends my own age with exciting careers and great apartments, who had assistants and expense accounts, or who were making down payments on their first condos or houses. There were times when I arrived home so exhausted I could cry, with nothing more to show for my day's efforts than the bag of catnip I'd picked up on the way home for Scarlett, Vashti, and Homer.

Homer, by now, had officially transitioned from kittenhood into a full-grown adult cat—although he'd stopped growing around the time he was neutered at seven months, weighing in at a slight five pounds. Homer wasn't short so much as he was narrow and delicate of bone structure. He was lean and sleek, and he walked with a sinuous, leonine grace. When carrying his stuffed worm, Homer would clamp his jaws around what would have been its neck, allowing the rest of its body to dangle between exquisitely formed, exquisitely tiny front paws, making him look like a very small and very dark tiger dragging home a fresh kill. His fur was always groomed to such a high gloss that he seemed to cast light instead of a shadow. Lying in a patch of sunlight, its blackness gleamed cobalt. In response he was like a sculptor's vision of the archetype of a cat, chiseled in perfect black marble.

He was still active to the point of hyperactivity, still in love with running in circles and bouncing off the walls, causing my mother to refer to him affectionately as "a little goofball." He still loved to leap, climb, and explore. But whereas he used to do these things with the reckless imprecision of one who might miss his mark but doesn't care, Homer now moved with the supreme physical confidence of one who knows that falls and failures simply aren't possible—like a ballet dancer who, after years of training, doesn't have to think about how to land flawlessly.

It was Homer's confidence that, in my most disheartened moments, also made me feel the most ashamed of myself. Wasn't Homer the cat who wasn't supposed to be able to do anything? To meet new challenges or be independent? Wasn't he the one who'd inspired me once with his willingness to climb as high as he could without knowing exactly how high he was going, or how he would get back down? Every leap Homer took was a leap of faith. Homer was living proof of the adage that fortune favors the brave, that just because you couldn't see the light at the end of the tunnel didn't mean it wasn't there.

I remembered how, when I'd met Homer for the first time, I'd been impressed with the idea that it was possible to have something within yourself that was strong enough to persevere no matter what. It was an idea that kept me going, even when professionals in my chosen field told me that I had the wrong kind of background and not enough experience, and that despite having a talent for the work, it would be years before I'd land the kind of permanent position I was hoping for. I would struggle against a feeling of panic—if I couldn't support myself doing this, and I couldn't support myself doing what I'd done before, then what was I going to do? *Screw that*, I would think grimly, and there was comfort in the thought. *Nobody could tell Homer what his potential was, and they can't tell me.*

One of the best things I could do to advance my own cause was to make new friends and network. Who knew where word of a great job opening might come from? But sometimes I hated meeting new people during that time. I never liked to admit that I was living with my parents, and the further disclosure that I had three cats (I had friends who delighted in adding this tidbit to my verbal curriculum vitae) drew looks of amazement. Three cats might not sound like a lot to any diehard pet person, but among people my own age in a place like South Beach I was an eccentric. "*Three* cats?" people would say. "*Three*, really?" Even my closest friends sometimes referred to me as "the crazy cat lady," and I could tell that newcomers were mentally deciding that there was nothing less sexy than a twenty-seven-year-old girl who lived with her parents and was, apparently, some kind of fanatical cat collector.

"Well, the first two were planned," I'd say in a breezy fashion. "The third one was an accident." This naturally led to descriptions of Homer and his "special circumstances," always to an enraptured audience. Inevitably, they would ask if Homer could get around on his own, whether he was able to find food and litter, and then they'd speculate about how unhappy an eyeless cat must surely be. Some would even add, probably not meaning to be unkind, that it might have been better had Homer been put to sleep as a kitten.

Something inside me would flare up at such displays of ignorance, but ignorance was better fought with education than anger. "He's a terror," I would tell these people, with enormous pride. "You've never seen such a sure-footed ball of energy in your life." I had vowed not to be the person who talked too much about her cats, not wanting to be the crazy cat lady people suspected me of being. But as soon as I had recounted one of Homer's adventures, listeners wanted to hear more, and then even more.

I tried to remain upbeat during this period in my life, although it often wasn't easy. Homer could sense when my mood was down. He always paid such close attention to the sound of my voice, listening for the slightest change in pitch and cadence, and he knew the difference between how I sounded when I was happy, and how I sounded when I was only pretending to be. He didn't scamper about the way he normally did, choosing instead to rub his face hard against my chin and curl up with me in a spoon position, burrowing as tightly as he could into my midsection, as if he knew my core was where I felt the most hollow. "If it weren't for you, I wouldn't be in this mess, you know," I'd say, only half joking. Homer would crane his neck around to lick my nose with his raspy tongue, purring all the louder.

Sometimes it's possible to know two completely contradictory things at the same time, and to believe with equal certainty that both of them are true. I knew that I loved Homer to an extent that frightened me, that if somebody could wave a magic want and give me a million dollars tomorrow in exchange for Homer, I wouldn't so much as consider taking the deal.

But I also knew that I'd ended up changing my life for him far more than I had anticipated the day I adopted him. I wanted a life with Homer—a life that afforded him absolute safety and freedom in a home of our own. But I also wanted to have the kind of life most of the friends my age had, the kind that was only semi-responsible—where I paid my bills on time and was conscientious about my job, but beyond that was just a kid in my twenties, throwing parties in my apartment and dating a succession of inappropriate, but nevertheless entertaining, men.

Perhaps that was why, on occasion, I lost my temper with Homer. If I came home after an eighteen-hour day, for example, to find that he'd broken some treasured knickknack I'd placed on a shelf I'd believed too high for him to reach; or if I discovered that he'd tossed half a bowl's worth of cat food from its dish into the water bowl—food I'd paid for out of the virtual nothing I scraped by on after putting money into savings for the home we would someday have, food that was wasted and that clotted up the water so Scarlett and Vashti had nothing to drink all day.

My parents, still half convinced by Vashti's shenanigans that I wasn't changing the cats' water frequently enough, would sometimes sneak into my room while I was out and refill the water bowl for them—never remembering to place it far enough away from the food bowl to prevent these incidents. "You have to separate the bowls," I'd remind them, in a tone I meant to be patient but that, when I heard it aloud, sounded anything but. I emphasized the word *separate* and held my hands wide apart, as if I thought visual cues were the only way to drive this point home.

I never yelled at Homer, not wanting to squander the currency I had in being able to stop him in his tracks if he was about to do something dangerous. If I raised my voice too often, about things he couldn't understand and that weren't related to his safety, my authority would, I knew, eventually diminish.

And even at my angriest, I realized he hadn't known he was doing anything wrong, that he was only engaging in the antics I loved him so dearly for most of the time. He couldn't help it if, when exploring a shelf he'd never climbed up to before, he couldn't see that he was about to knock something over and break it. When he was bored, he couldn't sit at a window and watch the world go by the way my other two cats loved to do. Climbing furniture or listening to the sound of food hitting the water kept him entertained, and who was I to begrudge him that?

I never yelled. But when he came bounding over, overjoyed that I was finally home, I would push him brusquely aside. "Why do you have to be so hyper *all the time?*" The tears of frustration that I knew were too ridiculous to allow myself were nonetheless audible in my voice.

Homer didn't understand, but he was perceptive enough to realize I wasn't happy with him at moments like these. He would hang his head and edge toward me meekly, pawing at my leg with a series of anxious *mews*. Nothing put an instant damper on all Homer's joyous high spirits like sensing that I was displeased with him.

Seeing how crushed Homer was always made me feel like a monster. I would relent within a few minutes, reaching down to rub him under his chin and behind his ears. As soon as I touched him, he would crawl into my lap and all over me, unable to purr or nuzzle enough to indicate how ecstatic he was that we were friends again.

"It's not easy being a parent, is it?" my mother said, with a healthy dose of irony, upon finding us in the midst of one of these reconciliations.

"No," I agreed ruefully. I looked up at her. "I guess I didn't always make things easy on you and Dad, did I?"

My mother smiled. "No, you didn't," she said. "But you got better."

My parents had fallen hard for Homer by this time. I would hear my father on the phone with friends and business colleagues, boasting of Homer's latest exploits. "And he's *blind*," he'd add at the end of each anecdote, as if he were positive the person on the other end had never, in all his born days, heard of anything so extraordinary as a blind cat who could play fetch or find his way to a can of tuna located all the way at the top of the kitchen counter. My mother loved to compare Homer with her friends' cats. *He has so much more on the ball than Susan's cat*, she would say, referring to some cat-owning acquaintance of hers. *Susan's cat never knows what's going on*.

"Your father and I always say that if anything were to happen to you, and you couldn't take care of the cats anymore, we would take Homer," my mother informed me, out of nowhere, over a Sunday breakfast.

I furrowed my brow quizzically. "Like what?"

"Oh, I don't know," my mother replied. She buttered a piece of toast. "I'm just saying if, *God forbid*, something happens..."

"If something happens, like...*what?*" I repeated. I tried to envision the calamitous accidents and life-threatening illnesses my mother was so obliquely referring to.

Or maybe she meant that I might decide Homer was too much trouble, that I might not *want* to take care of him anymore. Perhaps she and my father were doing that thing parents do—trying to relieve me of a larger responsibility than

I should, in their minds, have to cope with at this point in my life. Maybe they were attempting to give me a graceful way out.

In my own childhood, my parents had often snapped at me or lost their tempers in ways I had found inexplicable and bewildering. Sometimes, I thought, you could end up resenting someone in direct proportion to how important it was to you to make them happy. The resentment was second only to the devastation you would feel if you lost that someone altogether.

Homer and Casey were sitting a few feet away from the breakfast table, side by side, at rigid, rapt attention. They tried not to appear conspicuously as if they were begging, but they were obviously hopeful that a few table scraps might find their way over.

I had referred to Homer as an "accident." What I believed in my heart, however, was that Homer had been a surprise. An accident was something you would go out of your way to avoid if you had the chance to do things over. A surprise was something you hadn't even known you wanted until you got it.

I clearly wasn't the only one who felt that way.

"Sorry." I picked up the front section of the Sunday paper. "You and Dad will just have to find your own cat."

My mother grimaced. "As if *that* would ever happen."

11 • A One-Bedroom of One's Own

It rests with heaven to decide who shall be chief among us, but you shall be master in your own house and over your own possessions.
– HOMER, *The Odyssey*

THE DOTCOM REVOLUTION CAME eventually to Miami—albeit several years later than it had arrived in cities like New York and San Francisco—and with it a sudden surge in job opportunities. Start-up companies set up shop in the aging office buildings of South Beach, with apparently limitless budgets and a need to staff up as quickly as possible. Because most of these companies couldn't fill positions as rapidly as their needs were growing, they required employees who were, in the parlance, able to "wear a lot of different hats."

One company, for example, needed someone to be their director of event marketing, able to produce large-scale corporate events, cocktail parties, and trade shows. Since they didn't have a press representative yet, it would be great if that same person also had a working knowledge of the city's press contacts and how to mobilize them. As they also hadn't yet found a fulltime copywriter, it would be helpful if this new hire had a degree in English or creative writing and could pinch-hit with copywriting responsibilities as necessary. And because the mission of this particular company was to produce a local, online directory replete with information about community activities and volunteer efforts, it would be ideal if they found someone with strong connections in Miami's nonprofit orbit.

"They know they're asking for a lot," the friend who tipped me off to this position told me. "So they're willing to pay a pretty high salary for the right person."

My hands trembled over my computer's keyboard that night as I updated my résumé, so nervous was I that I might submit it too late, or that they might not want me for the position. But I didn't, and they did.

It was just under two years since I had moved back into my parents' house. Finally, after so much time spent in what had often felt like a fruitless struggle, I had attained a job and a salary that would more than cover the bills I already had—plus a place of my own.

Every second when I wasn't working over the next couple of months, I devoted to reading real estate listings. I eyed them with the close, loving attention to detail that a shut-in lavishes on reading pornography.

I had never lived in an apartment of my own. After college, I'd moved in with Jorge. After Jorge, I'd lived with Melissa, and then with my parents. So each four-line description in the apartment listings was a window into a glittering, glamorous new life. I could be the fashionable young tenant of a sleek new high-rise on Brickell Avenue, with ocean views, doormen, and concierge service. A converted guesthouse on one of the sprawling older estates on Pine Tree Drive, with palazzo floors and a spiral staircase, would be my entrée to ramshackle bohemia. I could be part of the trendy, cutting-edge set with a garden apartment in Miami's burgeoning Design District. If what I wanted was SoBe cachet, a charming duplex in a restored Art Deco building was the way to go.

I had a price range in mind, but I didn't want to spend all the way to the top of it. One never knew what the future held, but what I knew for certain was that I never wanted to be forced again, for financial reasons, to live with my parents.

There were other considerations as well. Anything on the ground floor—like the Design District garden apartment—struck me as unsafe for a woman living alone. And if Homer were to inadvertently scurry his way out the front door, I didn't want him in a position to run straight out onto the street. The gaps between the metal steps in the spiral staircase of that converted guesthouse were dangers for a small blind cat who could easily, in a fit of playfulness, slip between them and plummet to the ground floor. The balcony of the Brickell Avenue high-rise was a death trap. Homer had no idea that solid ground could end suddenly, and with the speed at which he moved he could be out a balcony door, onto the balcony itself, and over the side in a matter of seconds.

I finally settled on an eleventh-floor, one-bedroom apartment—light-filled and spacious—in a gargantuan complex on South Beach's West Avenue. It didn't convey much in the way of personality or lifestyle, but it was sensibly priced in the middle of my range. The apartment featured walk-in closets, an enormous bathroom that could discreetly accommodate a litter box, and a large balcony with sweeping views of Biscayne Bay to the west and the Atlantic Ocean to the east.

I had been deeply conflicted at first, wanting that apartment but also worried about Homer and the balcony. But South Florida living was all about taking advantage of our balmy climate, and just about anything that wasn't ground-floor had some sort of balcony or adjoining patio. At least this apartment featured a screen door behind the sliding glass door that led to the balcony. A sliding door was in itself a great safety measure, taking longer to open than a hinged door, which meant I had additional seconds to stop a death-defiant Homer from working his way past me outside. Even if Homer did manage to slip by, there would be a screen door behind the door—one he couldn't squeeze through unless I unlocked it.

The apartment was unfurnished, and I was starting from scratch since I owned nothing beyond my clothes, my books, a small television, and the CDs that had been gathering dust in boxes; I hadn't wanted to revert to my teenage habit of playing loud music in my room and annoying my parents. Here too, though, in selecting the things that would convert my apartment from anonymous rental unit to comfortable home, were countless hours of joy.

I was as mindful of the cats in selecting furniture as I had been in selecting an apartment. They were all good about using scratching posts, but since Homer didn't so much leap to the top of tall furniture as climb it, his claws inevitably found their way onto things. A leather sofa was out of the question—too many snags, not enough options for covering them. But a cloth sofa made from too delicate a material was equally impractical. I ended up with a neighbor's red velvet sofa and love seat, which were both appealingly risqué—appropriate, I thought, for the first apartment of my own that I would eventually bring "boys" over to—and made of a fabric surprisingly strong and snag-proof.

A friend suggested declawing Homer, since I was so concerned about the impact of his claws on household furnishings. It was something I couldn't even bring myself to consider. Not only was I opposed to declawing any of my cats, but Homer's claws were too much a part of his sense of confidence. He was so comfortable climbing and leaping in part because, even if he couldn't see that he was about to slide down or tumble backward off something, the quick deployment of his claws would save him from a fall like a mountain climber's grappling hooks.

"I'm going to miss him," my mother said, when our moving day finally arrived. Her eyes were suspiciously bright. "I've really come to love this stupid little cat."

"Hey!" I protested, but I smiled. "Who are you calling 'stupid'?"

"Casey and Brandi aren't going to like it," my father glumly predicted.

I couldn't resist teasing him. "Do you think maybe they'll offer to take care of Homer if, *God forbid*, something happens to me?"

Leaving this time felt different than it had when I'd first left for college. Back then, I'd known I would return for school breaks and summer vacations. There had never been a single, definitive moment of rupture or leave-taking. This time was different, though. This time, we all knew I wasn't coming back.

Returning to live in my parents' home had seemed, at times, like a demoralizing descent back into childhood. All that was already receding, however. Now it struck me that circumstances had brought me closer to my parents, had allowed me to get to know them as an adult in ways I never would have otherwise.

The cats struggled frantically in their carriers as I loaded them into the car. As far as they were concerned, nothing good was ever on the other end of a trip in the carrier. It always meant either a vet visit (bad) or a new home to get used to (even worse).

"This time we're going to a better place," I whispered to them. "You'll love our new home. I promise."

"Call us when you get there," my mother said. She pulled me into a hug. "Maybe we'll bring over bagels or something tomorrow morning, so you don't have to worry about food while you're getting settled."

"That sounds great," I told her, returning the hug.

The last thing I heard, as I shut the car doors behind the cats and prepared to drive away, was the sound of Casey howling from inside the house.

12 • Pet Sounds

A servant presently led in the famous bard Demodocus, whom the muse had dearly loved, but to whom she had given both good and evil, for though she had endowed him with a divine gift of song, she had robbed him of his eyesight.

– HOMER, *The Odyssey*

HOMER HAD A MILE-LONG to-do list as we settled into our new home. There was a whole new floor plan to memorize, and I ensured that Homer would learn it in relation to his litter box by placing him there first when I released the cats from their carriers. After an hour of hugging the walls as he ran from room to room, he had the layout down cold. There were also new hiding places to be discovered and claimed, new furniture to be climbed and categorized. The apartment was filled with moving boxes, and Homer personally inspected each and every one. He excitedly shredded and tossed paper wrappings, plastic bubble wrap, and Styrofoam popcorn, until the air around him resembled the chum you see in the water after a piranha attack.

Homer loved to climb into the boxes and leap out from them unexpectedly. He had never been as successful at hide-and-seek as he now was with the boxes to provide well-concealed hiding places. He would hunker all the way down, making sure the flap of the box was closed over his head, and spring out like a Jack-in-the-box when Scarlett or Vashti or I walked past. I don't know if he connected the actual invisibility of hiding in a box with his previous failed attempts at "sneaking" up on the three of us in plain sight. But there was now a satisfaction in the game he'd never found before, and I wound up keeping a few boxes around for weeks after they'd been emptied, unwilling to deprive him of such an easy source of happiness.

Homer also made it his business to greet all deliverymen or phone and cable technicians who passed through our front door. Scarlett and Vashti would hide—Scarlett not caring to meet new people, and Vashti perfectly happy to meet new people but terrified by the noise these men made bumping into things with heavy crates, or rattling metal tools around in a toolbox.

Homer was fascinated by these visitors for the exact reasons, and to the exact degree, that Scarlett and Vashti avoided them. They were new *and* they made interesting sounds! Where Scarlett and Vashti flew from any noise that was too loud or unusual, Homer was invariably drawn toward it like a compass needle spinning north.

You would think that a blind cat would be more, not less, intimidated by sharp or sudden sounds, that they would be less comprehensible to him than to other cats. But in a world where no sound was expected—where you couldn't see the book about to thud on the floor tumbling from the bookshelf, or the vacuum cleaner that would soon begin its wail being pulled from the closet—then no sound was unexpected, either. Sound, in fact, was the thing that explained most of Homer's world to him. An unanticipated noise, perceived as a potential threat by Vashti and Scarlett, was for Homer one more puzzle piece that made his unseen universe comprehensible. He found comfort in the rhythm and pulse of sound, no matter how jarring or abrasive, the way my other two cats did in silence.

It was Homer's habit to trot closely behind the men who arrived with a clanging metal bed frame or several feet of television cable that dragged noisily on the floor. Frequently, I had to keep Homer—who was eager to poke his nose and ears into whatever mysterious things they were doing—at heel, so he wouldn't interfere with their work. Most of them would regard him in a friendly enough manner, although the inevitable question always came up after a moment or two of puzzled scrutiny.

"Something happen to your cat's face?"

"He's blind," I'd answer shortly.

"Aw, poor little guy." Homer, knowing that this sympathetic tone was directed at him, would leave my side to climb up their legs or jump into their laps. He often dragged along his stuffed worm (whose recovery from the moving boxes he'd been very anxious about), hoping to engage one of these strangers in a game of fetch.

It was a momentous day when I was able to squeeze enough from my paycheck to purchase a stereo system, and the man who delivered and installed it was the deliveryman who had the greatest long-term impact on Homer's life. Homer hadn't been exposed much to music. Once my CDs came out of their boxes and found their way into the new CD player, a further audio vista opened before him. I learned that music had a tremendous impact on Homer's moods. Anything with a hard, driving tempo—rock or clubby dance music, for instance—sent him into a tizzy. Hole's *Live Through This* made him hyper almost beyond the telling of it. He'd tear around the living room, leaping manically on and off the couch or flinging himself to the top of his six-foot cat tower, while uttering a low whine as if his body held so much energy, the containment of it was painful.

The first time I played the Brandenburg Concertos, however, Homer fell into a deep sleep right in the middle of chasing a paper ball around. It happened as swiftly as if he'd been shot in the neck with a tranquilizer dart.

My friend Felix was vising that day. "Guess Homer doesn't like your taste in music," he said.

I shrugged. "Everyone's a critic."

HOMER WASN'T A CREATURE who was moved simply by the sound he heard around him. He was equally concerned with the sound he himself produced. It was important to Homer to feel that he and I were in constant communication with each other, and he was never content—as my other two cats were—to incorporate silent gestures or postures into our vernacular. Scarlett, for example, would sit pointedly in front of the litter box when she thought it was time for me to clean it, and Vashti had a bizarre, ritualistic dance that she did in circles around her food bowl whenever she was hungry.

But Homer—who, of course, had no understanding that he was visible generally or visible to me, specifically—eschewed such imprecise methods of getting his point across. At three years of age, he had developed a full, incessant range of meows and yelps that bordered on the human in its nuance and complexity.

Homer was still convinced that as long as he made no sound, I couldn't "see" him, and he never tired of trying to get away with things right under my nose that he knew he shouldn't. As a kitten, he had accepted my command of "No!" with nothing beyond a look of confusion. *How can she always know what I'm doing?!* These days, he argued with me—with a long, high-pitched *meeeeeeh* I thought of as his way of saying, *Awwwww...c'mon Ma...*

He had a very specific meow that meant, *Where's my worm? I can't find my worm!* and another, slightly more prolonged meow that meant, *Okay, I found my worm, now I need you to throw it.* Then there was a low, guttural, drawn-out kind of cry that I heard if I was thoroughly engrossed in something—watching a movie, say—and hadn't paid attention to him in a couple of hours. It was a meow that very clearly said, *I'm booooooored*, and it would only be discontinued if I hauled out something for him to play with.

There were happy, half-swallowed little yips that greeted me whenever I came through the front door. *Yay, you're home!* A tiny, plaintive *mew?* that went up at the end, like a sentence punctuated by a question mark, meant Homer had fallen asleep in a room I was no longer in and, now that he was awake, wanted to know where I was.

A piercing, persistent kind of *mew* that I rarely heard strummed a fearful twang in my stomach, because it meant Homer had gotten himself stuck in or on top of something and didn't know how to get back down. "Where are you, Homer-Bear?" I'd say, following the sound of his cries through the apartment until I located him. The one that drove me to distraction was a repetitive, atonal, *mrow, mrow, mrow, mrow,* which Homer produced if I'd been talking on the phone for a while. It was like a small child's relentless chanting of *Mommy, Mommy, Mommy, Mommy,* until, exasperated, I'd put one hand over the receiver and say, "Homer, can't you see I'm on the phone right now?"

Hey—most people forgot Homer was blind once they'd spent enough time with him. I occasionally forgot, too.

ONE OF THE LUXURIES I now indulged in was a subscription to the newspaper—the first I'd ever had in my own name. The leisurely perusal of the paper over a light breakfast was a treasured and essential component of my morning routine.

Delivery of the newspaper soon became a highlight in Homer's schedule as well. This was not because he'd developed a sudden, passionate interest in current affairs. It was because the good people at the newspaper production plant saw fit to churn out and deliver the paper to my door every morning—wrapped in a rubber band.

Homer had never been interested in rubber bands, even though most cats love them. Generally, what they like to do is eat them—a dangerous, and sometimes fatal, habit. If I happened to lose track of one and it made its way into Scarlett's or Vashti's paws, she'd bat it around and munch on it happily until I saw it and took it away. Homer would sit nearby, straining his ears for some clue as to what, exactly, made this game so interesting. *I don't get it, you guys. What's the big deal?*

But that was before Homer learned that a rubber band, stretched taut around a rolled-up newspaper and plucked by a single claw, would produce *a sound*.

As with so many great discoveries, this one was an accident. I had left the paper, with its rubber band, on the coffee table one morning while I retrieved my toast and juice. Homer leapt onto the table to investigate. From the kitchen, I heard a *ping!* There was a pause, then another *ping!* The next pause was shorter than the first, and it was followed by a *Ping! Pi-ping ping! Ping!* I came out from the kitchen to find Homer cocking his head curiously from side to side, as enthralled by the reverb of the still-vibrating rubber band as he'd been by its initial sound. He plucked the rubber band again and pressed his paw over it while it vibrated. Upon realizing that doing this made both sound and vibration stop, he plucked at it once more.

"I'm sorry, kitty," I said, and I really did feel bad. He was having such a good time! But I wasn't about to forgo my morning paper fix—and I certainly wasn't leaving Homer in possession of a rubber band. I unrolled the newspaper and threw the rubber band in the trash. And there, I thought, was the end of it.

Like most cats, Homer was a creature of habit. Being blind, he was even more wedded to his habits than the average cat. Homer, for example, would only curl up next to me on my left side. He might not have even known I had a right side, so ingrained was his habit of sitting to my left. If I adopted a position on the couch that made only my right side available, Homer would wander around, meowing in nervous confusion, until I shifted over.

When I added a set of squat wooden candlesticks to the coffee table, it took Homer weeks to learn not to bump into them. This wasn't because he was slow in figuring out how to avoid solid objects; he'd learned his way around the entire apartment in under an hour. It was because once he'd learned the exact number of steps left and right that took him from one end of the coffee table to the other—like learning where immovable things such as walls and doorways were—it was difficult for him to get past the ingrained habit of memorized routine. When I tried to replace Homer's stuffed worm—which was, by now, hardly more than a few tufts of fabric clinging to a tiny, dented bell—with an identical new one, he sniffed it once, gave it a single toss into the air, and stalked away in disgust. He slept in the same spot on my bed every night, for exactly as long as I slept. Scarlett and Vashti would also pile into bed with me, but they would leave in the late-night hours to scamper around the apartment together. Homer had trained himself to sleep as long as I slept, and to remain there until I awoke.

Waiting for the predawn *thonk!* of the newspaper against our front door immediately became a new Homer habit. The joys he'd discovered in making his own music were so great that they overrode his three-year-long old habit of sleeping as long as I did. No matter how I tried to wean him from the newspaper and its rubber band, no matter how I tried to distract, cajole, or plead with him, he would wait with his nose flush against the crack of the front door at exactly five thirty every morning. Once he heard the paper land, he'd paw at the door and meow frantically (*The paper's here! Mom, hurry, the paper's here!*) until I stumbled out of bed long enough to bring it in and drop it at his feet. My reward for this act of mercy was a solid hour of *Ping! Ping! Ping! Pi-ping pi-ping-ping!*

It was maddening.

Finally, to preserve both my sleep and my sanity—because the constant strumming of that single note, over and over again, was killing the latter as surely as it was the former—I did something I remembered my grandmother doing for me when I was a child. I took an empty Kleenex box and wrapped five rubber bands of varying thickness around it. I then handed this impromptu guitar over to Homer.

He was utterly enraptured. Each rubber band played a completely distinct note. The hollowness of the empty Kleenex box added depth and resonance to these notes. The best part was that, since this toy was available all the time, I was able to put it away while I slept and Homer resumed sleeping the whole night through with me, knowing it would be there waiting for him when he woke up. If I was reading or talking on the phone, Homer entertained himself with it for endless, rhapsodic hours. Our home became a veritable philharmonic, where ad hoc concertos of *Ping! Ping plong BOING!* could be heard.

The only thing that interfered with this affair of the heart was the occasional breaking of a rubber band. It would snap up into Homer's face so suddenly, and with so little warning, that Homer leapt back a good foot and a half, grimacing horribly, his fur standing straight up on end. *What the...?!!?* He would approach the box again cautiously, cocking his head from left to right, and smack it quickly and firmly with his paw. *Hit me and I'll hit you back.* Then he'd leap away once more, as if afraid what the consequences of his own daring might be.

Homer would sulk for hours after an incident like this, refusing to so much as go near the thing after he'd smacked it into submission. I couldn't help but laugh. "Art is suffering," I'd tell him. But he loved his tissue-box guitar too much to stay angry with it for very long. The next morning would find him plucking away as if nothing had gone awry.

I wish I could conclude this chapter by saying that Homer eventually learned to play something recognizable, like "Oh! Susanna" or anything from side one of *Led Zeppelin IV*.

But if he had, you almost certainly would have heard of him before this.

13 • Lord of the Flies

**He looked like some lion of the wilderness
that stalks about exulting in his strength and
defying both wind and rain.**
— HOMER, *The Odyssey*

ASIDE FROM THE SAFETY considerations I'd had—for myself as well as for Homer—in eschewing garden and ground-floor apartments, there had also been that secondary, but persistent, reality that dominated so much of Miami living.

I'm talking about the insects.

To live in Miami is to learn, the hard way, that the human population is on the losing side of a never-ending war with the insect kingdom. It's a battle in which you know you'll never gain any ground; the most you can do is shore up your defenses and try to hold the line. I might as well have set out cookies and featherbeds for six-legged intruders if I'd decided to go the garden-apartment route.

It was spring when we moved into our new apartment, and now we were in the thick of summer, that buggiest of all South Florida seasons. It was particularly rainy that summer, with thunderous tropical systems moving through practically on a daily basis. It was the kind of weather that drove outdoor critters in, looking for relief.

Living on the eleventh floor went a long way toward controlling my apartment's wildlife population, but there were always those hardy souls who were more than equal to the climb. Chief among these were the flies—huge suckers bigger than my thumbnails and excruciatingly annoying.

For Homer's sake, I made something of a religion of getting in and out of the glass door leading to my balcony as quickly as possible. But—no matter how quickly I slid the door shut behind me—flies always managed to get in. If an influx of flies ran the risk of compromising my enjoyment of our new apartment, however, they added immeasurably to Homer's. Once all the boxes had been unpacked and thrown away, Homer again found himself unable to launch a successful frontal attack against Scarlett or Vashti. With the influx of flies, finally, there was something Homer could track and hunt without having to encounter either Vashti's passivity or Scarlett's scorn.

The first time Homer caught a fly was a few months after we'd moved in. I was shelving some new books in the living room when I heard a loud, angry buzzing from somewhere in the vicinity of just over my head. Looking around, I saw all three cats lined up—as if in formation—trailing slowly behind a fly zigzagging madly about five feet in the air.

Homer's head was raised and it pulsed rapidly back and forth in perfect time with the fly's irregular movements, his ears pricked up as high as they would go. Scarlett and Vashti's pupils were hugely dilated, so that their eyes seemed to be all pupil. They didn't unfix their gazes for even a second. It looked like they were making up their minds to pounce—but while they were still thinking about it, Homer, without any warning, was airborne.

He sprang straight up, rising and rising until the top of his head was higher than mine. The lower half of his body curved beneath him in a graceful arc. He hung in midair for a moment, an Olympic gymnast at the crest of a dismount, and I heard his jaws snap shut. He landed nimbly on his hind legs and rested on his haunches.

The buzzing had stopped. The fly was gone.

"Oh my God!" I exclaimed involuntarily. Even Scarlett and Vashti blinked, looking impressed despite themselves. *Did we just see what we thought we saw?*

The only one who didn't seem surprised was Homer himself. His jaws worked furiously, like a child chewing taffy, and I realized that—having never successfully captured anything before—he hadn't considered that catching a fly in his mouth would mean he'd...well...end up with a fly in his mouth.

I'd bought a swatter and some fly strips when I first moved in, but they were destined to remain unopened, gathering dust in a kitchen drawer. I didn't have the heart to deprive Homer of the joys of what soon became his favorite pastime. And to be honest, any efforts I might have made in the direction of fly control would have been superfluous anyway.

Homer honed the catching of flies into an art form, experimenting with different styles and strategies as necessity, or boredom, dictated. Sometimes he would leap up, as he had that first time, but rather than catching the fly in the air, he would slap at it energetically with his front paws, like a swimming doing a doggy-paddle, until the fly was forced to the ground. Then, while the fly was struggling to take off again, Homer would back up a few inches and pounce on it. Sometimes he would chase a fly toward the balcony until it hit the sliding door. As it banged helplessly against the glass, Homer would press one paw against the hapless bug and slide it down into the corner where the door met the floor and hold it there until it stopped moving.

If a fly landed on the wall behind the sofa, Homer would stand on top of the back of the sofa with his hind legs and, lightning-fast, whap out a front paw to pin the fly against the wall. Then he'd lift his paw just enough to wedge his head in and scoop the fly up in his mouth. One time, I saw Homer dart up the back of a chair in pursuit of a fly. Balancing on three legs on the back of the chair, he used the fourth one to swat at it feverishly. But it flew to a spot just behind Homer's head. Homer—I swear—propelled himself off the chair into a spectacular back-flip, a head-over-tail pinwheel of a cat, catching the fly in the air and twisting his body around so that he landed, perfectly, on all fours.

"Okay, now you're just showing off," I told him. But I couldn't help laughing at how remarkably pleased he looked with himself.

It got to the point that I didn't have to hear any actual buzzing to know there was a fly in our midst. Out of the corner of my eye I'd catch a black blur of speed and sinew zipping by, and I'd know.

I used to entertain myself sometimes by imagining conversations among those flies who observed the particular indignity of their compatriot's being caught by a blind cat. In my head, the dialogue went something like this:

> ***First fly:*** *Did you see Carl get caught by that eyeless cat? And Carl had, like, a hundred eyes!*
> ***Second fly:*** *Yeah, well, Carl was an idiot.*

It wasn't only the flies that Homer felled in his new capacity as our home's head gamekeeper. He proved himself equally adept at dispatching all manner of pests: ants (which were so easy for him to catch, it was almost an insult to his abilities), mosquitoes, and the occasional moth.

And then there were the roaches. I live in New York now, and I've seen what passes for a "roach" here in the Northeast. But let me tell you—some of those southern bad boys were so big, you could saddle them up and ride them in the Kentucky Derby. Living on a higher floor meant we weren't plagued with a full-fledged infestation. Given, however, that the larger ones—the ones we call palmetto bugs in the South—were able to fly, more than a few managed to creep their way in. And the ones that did always lived (briefly) to regret it.

Even big roaches are fast, but none of them were as fast or difficult to pinpoint as the flies Homer routinely caught. So the only thing that made catching roaches a real challenge for Homer was that flies announced their presence with loud buzzing, while the roaches were soundless. Or so I thought. But Homer's hearing was infinitely more sensitive than mine, or even than Scarlett's and Vashti's; on numerous occasions, I'd catch Homer cocking his head to listen to something I couldn't discern. Then he'd leap toward a particular spot where a bookcase met a wall and, sure enough, an enormous cockroach would come scuttling out.

Homer tended to eat everything he caught, except for the roaches. Those he saved for me. During a particularly rainy two weeks, I woke up every morning to find a neat pile of two or three palmetto bug corpses stacked in front of my bed.

As soon as he heard me stir, Homer would jump from the bed to stand over the pile of dead roaches, meowing in an inviting, anxious sort of way. (It would have been irrational in Homer's worldview to assume I would find, unassisted, anything soundless.) *Look, Mom! Look what I brought you! Do you like them? Do you?*

"Thank you, Homer," I always said, grateful he couldn't see my reflexive grimace of disgust. "You're a very thoughtful kitty. Mommy loves her new roaches." Homer would stretch up his front paws and clutch my shins in a gesture that meant he was eager for me to pet and praise him, which I did—lavishly.

Now that I had my own place, I was entertaining friends on a fairly regular basis. Homer would always greet them with his customary friendly interest, but nothing ever diverted his attention from a six-legged intruder on the loose. "That is *so crazy!*" people would say upon seeing Homer snatch a fly out of five feet of air. "I mean, he's *blind!*"

"Don't tell him that," I'd reply. "I don't think he knows."

"He's like Mr. Miyagi catching flies with chopsticks in *The Karate Kid*," my friend Tony observed once. "I wish I had a whole box of flies and roaches I could release in here just for him to catch."

I shuddered at the hideous prospect. "I'm incredibly glad you don't."

Homer hadn't yet bagged his biggest game, however. That was an honor still to come.

14 • Mucho Gato

Ill deeds do not prosper, and the weak confound the strong.
- HOMER, *The Odyssey*

It was an uncomfortably hot night in mid-July when I awakened, startled, at four o'clock in the morning, to a sound I'd never heard before.

It sounded like a cat growling, but the only one of my cats I'd ever heard growl was Scarlett. I knew it wasn't her, though. And it couldn't possibly be Vashti—Vashti who was so polite and unassertive that her meows came out as tiny squeaks; Vashti didn't have it in her to growl at anyone.

That could only leave Homer.

The mere fact of Homer's growling—Homer, who was friendly as a puppy, who was always so happy-go-lucky that I'd never known him to be so much as grumpy—already had me frightened. I squinted and struggled to see him in the darkness.

Faint light streamed in through the blinds from the streetlights outside. But Homer, black and eyeless, was completely invisible. I could tell, though, that he was close by, somewhere on the bed. I sat up and reached over to flip on my bedside lamp.

The first thing I saw was Homer, standing in the middle of the bed, puffed up to about three times his normal size. His back was completely arched, and every hair on his body stood straight up, his tail bristled and stiff as a pipe cleaner. His legs were set wide apart, and although his head was tucked down low, his ears were at full attention. He moved his head and ears evenly from side to side with the precision of a sonar dish. His front claws were extended farther than I'd ever seen them, farther than I would have thought physically possible. His growl continued, low and unbroken—not completely aggressive yet, but a definite warning.

Beyond Homer, standing at the foot of my bed, was a man I'd never seen before in my life.

In the disoriented way you think when woken out of a sound sleep, my mind rapidly considered and discarded all innocent explanations for this man's presence. Visiting friend? No. New boyfriend? No Drunken neighbor who'd stumbled into my apartment instead of his own?

No, no, and no.

I felt every muscle in my body stiffen and tense, my very eyelids snapping open so wide and so fast that the muscles twinged in pain.

All I could think was that the buried nightmare of every woman living alone—the doomsday scenario that had spawned a thousand horror movies—was playing out right here, right now, *in my bedroom*. I also realized that, having never really believed it could happen to me, I had done nothing in the way of arming myself against such an encounter. My eyes plunged wildly around the room, considering what value each object I saw might have as a weapon.

The intruder looked as startled as I felt and, for a crazy moment, this struck me as ridiculous. Surely, among the three of us, he must have been the most prepared for whatever was about to happen. I mean, who had broken into whose apartment?

But then I realized he wasn't looking at me. He hadn't taken his eyes off Homer.

Like me, he had obviously heard Homer growling but, also like me, been unable to distinguish any visual evidence of Homer's presence. Unlike me, however, it was taking him a second to figure out *why* this cat—who gave every indication he was preparing an attack—had been so completely invisible. There was something weird going on here, something off about this cat, something wrong with this cat's *face*...

Under more benign circumstances, I would have been deeply offended by the look of horror that broke over the burglar's own face when he realized what it was.

Homer may have been alarmed at how rigid my body had become, or perhaps by the fact that I was awake, yet not speaking to him in my usual reassuring tones. His growl rose drastically in both volume and pitch.

Some cats growl and bristle as a way of avoiding a fight, slowly backing up while maintaining an intimidating posture in the hope their adversary will back down first. But Homer wasn't backing up. With a slow precision I instantly recognize from all those failed attempts at stalking Scarlett, Homer was creeping forward, *toward* the intruder.

It's going to sound foolish (keep in mind that, about five seconds earlier, I'd been deeply asleep), but for a split second I was worried for the burglar's safety. It was simply my first, unthinking instinct when faced with an aggressive pet squaring off against somebody in my home. If anybody had asked me half an hour earlier, I would have told them that Homer would *never* attack anybody in my presence, that—even if for some impossible-to-imagine reason, Homer took it into his head to depart from his general friendliness toward everybody he met—the sound of my command *"No!"* would have stopped him instantly. Homer was a troublemaker and a daredevil, but he never disobeyed me outright. I knew this for an absolute, positive fact. It was one of the cornerstones of the relationship I had with him, one of the fundamental things, aside from his blindness, that set Homer apart from other cats.

In that moment, though I knew—*knew*—that if Homer indeed decided to attack this man, I wouldn't be able to stop him. The snarling, furious animal on my bed was a cat I'd never seen, didn't know, had absolutely no control over. The only question was how clawed-up and bloodied the burglar, or I, or both of us, would get in the process of my subduing him.

It had been only a matter of seconds since I'd first switched on the lamp, and now my next move seemed so painfully obvious, I couldn't believe I wasn't already doing it.

I picked up the phone next to my bed to dial 911.

"Don't do that," the man said, speaking for the first time.

I hesitated for the briefest instant, and then I looked over at Homer. *Do what he's doing,* a voice in my head urged. *Act bigger than you really are.*

"Fuck off," I said to the man, and I made the call.

Then a lot of things happened at once. The 911 operator answered and I told her: *"There's somebody in my apartment!"*

"There's somebody in your apartment?" she repeated.

"Yes, there's somebody in my apartment!"

Homer, meantime, had finally galvanized into action. He might not have understood relative size, he might not have realized how very much smaller he was than this man standing menacingly over the bed, but if there was one thing Homer *did* understand it was pinpointing a location based on sound.

The intruder, in speaking, had let Homer know precisely where he was.

With a loud hiss that bared his fangs (prior to this, I'd always thought of them as "teeth"), Homer thrust the whole weight of his body forward and brought his right front leg into the air, stretching it up and out so far that it looked, bizarrely, as if the bone connecting his leg to his shoulder had come out of its socket, held in place only by muscle and tendons. His claws extended even farther (good God—how long *were* those claws?). Glinting like scythes in the lamplight, they slashed viciously at the man's face.

Homer missed by the merest fraction of an inch—and only because the man had reflexively snapped his head back.

"Okay, ma'am, I'm dispatching officers now," the 911 operator said. "Stay on the phone..."

I never heard the rest of her instructions, however, because at that point the intruder turned and ran. Homer, his tail still bolt upright, leapt from the bed and raced after him.

"HOMER!" My shriek was unlike anything I'd ever heard coming out of my own mouth. It tore the inside of my throat till it felt bloody. *"HOMER, NO!"*

I threw down the phone and ran after them.

Like two competing runners panting toward a finish line, two separate and distinct fears vied for prominence in my head. The first was that Homer might actually catch up to the intruder. Who knew what that man would do if he saw Homer's talons coming at him a second time?

I was also terrified that Homer might chase the burglar out the front door and into the long, labyrinthine corridors of my apartment complex—and, unable to see his way back home, be lost to me forever. As this picture played vividly in my imagination, I was shocked to realize how deep-seated it was, how a fear of Homer's getting lost had always lain in the background of my thoughts, coiled and silent but ready to spring up and bite me at a moment's notice.

Homer had made it out the front door and about six feet into the hallway before I caught up with him. Looking around—to make sure neither of the other cats had gotten out as much as to confirm that the burglar was gone—I saw the emergency exit door at the far end of the corridor swinging closed.

I scooped Homer up in one hand. The staccato pounding of his heart alarmed me, although my own chest cavity felt molten, as if it were full of liquid fire. Homer resisted mightily, flailing out his front claws at random and catching the skin inside my forearm with his back claws, raising a trail of angry red welts. It wasn't until I'd reentered the apartment, slamming the locks shut behind me and throwing Homer roughly to the ground, that he seemed to come back to himself.

"*When I say no I mean no, god dammit!*" I screamed. "You're a bad cat, Homer! *A bad, bad cat!*"

Homer was panting heavily, his rib cage expanding and shrinking in rapid succession. I saw him take a deep breath, and he cocked his head slightly to one side.

One of the things about Homer that always clutched at my heart was the way it seemed like he really tried to understand me when I talked to him. Like right now, as he tilted his face up toward the sound of my voice, struggling to make sense of my yelling. On the one hand, every instinct in his body told him he had just done the exact right thing: There had been a threat, and he had defended his territory and chased the threat off. What could be wrong about that?

But here was Mom, yelling at him as he'd never been yelled at before, obviously of the opinion that what he'd just done was very, *very* wrong. So which of us was right?

Homer didn't creep toward me apologetically the way he usually did when I was angry. He just sat there on his haunches, his tail curled lightly around his front paws like ancient Egyptian statues I'd seen of the cats who guarded temples.

I found myself remembering a scene from the novel *For Whom the Bell Tolls*. A ragged group of peasants had just done battle with Fascist soldiers in a Spanish Civil War skirmish, and had suffered grievous losses. Among the dead was the loyal horse of an elderly farmer who'd joined the fight. Kneeling over the body of the fallen horse, the farmer whispered in his ear, *"Eras mucho caballo,"* which Hemingway had translated as: *Thou wert plenty of horse.*

It was a line that always stuck with me, because it was a single sentence that had seemed, to me, to contain multitudes. What the farmer was saying was that this horse had been a horse beyond all other horses, a horse who had fought like a man and died like a hero. For sheer valor, he was worth an entire herd of horses, so much horse that the body of a single horse had been barely sufficient to contain him.

Homer looked even smaller than usual as he sat there, his head still bent to one side as his fur sank quietly back into its normal patterns.

Such a little boy, I thought. *He's such a tiny boy!*

"Oh, Homer," I said, and my voice was ragged. I knelt down and rubbed him behind the ears. He purred softly in response. "I'm sorry I yelled at you. I'm so sorry, little guy."

There was a sharp rap at the door, followed by an extremely welcome: "Police!"

"I'm okay!" I called back. "I'm coming!"

I picked Homer up again. Homer loved to cuddle, but he hated to be picked up and would squirm and wriggle in a desperate attempt to regain the ground. Now, though, he rested quietly in my arms. I buried my face in the fur of his neck.

"*Eres much gato*, Homer," I whispered. *Thou art plenty of cat.*

I placed him gently back on his own legs.

15 • My Homer/My Self

A second ago, you were all in rags, and now you are like some god come down from heaven.
— HOMER, *The Odyssey*

LIGHT TRAVELS AT 186,000 miles per second, but slows to about two-thirds of that speed when it hits the lens of your eye. If this didn't happen, we would be functionally blind, unable to distinguish more than shadows interspersed with vague patches of brightness. It's this slowing down that allows our brains to interpret and relay back to us what light reveals. But our minds go even further, imposing logic and regularity, smoothing over distortions and filling in the occasional gaps that open in our visual field. It's the reason why, for example, an object traveling almost too fast for our eyes to follow is seen as a blur. The object isn't really a blur; the blur is simply our minds' way of creating order where otherwise there would be confusion.

The lesson here, I suppose, is that what we think we see isn't precisely the way things are in the objective reality that exists outside our own heads. Or, to put it more simply, things aren't always what they appear.

I wandered around in a kind of shock for days after the break-in. (*I could have died*, I told myself repeatedly. *I could have been raped and murdered and* died!) Nothing looked or felt or sounded the way it should. Music was too jarring; sunlight grated on me like sandpaper with its too-brightness. But silence and darkness squeezed the breath out of me with the terrors they held. Familiar things offended me by pretending to be ordinary when nothing, clearly, could be taken for what it seemed. My home was not the safe haven a home was supposed to be, and unknown horrors skulked beneath the surface of everything.

Homer returned to his customary cheerfulness far more quickly than I did. By the next morning—as red-eyed a sunrise as I'd ever stayed up to witness—his attitude about the incident seemed to be, *Boy, that was weird, huh? Let's play fetch!* It was as if the fierce defender he'd morphed into so breathtakingly and unexpectedly had been merely a trick of the eye. I found myself calling just about everyone I knew and telling them about what Homer did, not so much to brag about him (although bragging certainly seemed warranted) but because I felt the need to cement a memory that was hard to maintain in light of Homer's unruffled complacency a mere five hours later.

Most of us with pets will come to feel eventually that we know everything about them—that we can predict with near certainty what they'll do or how they'll react in any given situation. My father had famously walked some of our dogs without a leash on occasion because, "Tippi will *always* stop when I say *no*," or, "Penny would *never* run away from my side."

But my father, who understood pets better than anybody, was also always the first to say that a pet was an animal first and foremost, and that with animals—as with people—there was always room for the unpredictable.

I had thought that I knew Homer as well as my father knew our dogs. If Homer nosed around an empty tuna can—sniffing it, turning it upside down, digging inside it with his front paws in a frustrated manner—I would say to an observer, "He doesn't understand how something can smell so strongly of tuna and not *be* tuna."

I've already noted that Homer slept with me every night, falling asleep precisely when I did and sleeping for exactly as long as I slept. But it was more than that. When I ate, Homer trotted off to his food bowl. When I was in an especially good mood, Homer ran zanily around the apartment, his cartwheels and caperings the physical manifestation of what I was feeling. If I was sad, Homer curled in a tight little ball in my lap and couldn't be persuaded out of his funk even when presented with a favorite toy or fresh can of tuna. When I walked from room to room, Homer might charge in front of me or lope behind me or weave in and out of my legs, But the rhythms of our steps had so completely adjusted themselves to the other's that neither of us ever missed a beat, never faltered, never tripped the other one up. I could walk down an unlit hallway with Homer darting around my feet and, without being able to see him, never come close to stumbling or falling over him.

But Homer was also clearly capable of things—courageous, extraordinary, heroic things—that none of us could have predicted when I'd first adopted him as a helpless blind kitten, or that even I could have predicted now, having spent three years with him. I was proud of him. How could I not be? I had always been the one to insist that Homer was just as "normal" as any other cat. But this was something else altogether. Regarding him as *heroic* rather than *blind* or even *ordinary* required a slight adjustment in my thinking.

A long-married friend, on the eve of my own wedding years later, would tell me, "Never forget—you're still going to bed with a stranger every night." By then, though, this was something I had known for a while. It was the second important lesson about adult relationships that Homer taught me.

They never did catch the man who broke into our apartment. A police report was filed and I went down to the Miami Beach Police Department to look through their big book of mug shots. I saw a couple of pictures that might have resembled my burglar, but I was afraid to identify anybody. Whenever I remembered that night, the only thing I saw in my mind's eye was Homer; there was no way I would have sworn in court that anybody I picked out of a lineup or a mug-shot book was the right man.

Still, it was weeks before I could sleep. But where my fear and outrage stayed with me, those feelings on Homer's part had clearly been the work of a night. Homer slept like a baby next to me on those long, sleepless night, while my eyes popped open at every wisp of sound.

I had always envisioned myself as being the one who would make the world intelligible for Homer. I would be the eyes he didn't have, the one who would soothe his fears in the dark. But Homer was far more comfortable in darkness, in the world of random sound, than I was. I'll admit that, in the aftermath of the break-in, it was I who felt safer knowing Homer was sleeping next to me.

It occurred to me as I lay there, battling my newfound insomnia, that what I had always taken to be Homer's fearlessness despite his blindness was perhaps the opposite. Homer had known there were things to fear in the dark; he wouldn't have reacted so aggressively if he hadn't known there was cause to be afraid. But what could you do with that fear? You had to live your life, didn't you? Where another cat might have spent his life hiding and hissing, forever anticipating dangers that might or might not be there, Homer simply went about his business, confident on some instinctive level that he could deal with threats if and when they arose.

I didn't tell my parents about the break-in. There was nothing they could do after the fact, I reasoned, other than worry—and if I was having trouble sleeping, who knew how long it would be before my mother was able to close her eyes again? But Homer was made much of in the following days by our friends. "No way!" they said. *"No. Freaking. Way!"* They, too, looked at Homer as if they'd never seen him before. He was our Daredevil, our real-life superhero, although he probably never connected his bravery of that night with the endless cans of tuna, pounds of sliced turkey, and tubs of inexpensive caviar (which he chewed so thoughtfully—intrigued by its fishy smell but unfamiliar with its texture) that he received. Scarlett and Vashti, who were given their share of this bounty, also seemed to accept it unquestioningly, content to enjoy the goods the gods had seen fit to provide.

I think the thing that drove me craziest was wondering *why?* Why me, why *my* apartment? The most maddening thing to accept is that there usually isn't a *why*. Or there probably is—because effects have causes—but you'll never know what it was. Not knowing makes it impossible to avoid having the exact same thing happen again. But it's also liberating. The world could be dangerous and bad things sometimes happened, but there was thing you could do except live your life. And it would be foolish if, in the process of living it, you didn't also enjoy it.

Homer, in his own way, had known this all along.

In the end, after the shock and the fear and the anger had subsided—when Homer was again an ordinary cat who loved rubber bands and organized daring raids on bookcases and pantry shelves—I was left with two things. I realized I had succeeded in "raising" Homer as I had long ago resolved to. Homer was, indeed, brave and independent, uncrippled by self-doubt. I had been emphatic in insisting that Homer could take care of himself—just like any other cat. And so he could. He had proven that, under the right circumstances, he could take care of me as well.

And I was also left with a gratitude so profound and solid that it was like a third living presence in whatever room Homer and I were in together. In the dark hours of five a.m., when even a town like South Beach had quieted down for the night, thoughts of how that other night could have ended rose like a wave to drag me under. My eyes would well with tears, and I would pull Homer closer to me, murmuring, "Thank God for you. Thank God for you, little cat!"

Homer may have surprised me, but there was no denying this new, deeper symmetry between us. Once upon a time, I had saved Homer's life. And now, years later, he had saved mine.

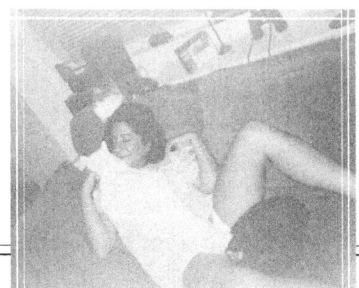

16 • Cats and the Single Girl

The sons of all the chief men among you are pestering my mother to marry you against her will.

– HOMER, *The Odyssey*

PRIOR TO THE BREAK-IN, I had been on exactly one date where the man in question made it past the front door of my apartment and into the apartment itself. He'd arrived on a Thursday evening to pick me up, and I'd invited him inside for a drink before we set out. I went into the kitchen to mix us some cocktails. When I came back into the living room, I found Homer trapped in a corner by my date, who was standing in front of Homer and hissing loudly at him. There was a wild, terrified look on Homer's face as his ears turned rapidly back and forth, as if he were trying to hear his way into an escape route.

I nearly dropped the glasses I was carrying. "What the…?"

"He came over to me," my date explained. "Black cats are bad luck."

Most people made a point of being kind to Homer. A small few were indifferent and simply left him alone. But I had never witnessed anybody going out of his way to *frighten a blind cat*. The voice I heard in my head sounded a lot like my mother's. *What kind of a person does such a thing? Who raised this man?*

It may have been the one time in my life when I wished I were a man, because what I wanted more than anything in that moment was to haul off and belt that guy in the face. I had a delightful vision of myself smashing the glass I held, *Sopranos*-style, against the side of his skull. My hands clenched into fists around the ice-filled glasses until I thought frostbite would set in, but my voice was measured.

"The cat lives here," I said. "You do not. Please *get the hell out* of my apartment."

He was the first and last man, other than my male friends, who would be invited into my home for many a month. *See what can happen?* I would think. Even people you met through work or through friends could be scary in all kinds of ways you couldn't possibly know about beforehand.

One of the things I had looked forward to when I moved out of my parents' house was dating. It wasn't that I hadn't gone out on dates when I'd been living with them; but, once you're out of high school, the idea of sitting on your parents' couch with a guy you like loses its appeal. Finding a serious boyfriend—one whom I spent more days with than without—would have meant spending most of my time at his place, which would have required far more time away from my cats than I would have found acceptable. The whole situation had hampered me in ways that I expected to free up once I was living on my own.

Things didn't work out exactly as I'd envisioned as the months in my apartment passed. Sometimes it almost felt as if I'd had more of a social life when I lived with my parents. Now that I no longer had my parents' presence to fall back on as a pretext for not bringing somebody back to my place, I seemed to be avoiding the my-place-or-yours discussion altogether by limiting my social activities to evenings out with groups of friends. Occasionally, these outings included a guy who I might or might not like, who might or might not like me back, but that was about it.

My job—the job that enabled me to live in my own apartment—was very demanding. I worked long hours and told myself that my career was more important right now than "boys."

But that wasn't the whole truth. I was a part of the *Sex and the City* generation. The entirety of popular culture—television, movies, magazines—was united in assuring me that a challenging career combined with a decadent love life was my birthright, practically an obligation for a girl my age.

I liked men, and I liked getting to know better the men I found interesting. But I also enjoyed living on my own for the first time in my life. I wasn't anxious to fall into a relationship and end up with somebody in my home four or five nights a week, or—an even worse scenario—discussing the possibility of moving in together.

And I was fiercely protective of my cats, particularly Homer. I didn't want to bear the scrutiny of somebody who might not like cats very much, or who might judge me as less desirable for having three of them. I wasn't willing to form the slightest emotional attachment to anybody with whom I might have an *it's me or the cats* conversation somewhere down the road. After my experience with Hissy the Wonderputz, I was reluctant to go out on a second date with anybody who so much as frowned when the word *cat* was mentioned.

Most of my friends went out with men, brought them home impulsively, and figured out as things went along how mature, compatible, and commitment-oriented the man in question was. The whole point of relationships in your twenties was supposed to be about making mistakes, learning from them, and establishing the criteria that would eventually lead you to The One.

But I had be satisfied as to a certain basic level of responsibility and cat-friendliness before I even thought about bringing a man into my home. A visitor might decide to go out onto my balcony and forget to close the balcony door behind him. It was an easy enough mistake to make—but the rapidity with which such a mistake could blossom into full-blown tragedy, ending with Homer plummeting eleven stories, was unbearable to contemplate. Turning a back, even for a second, on an open front door while accepting a Chinese food delivery would allow Homer all the time he'd need to dart outside to "explore." Another girl might wail in irritation over boyfriends who always left the toilet seat up or consistently cracked the bedroom window open too wide. My friends and I laughed about such minor lapses—the silly thoughtlessness that crops up in even the best relationship—but in my world, there was nothing funny or minor about the consequences a moment's thoughtlessness could bring.

"You're a control freak," my friend Tony frequently informed me. "You want to try to control everything, and you're using Homer as an excuse."

He wasn't entirely right. Homer did require more consideration than another cat would. The carefree irresponsibility I'd longed for when living with my parents, of being able to say *I have no one to please but myself*, was a moment in my life that had come and gone, if it had every existed at all. I didn't regret it; the rewards of living with Homer far outweighed the limitations. Nevertheless, the limitations remained.

But Tony wasn't entirely wrong, either. I could make a good argument for doing a better job than most of my friends did of vetting dates before I brought them home. But there was no argument I could make for refusing involvement altogether.

During those weeks of insomnia after my apartment was broken into, I thought about my life and where it was going. I spent hours weighing and reviewing every major decision I'd made since leaving college, and innumerable trivial choices—a dress I'd loved but hadn't bought; my decision not to visit the Louvre during my one day in Paris a decade ago, because I'd wanted to experience the city outside of museums—came under scrutiny. In the aftermath of what had felt like a near-death experience, it seemed important to be able to assure myself, *If I had died that night, I wouldn't have had any regrets about how I lived.*

Overall, I was pleased with the progress I'd made over the past couple of years. I was self-sufficient for the first time, and I was proud of myself for getting there. I had created what I felt was a reasonably happy life for myself and my feline brood.

It was the little things, I realized, that had a way of getting away from you and never coming back—the afternoons in a city you might never visit again, or the nights when a group of friends, having been out later than anyone had intended, decided to stay up to watch the sun rise over the ocean, but you went home because it was late, after all, and there was work the next day. Adopting Homer had made me feel older than my age in many ways. But I wasn't old, not really. And I wouldn't be young forever.

There were whole areas of my life that I was cutting myself off from. I didn't necessarily subscribe to the notion that said, *What is it all worth if you have no one to share it with?* If you had work you enjoyed, a home you loved, friends you could laugh with, you were already luckier than probably 90 percent of the world's population.

I knew this to be true. But I also, in a very basic and primal way, wanted to love someone. I wanted someone to love me.

I wasn't a risk taker by nature. Blind leaps into the unknown were Homer's province, not mine. But risk was an inescapable fact of life. Sleeping alone in your own bed in your own home behind a locked door could be risky, as I'd learned. There was something to be said for being young and romantic, for bubbling up with breathless excitement when the phone rang and bemoaning your ill fortune—over a pint of ice cream and a stack of romantic comedies—when it didn't.

And so what if I wasn't looking for somebody to spend the rest of my life with right now? Not everything had to be so goal-oriented. Look at Homer. He had no idea where he was climbing or running or jumping to half the time. Simply to be in motion was a joy undertaken for its own sake.

I BEGAN TO APPROACH dating with the resolute intention of finding a few brave souls who would pass what I came to think of as "the Homer test." I didn't have anything so formal as a written questionnaire (I was a touch neurotic when it came to Homer's safety, but I wasn't *crazy*), but I listened closely to anecdotes and asked probing questions. Was the man in question absent-minded? Was he forever fumbling around for keys or his wallet, or did he have a sharp memory for small details? Had he ever had a beloved pet, one who perhaps had required close attention and long-term care? Was he the kind of guy whose siblings entrusted him to take nieces and nephews to ball games or on camping trips, confident they would return in one piece? I figured someone who could remember that Jonny couldn't so much as inhale a whiff of any food containing nuts, or that Sally couldn't spend more than fifteen minutes in the sun without exploding into hives, was up to the task of remembering the very few rules I'd established in my own home to keep Homer safe without having to think about it constantly.

Homer was as fascinated with these men as he was with every new person he met, and they were no less fascinated by him. Usually, they started out being skeptical about taking on a woman with three cats. It wasn't that they disliked cats per se, but three seemed excessive, and one had to wonder about the owner of such a horde.

After a few visits to my home, however, most of them became devoted members of the cult of Homer.

Homer was certainly a very "boyish" little cat, and I think the men who met him were taken with how scrappy and rough-and-tumble he was. Homer still loved to wrestle around and play spirited games of tag or fetch as much as he had back when he'd stayed with Jorge and his friends. It's said that most men prefer dogs to cats, and maybe that's true, but Homer was about as puppyish as a cat could be when it came to instant affection and playful high spirits.

Living with Homer, it was easy to forget the things about him that were so astonishing to others. The mere idea of meeting a cat without eyes struck most people as a once-in-a-lifetime novelty. I think they expected Homer to look gruesome or malformed, because most of them made a point of noting, with surprise evident in their voices, how normal Homer looked. "Like he just has his eyes closed," they said. That Homer moved with such graceful self-assurance, that he was able to feed himself, groom himself, and navigate around the walls and furniture in my home, struck newcomers as nothing short of miraculous.

Homer was uniformly friendly with nearly everybody, but the small band of men who were granted access to him were sure that they—and only they—had a gift, some extraordinary inner quality that drew this blind creature to them. People loved Homer as much for how he made them feel about themselves as for his love of mischief and play. To forge a bond of trust and friendship with this sightless little cat could only mean that one possessed a streak of goodness, a purity of spirit that might ever have been detected before this, but that was obviously real. (Homer saw it, didn't he?) In fact, I never had a single boyfriend who wasn't convinced he had a unique and special relationship with Homer.

"Homer's my buddy!" they all claimed.

"Homer's everybody's buddy," I would reply fondly—not meaning to undercut them, but speaking from the pride I always felt at how engaged and outgoing my little guy had turned out to be.

"Yeah, but it's different with Homer and *me*," they would say, with the kind of confidence that admitted no room for dispute or doubt. I never corrected them a second time; who was I to argue with anybody who loved Homer?

Homer may have had similarly unique relationships with each of these men, but the particular forms the relationships took were always different. One such boyfriend, a pillar of Miami's international finance community who'd played guitar with a garage band back in high school, discovered Homer's love of the rubber-band-wrapped tissue box and pulled his real guitar out of storage to "jam" with Homer. He even let Homer strum on the real guitar a few times, declaring him a prodigy. A chef at one of the local restaurants enjoyed preparing different recipes and watching Homer's varying reactions depending upon what was cooking. Beef was mildly interesting to Homer, fish was *very* interesting, and anything with turkey made him absolutely frantic. Homer developed a wild attachment to a specific kind of fresh-roasted-deli-sliced turkey, and was able to distinguish it—while it was still wrapped in plastic and waxed paper—from lesser turkeys and deli meats. "He has the nose of a gourmet," this man proclaimed, and I didn't have the heart to tell him that Homer was equally passionate about the occasional Friskies that came his way. The boyfriend with fond memories of building pillow forts as a child delighted in bringing over boxes, large shopping bags, and anything else he and Homer could use to construct cat-sized caves, engaging in elaborate games of hide-and-seek that lasted for hours.

I wish I could say that I thought these men were overstating their interest in Homer as a way of getting closer to me. Deep down, I suspected that, if anything, the opposite was the case. Many a crestfallen boyfriend over the years, upon being broken up with, would tremulously ask, "Does…does this mean I can't see *Homer* anymore?"

I REMEMBER ONE MAN I dated, a man who met Homer a few times and whom I became well and truly infatuated with. He was brilliant, handsome, wildly funny, and one of the greatest kissers I'd ever encountered. We went out on a few progressively intense dates, and had just reached the shy-confessions stage of our burgeoning relationship, (*You're the most amazing*

woman I've met in years... that sort of thing) when he abruptly canceled three dates in a row at the last minute.

Anybody who's been there knows the thoughts that start crowding your head in a situation like this. You're simultaneously angry at the lack of consideration, and hurt by the inevitable conclusion that you must have done something wrong—surely, you must have become less interesting, or been too obvious about your feelings, for things to change so rapidly.

When I finally questioned this man about what was going on, he told me that his father had been an alcoholic, that the trauma of his childhood remained with him, and that while he liked me more than he could say, he needed me to understand that he was the kind of guy who had to take things slow—but there was no doubt in his mind that we could get through this and end up stronger as a couple, that having "shared" we could only know each other better than we had before this conversation.

I told him never to call me again.

I didn't make that statement thinking, *If he treats you this way now, early in the relationship, it's not going to get any better.* I didn't tell myself, *He couldn't possibly like you as much as he says he does if he stands you up three times in a row.* That was all probably true, but it wasn't what I was thinking.

What I felt was disgust. Following the logic of his argument, he was saying that it was okay to hurt me now (surely, he must have known that standing me up three times would hurt my feelings) because, some twenty-odd years ago, somebody else had hurt him. It was bad behavior masquerading as self-knowledge. He saw himself as a man who'd made a brave confession, who'd been honest—and honesty was an indisputable virtue. I saw someone who thought it was okay to transfer his own pain onto others because it was easier than handling it himself.

It wasn't that I thought it was wrong. It was worse than wrong. It was unmanly.

Like any woman who's spent enough years dating, I could fill a whole book with stories like these. But I come here neither to praise nor to bury the men I dated yet didn't end up with. They had their admirable qualities, and if they made mistakes, well, so did I. We were only human, after all.

Since adopting Homer, however, my standards had changed. You could argue that comparing men with a cat would be ridiculous, and I wouldn't disagree. But Homer had, without thinking, thrown himself between me and a threat to my life. I didn't expect many such scenarios where a boyfriend would be called upon to do the same thing. But I admired Homer—I wished, almost every day, that I could be more like him. I wanted his strength, his courage, his reflexive loyalty. I wanted to be as cheerful as he was in the face of adversity. And I wanted a man with those same qualities. I realized that I couldn't be with anybody long-term if I couldn't admire and look up to him. Intelligence, attractiveness, a sense of humor—these were all important things.

By themselves, though, they weren't enough.

Back when I first adopted Homer, that first time I saw him in my vet's office, I was struck by something about him that had seemed stronger and braver than other cats, or even most people. Before that, my criteria—the criteria I never thought about specifically, but responded to unconsciously—for evaluating both pets and people had been roughly the same: cuteness, intelligence, personality, how entertaining I found them to be, and so on. I was also—as should surprise nobody who knows I began my career in the charity sector—a sucker for feeling that I was needed. Scarlett and Vashti had been adopted because they so clearly needed me, and loved after that simply because they were mine.

It had been different with Homer. I had fallen in love with Homer because he was cheerful and brave, and not at all needy, despite the pain and loss of his earliest weeks of life. You can say that Homer was a cat and didn't know any better, that it wasn't as if he said to himself, *Well, now, there's no point in being miserable over this disability that I can't change anyway.* And you'd be right. But I had worked with enough abused, injured, and traumatized animals to know that a great many of them never got over it and spent their lives cringing or snapping whenever anybody tried to get close. It was heart wrenching and certainly not something you blamed the animal for. They didn't know any better. But Homer didn't any better, either. Homer's courage and optimism were innate—things that could be reinforced, but never taught. Bravery was Homer's reflex, just like catching flies or crouching down before he pounced on something.

Adopting Homer was the first time in my life when I made a decision about a relationship based on what I would have called essential character, if I had thought about it clearly at the time. It wasn't Homer's charm or his need that had drawn me to him. It was the something about him that I would have respected in anyone—even in any human—if and when I found it.

As it turned out, the one romantic relationship that had the most profound impact on my life was also one of the shortest. He lived in New York, and long-distance relationships almost never work. This one was no different. But I did spend a few long weekends with him in Manhattan.

My best friend, Andrea, had recently moved to New York from California with the boyfriend she would undoubtedly soon be engaged to. Andrea's entire family lived in New York, so it seemed likely that, even though Andrea's job had relocated her to five different cities in the last eight years, this move would be permanent. Whenever I went to visit my boyfriend in New York, I spent time with her as well.

I may not have fallen in love with the man, but I did fall in love with the city. To be a person who loves books is to be half in love with the idea of New York. After only a few days spent in the concrete reality of it, I was hooked.

"You should move here," Andrea would say when I saw her. "Think how much fun it would be if the two of us were in the same city together again."

It was an appealing idea, but it was also a scary one. I had my family and friends to fall back on in any worst-case scenarios as long as I stayed in Miami—and, as I had learned, worst-case scenarios had a way of cropping up. In Manhattan, I would be truly on my own for the first time in my life.

"What do you guys think?" I asked Scarlett, Vashti, and Homer. "How would you feel about being New York City cats?"

Scarlett and Vashti were watching Homer with lazy interest as he tried to find a trajectory that would allow him to leap directly from the top of his six-foot cat tower to the top shelf of the closet. He'd landed flat on his face three times already, but that hadn't deterred him from attempt number four.

Fortune favors the brave, I thought.

17 • "The Pussy Galore Tour"

Zeus takes all travelers under his protection, for he is the avenger of all suppliants and foreigners in distress.
— HOMER, *The Odyssey*

By January of 2001, my thirtieth birthday loomed on the horizon (technically it wasn't until October, but milestone birthdays cast long shadows), and dark days had descended on the dotcom industry. Internet companies everywhere were shedding employees or shutting down altogether, and Miami was no exception. The company I had originally gone to work for had closed its doors months earlier. I had quickly found a position with another firm, but a mere three months later, they shut down as well. I'd found yet another job within six weeks, but they soon lost their funding and cut my salary in half. I was hemorrhaging savings as I struggled to make ends meet.

It was a state of affairs that couldn't continue indefinitely. I began to send résumés everywhere I could think of, but hiring in Miami had all but frozen solid. The fallout of the dotcom failures had spread its misery across most of Miami's other industries—tourism, real estate, finance—and nobody was hiring staff for marketing positions. I didn't get a single call for an interview.

The beauty of having nothing to lose is that you have everything to gain. My vague soap bubble of an idea about moving to New York had drifted aimlessly in the background of my thoughts for some time, but it had always seemed too impractical for serious consideration. For one thing, why would anybody in New York hire me in Miami? Moving would be expensive, not to mention how much more expensive it was to live in New York City than South Florida. And wasn't I getting a little old for such a major life change? Starting over in Manhattan seemed like the sort of thing one did straight out of college, not when one was approaching thirty.

But as the Miami job market continued to dry up, I started emailing my résumé to companies in New York. *Why not?* I asked myself, and couldn't think of a single good reason.

It was a shot in the dark, one that I didn't really expect to hit its target. Within three weeks, however, I had requests for interviews with five firms in New York City. I flew up the following week to meet with them, and by the end of that week I had three written offers of employment. One was for a director of marketing position with a large technical recruiting firm located in Manhattan's Financial District, six blocks from the World Trade Center. In addition to the generous salary they offered, they were also willing to offset my moving expenses. I had a friend who lived in an apartment building only a block away from this company, and he pulled some strings with his leasing office. Twenty-four hours later, I'd landed an apartment without any of the drama one normally hears associated with apartment hunting in New York.

It was almost disconcerting how easily everything had fallen into place. By mid-February, my whim of only a few weeks ago was a reality.

I was moving to New York.

ALL THE ARTICLES I'D read over the years on the subject of caring for a blind cat were united on one point: The most important thing was to create a stable and permanent environment for the cat. You were advised not to do things like move furniture around or change the litter box's location. Moving homes altogether is unsettling enough for any cat—cats not being creatures who regard change favorably—and is especially to be avoided when the cat in question is blind.

Homer was about to undergo his fifth move in less than five years. Like the hero Odysseus, imagined by the poet for whom Homer had been named, perpetual journeying seemed to be his destiny.

I considered various options for getting my three cats to New York with a minimum of trauma for all concerned. I could drive the four of us up, but was reluctant to subject the cats to two full days in their carriers—which they hated—not to mention the logistics of litter breaks, finding motels along the way that would be willing to accommodate three cats, and so on.

Flying up would make the most sense—at least it would get the whole thing over and done with faster than any other option—but I flat-out refused to check my cats as baggage. The thought of them in a cargo hold, cold and terrified, was something I couldn't even stand to think about. Nor was I eager to become one of those news stories you sometimes heard about, where a checked cat ends up as lost luggage, flying around the world for days and surviving by licking the condensation that forms in his carrier.

So I called the airline to find out if it was possible to bring the cats onto the plane with me. The requirements were both straightforward and daunting. A cat boarding a plane had to be contained in a regulation-sized carrier that would fit beneath the seat. The cat had to have a recent health certificate, which had to be presented to security personnel at the metal detectors and again at the gate. Each cat had to travel with a ticketed passenger, and only one cat was allowed per passenger. Only two cats were permitted in a cabin, and only four cats were permitted on the entire plane.

The carriers I already had, and the health certificates wouldn't be a problem since all three cats were in perfect health and up-to-date on their shots. But if I wanted to bring the three of them onto the plane with me, I would have to find two other people willing to fly up to New York with me.

Hard as I searched, I was unable to find a direct flight from Miami to New York that had room for three cats. There was a flight that connected through Atlanta, and if I cashed in all my frequent-flier miles I could just manage to upgrade one of the tickets to first class, in keeping with the two-cats-per-cabin restriction.

Then I called my friends Tony and Felix, two of the highest-energy people I knew and always up for an adventure. "How'd you guys like a free trip to New York?"

THE DAY WE MOVED was undoubtedly the most unsettling day of Homer's life thus far. Our morning began just after daybreak, when the moving company I'd hired arrived to cart away everything we owned. I locked the cats in the bathroom during this process, where Scarlett and Vashti curled up warily in the bathtub atop some old towels I'd laid out for them. Homer meowed and pawed frantically at the bathroom door, hating his confinement and desperate to know the source of all the noise in the other rooms. When I finally released him he prowled compulsively through the empty apartment, unable to settle down and complaining at the top of his lungs for over an hour. *Hey! Where's all our stuff?!* Homer had never been in a room completely devoid of furniture, and it was plain that he didn't like it. Nothing that caused every familiar smell and texture to disappear could possibly bode well.

He wasn't wrong.

The only things left in the apartment aside from a single suitcase were the three carriers for the cats. Scarlett and Vashti took one look at the carriers and fled, huddling defiantly in the farthest corner of a now empty walk-in closet. Fleeing at the sight of their carriers was something of a ritual, but I rounded them up within a few minutes and, cooing soothingly, loaded them in.

I always put Homer into his carrier last, because he was typically the easiest one to corral. Since he couldn't see the carriers, he didn't run as soon as they came out. And he was the one out of the three of them who was most likely to respond to commands like *No!* and *Stay!*

Maybe he was still unnerved by the mysterious disappearance of all our belongings, but Homer rebelled that morning in a way he never had before. *No, Homer!* I yelled. *Stay!* Even though there was nothing for him to hide under or behind, I still had to chase him for nearly twenty minutes. After I finally caught him he fought the carrier for all he was worth, clawing the fronts of my hands in the process. It wasn't that he was trying to claw *me* as he struck blindly at anything within reach. In fact, it was my involuntary cry of pain that ultimately subdued him just long enough for me to gently press the top of his head into the carrier and zip it up around him. Homer immediately began to wail.

By the time the cats were finally settled, and I'd cleaned and bandaged my hands, we were running half an hour behind schedule.

"Hurry, *hurry*," I said urgently to Tony and Felix in turn as I picked each of them up. We were driving to my parents' house, where ewe would leave my car and transfer to theirs so they could drive us to the airport. Scarlett and Vashti were mewling in their carriers in the backseat, but their cries were drowned out by Homer, who yowled at full volume from his spot up front next to me. He struggled, poked, and punched from within his carrier, so that it resembled a container of Jiffy Pop left on the stove.

"I'll take Vashti," Felix said, settling her carrier onto his lap. "I like her. She's the most glamorous."

"I don't have to take *that* one, do I?" Tony asked anxiously, eyeing Homer's roiling carrier.

"I'm taking Homer," I replied tersely. "Tony, you can take Scarlett."

I raced desperately over the causeway, trying to make up the time I'd lost fighting with Homer. I couldn't miss this flight.

I just couldn't. Trying to rebook for the six of us would be an unthinkable nightmare, and I was supposed to start my new job the following day. I was doing at least eighty, so it shouldn't have been a surprise when police lights appeared in my rearview mirror.

"Dammit," I swore in a loud whisper—although it was unnecessary to lower my voice. With all the noise Homer was making, nobody could have heard me anyway.

I pulled over, turned off the ignition, and rolled down my window. Homer was kicking up such a terrific racket, I could barely hear the police officer when he finally reached the car. "I'm sorry," I said in a slightly raised voice as I gestured toward my ear. "I can't hear you. Could you speak up?"

The cop raised his voice, too. "I said, *do you know how fast you were going?*"

"Oh!" I looked around helplessly as I handed over my driver's license, as if the right answer would somehow materialize out of thin air. "Pretty fast, I guess. We're on our way to the airport," I added, hoping this would gain me clemency.

The cop peered into the passenger seat, where Homer's carrier jostled around, seemingly of its own volition, like a thing possessed. "What's in there?" he asked.

"My cat," I replied. "It took me forever to get him in there and now we're running a little late."

The officer's gaze took in the two other carriers containing Vashti and Scarlett, which now rested on the laps of Felix and Tony, who smiled winningly. "You should have left a little earlier," he said, and trundled off to his car to write up the ticket.

"We're going to miss the flight," Tony said, as the minutes rolled by and the cop still hadn't returned with what I had to assume was a lengthy manifesto on the history and future of traffic tickets—because *why else was* it *taking him so long to write the damn thing?*

"We'll make it," I assured him. "We'll make it because we have to."

The cop finally returned with the ticket and an admonition to "slow down," which was wholly disregarded as I bore down on the accelerator once the police car had disappeared into traffic. Homer's cries were beginning to sound a touch hoarse, but they continued unabated all the way to my parents' house. Tony and Felix donned the headphones of the portable CD players they'd brought with them for the plane ride.

Probably the only person I know who's more compulsive about punctuality than I am is my mother. She flung open the front door as soon as she heard my car pull into the driveway, with a cry of "*David! They're here!*" to my father in the interior of the house. "You're so late," she clucked as I grabbed Homer's twitching carrier and got out of the car, followed by Tony and Felix. They pulled their bags from the trunk of my car and loaded them into my parents'. "Why didn't you leave earlier?"

I shot her a look. "Let's just go."

Scarlett and Vashti had apparently resigned themselves to their fate, for they remained silent on the car ride to the airport. Homer kept up his caterwauling, which had become a loud, continuous howl that only subsided when he ran out of breath.

Tony, Felix, and I were wedged in the backseat of my parents' car. My mother turned around from her position in the front passenger seat and, raising her voice over Homer's cries, said tearfully, "I can't believe you're leaving. I'm going to miss you so much."

"What?" I replied. "I can't hear you."

"I said, *I'm going to miss you so much!*"

"Oh," I responded. *"Me too!"*

My father made good time and, miraculously, we arrived at the airport within thirty minutes of our flight. "No time for big good-byes," my father said as he hustled our luggage to a skycap. I slung Homer over my shoulder and fiercely hugged each of my parents in turn. Then Tony, Felix, and I pulled out our tickets and ran through the terminal for the metal detectors.

The people around us in line gave us a wide berth as Homer continued to yowl and tear at his carrier from the inside. A few of them threw me openly disapproving looks, and I knew they were thinking, *I hope she's not on my flight.*

"That's a lot of cats you got there," the security guard observed as we prepared to load the three of them into the X-ray machine's conveyor belt. I dug around in my bag and retrieved the cats' health certificates, which I handed over to her for a cursory glance.

"We're the Pussy Galore Tour," Felix said brightly. "Maybe you've heard of us."

"Oh, yeah." A slow grin broke over the security guard's face. "That *does* sound kinda familiar." She peered into the carrier containing Vashti, who gazed back with abject misery scrawled on her face. "This one's a beauty! Is she the star of the show?"

"There are no small roles," Tony told the guard very seriously. "Only small cats."

I rolled my eyes as we passed through the metal detector. "C'mon guys," I said as I retrieved Homer. "We have to hurry."

We made a mad dash for the gate and were panting by the time we got to it. I reached again into my bag and produced a small vial containing the cat tranquilizers the vet had suggested I dispense before boarding.

Felix and Tony instantly perked up. "Are those for us?" Felix asked.

"No, they're for the cats," I replied.

"Don't you think it would be easier if we tranquilized ourselves and left the cats alone?" Tony said.

None of the cats were ever enthusiastic about taking pills, but Scarlett and Vashti swallowed their tranquilizers with a minimum of fuss. I was half convinced they had some inkling of what lay ahead, and figured the best way to face it was unconscious.

Homer was another story. As soon as I unzipped the top of his carrier, he made a desperate break for freedom. I had to fight to keep him contained, and finally Felix held the carrier closed around Homer's neck with both of his hands while I patiently pried Homer's jaws open, placed the tiny pill on the back of his tongue, and softly stroked his throat to encourage him to swallow. I held his mouth closed for a minute or two, then released him.

Homer promptly spat the pill onto the ground.

"Come on, Homer," I said. "Do it for Mommy." I once again opened Homer's mouth and inserted the pill. I once again held his mouth closed and stroked his throat.

Homer once again spat the pill out.

I was getting desperate. The events of the entire morning had frazzled me, to say the least, and if Homer was this unhappy now, I couldn't imagine what he would be like unsedated on the plane. I tried three more times to give him tranquilizer, holding his mouth closed for so long I was afraid I'd suffocate him. He turned his head vigorously from side to side in an attempt to shake me off. I sprinkled some catnip into his carrier, I rolled the pill into a small bit of turkey from one of the sandwiches I'd packed, I even tried dissolving it in a bottlecap of water, which Homer not only refused to drink it, but nosed it out of my had so that it spilled on the floor. *No! I don't want it!*

I'd always known Homer was stubborn, that he was a cat who knew his own mind, but this was the first time I'd seen that stubbornness turned full force against *me*. I had my agenda, and Homer had his, and the two were obviously not in sync.

But I could be as stubborn as he was. One way or another, the two of us were getting to New York that day.

By now, the plane had been boarding for several minutes and Tony, Felix, and I were the only ones left at the gate. "What should we do?" Tony asked uncertainly.

I took a deep breath. *Steady*, I told myself. "He'll have to fly without it, I guess."

The struggle over the pill had had the one benefit of quieting Homer's crying He wasn't even rattling his carrier anymore as we boarded the plane. But as soon as I stowed him beneath the seat in front of me, and he felt the thrum of the plane's engine through the floor, he started up again.

"Would you like a cocktail before takeoff?" the resolutely cheerful flight attendant asked as I buried my face in my hands.

"God, yes," I replied. She brought me a vodka with cranberry juice, which I downed in a single gulp, hastily requesting another. Thank the Lord for first class.

THE FLIGHT FROM MIAMI to Atlanta, where we would pick up our connecting flight to New York, was brief. Homer's cries by now had deepened into a low, mournful tone I'd never heard from him before. His ears were so much more sensitive than other cats' to begin with, and I could only imagine how painful the change in air pressure was for him as the plane ascended. As soon as the FASTEN SEAT BELTS sign was turned off, I pulled Homer's carrier out from under the seat in front of me and cradled it on my lap. I unzipped it just enough to reach a hand in, and Homer cuddled and nuzzled against it with a desperation that surpassed even the occasions he'd believed me to be angry with him. His cries took on the contrite yips he made when trying to make up with me. *Please let me out. Please make it stop. I'll be good! I promise I'll be good!*

If I could have stuffed myself into his carrier, given him my seat, and borne his pain for him, I would have considered it a fair trade. How could he know, how could he possibly understand, why I was subjecting him to all this? "Good boy," I murmured as I rubbed his aching ears. "Good boy, good boy, good boy…"

Once I'd had my third drink and the plane leveled, a soothing sense of inevitability descended on me. We were on our way now. I continued to stroke Homer's head, which calmed him a bit. I ignored the filthy looks a few of my fellow passengers shot us as Homer's cries continued, softer, yet unceasing.

The plane began its descent into Atlanta sooner than I would have liked. I tensed slightly; I had gone to college in Atlanta, and I knew how enormous the airport was. My hope was that our connecting flight wouldn't be too far from where we arrived. To my horror, when the flight attendant announced the gates for connecting flights, I discovered that we were landing at an A gate and flying to New York from Concourse D. We had roughly fifteen minutes between flights—how could we possibly make it?

My seat was closest to the front of the plane, and I waited impatiently, bouncing on the balls of my feet, for Tony and Felix to emerge. "We have to run, guys," I told them. "Like, seriously, we have to run *now!*"

Tony and Felix took off in one direction while I bolted in the other. "No!" I called to their retreating backs. "This way! *This way!*"

The three of us tore through the airport, each with a bouncing carrier slung over one shoulder. "Here's the train to Concourse D," Tony shouted, slowing down at the empty track.

"There's no time to wait for it," I said desperately. "We have to keep going. Hurry!"

We sprinted as if all the devils of hell were chasing us, past slow walkers and cleaning staff, and occasionally bumping into a hapless bystander who popped unexpectedly into our path. *Excuse me, excuse me*, we muttered breathlessly, over and over again. Vashti and Scarlett didn't budge inside their carriers, regarding the passing scenery through glazed half-closed eyes. Homer, who had never been in his carrier for more than forty-five minutes at a stretch, and who had certainly never been bounced around so vigorously, wailed piteously.

"Who schedules these things so far apart?" Felix wondered aloud, gasping painfully.

"Some sadist who works for the airline," I called over my shoulder.

We arrived at our connecting flight just as they were closing the gate. "Wait, we're here! We're here!" I announced to the woman behind the counter. I bent over to catch my breath and rub a cramp in my side as I shoved our tickets and the cats' health certificates at her. My brow was slick with sweat, and I inadvertently dampened the papers as I drew the back of my hand across my forehead, trying to keep the sweat from dripping into my eyes.

"You really should try to arrive at the gate at least fifteen minutes before departure," the woman at the counter informed me with cold asperity.

I was positive that my restraint in not decking her guaranteed me a spot in heaven.

This time, I was seated next to an older woman who was also traveling with a cat. "I see they put us together," she said happily as I settled into my seat and stowed Homer in front of me, still fighting to catch my breath. "You wouldn't believe how hard it was for us to get a seat on this flight! And I had to upgrade to first class! All the other spots for cats were already taken. Did you ever hear of such a thing?"

I mumbled something indistinct.

"This is Otis," she continued, indicating the dignified-looking ginger tabby who snoozed peacefully in the carrier at her feet. "He's a good flier. We make this trip twice a year to visit my grandchildren."

"This is Homer," I told her. Homer was once again struggling furiously within the confines of his carrier. He responded to the sound of his name with an agonized lowing that was so loud, we almost didn't hear the announcement to fasten our seat belts. "Homer's never flown before."

"Poor little thing," the woman said. She lowered her head a bit to get a better look at him through the mesh of the carrier. "Don't cry, Homer. It'll be over sooner than you think."

We chatted comfortably as the plane began its climb. I told her all about Homer, about his usual bravery and how out of character all the fuss he was making was. "I'm so sorry he's making all this noise," I apologized.

She laughed. "Wait till you're traveling with a baby." I suddenly realized, in a moment that had all the settling heaviness of a truth long known yet only now understood, that this wasn't just a trip I was taking. I was flying into my future, a future so indistinct and shapeless as to be completely unrecognizable to me. I had lived thirty years in the same city, and now, after only a few week's thought and planning, I was grafting the entirety of my life onto a new and strange place. I had a vision of myself, sometime years and decades from now, traveling with a cat who wasn't Homer to visit grandchildren of my own. I would pat the arm of some nervous young woman sitting next to me and tell her, *Dahlink, this is nothing. You have no idea what the years will bring...*

Homer wailed again, jolting me from my reverie. "Can't you shut that thing up?" demanded an irate man behind us.

"Have some compassion, sir!" the woman next to me snapped. She turned to fix a stern eye on him. "The poor cat's never flown before. What's *your* excuse for bad manners?"

My eyes filled with tears, and I impulsively seized her hand. "Thank you!" I said.

She squeezed my hand back in a motherly fashion. "Some people act as if a cat didn't deserve any sympathy at all."

The moment I saw the Statue of Liberty and the twin towers of the World Trade Center pass beneath my window was one of the happiest of my life. Even learning—after landing and waiting forty minutes at the baggage carousel—that our luggage hadn't made the connecting flight, and wouldn't arrive until sometime the next day, didn't faze me.

I felt as if I had spent the day being pummeled like a punching bag, but Felix and Tony were remarkably fresh. Scarlett and Vashti had been no trouble at all, they told me. I thanked them profusely for having made the voyage with me, and then they disappeared into cabs bound for the friends and relatives they'd be visiting while in New York.

I loaded my three cats into a cab of our own and directed it to our new apartment. I had purchased a litter box, food, and bowls when I'd been in New York two weeks earlier to sign the lease, and had left everything my building's doorman. I had also ordered an air mattress (a temporary stopgap until the movers delivered my furniture a week or two later) along with sheets and a blanket, and my friend Richard, who lived in the building and had helped me land the apartment, had supervised their delivery. The rest of my furniture wouldn't arrive for a few days.

The doorman provided a luggage cart and helped me wrangle the cats and all their apparatus to our apartment on the thirty-first floor. The second the door was closed behind me, I unzipped each of the cats' carriers. Scarlett and Vashti were still groggy from the effects of the tranquilizer, and they ambled around in a befuddled way before falling in a heap together in front of the radiator.

Homer appeared bewildered, but grateful to be out of his carrier and on solid ground once again. Every other time we'd moved, Homer had sprung from his carrier, eager to explore his new surroundings. This time, however, he was more cautious. Something felt very different about this move, and it wasn't just the day he'd spent in his carrier or the grueling trip he'd endured.

Once I'd set up food and litter, and carried Homer over to show him where they were, I tossed sheets and blankets haphazardly onto the air mattress and collapsed onto it face-first. *We made it*, I thought. *We're in New York*.

Homer was still creeping slowly about the room. The air was dry and cold, and his fur crackled with static electricity. From my purse, I pulled Homer's stuffed worm, which I'd wrapped up and carried with me. I hadn't wanted it to get lost in a moving box; I thought Homer would feel better if there was something immediately familiar he could reconnect with once we arrived.

For once, though, Homer wasn't overjoyed to greet his old friend. He gave the worm a perfunctory sniff and carefully dragged it next to his food bowl. Then he resumed his measured pace about the apartment.

It had been thirteen hours since the moving van had arrived that morning to start my day, and the only thing I wanted was another thirteen hours, uninterrupted, in the warmth and comfort of my bed. Vashti, Scarlett, and I dozed, but Homer had no intention of resting. There was still something about this place that didn't make sense, something that had to be figured out. He couldn't stop until he knew what it was.

He was a cat who hadn't slept in the city that never sleeps. Homer was already a New Yorker.

18 • Cool for Cats

**Strangers and foreigners are under Zeus' protection,
and will take what they can get and be thankful.**

– HOMER, *The Odyssey*

My Manhattan apartment was a studio—a large one by New York standards, at something like 750 square feet plus a tiny outdoor "terrace"—but a studio nonetheless. Studio-apartment living took some getting used to, although the transition proved easier for me than it did for my cats. Homer was particularly put out, unable to grasp the concept of a home that consisted of a single room. Scarlett and Vashti, much as they initially disliked their sudden space restriction, could plainly see that, indeed, their living area had contracted to the confines of four walls and a bathroom. But it took Homer weeks to settle down. He was more rambunctious than the other two, and suddenly found his play space unaccountably diminished. I think he believed there *must* be a door to another room somewhere, if only he could find it, and he would skim along the walls of the apartment, nose to the ground and ears high in the air as he tried to detect the slightest clue as to where the rooms that surely lay beyond were hidden. He would meow in a throaty, irritable sort of way, as if demanding, *Why won't anybody tell me where the rest of this place is?*

Looking for an outlet for Homer's energetic high spirits, I resorted to store-bought toys for the first time since Homer was a kitten. He was uninterested in most of them, naturally, except for one—a plastic wheel containing a plastic ball. There were slits along the top and sides of the wheel through which a cat could reach to push around the ball inside.

Homer was quickly obsessed. The ball made a satisfying whiz and rattle as it hurtled through the wheel, but Homer—unable to see how completely contained the ball was within the wheel—was convinced that he could figure out a way to liberate it. He would burrow under the wheel, turn it on its side, push it from one end of the room to the other, then sigh loudly in exasperation when the ball steadfastly refused to come out. Sometimes he would sneak up on it, crouching down and pouncing from clear across the room, as if hoping to surprise the wheel into relaxing its grip on the ball.

Scarlett and Vashti, who also found the toy intriguing, seemed perplexed at the sheer volume of hours that Homer could devote to this new pastime. Scarlett, especially, would observe him at work on the toy with a kind of amused disdain. *Clearly you can't get the ball out of the wheel*, she seemed to be thinking. *There's no point in being undignified about it.* Sometimes, Homer would creep out of bed at three or four in the morning to try it again, filling our small apartment with the sounds of the ball whooshing and the wheel flipping over and over as Homer butted it around with his head. It kept me up many a night, but I felt guilty about taking the toy away from him. *We only have the one room*, I would think. *Where else is he supposed to play?*

I paid dearly for that studio, more than I was comfortable claiming I could afford, but the location was unquestionably convenient. Not only was I within a block of my office, but living all the way down at the southernmost tip of the island as I did, just about every subway line in the city came right to my door. I could be all the way up on the Upper East Side or the Upper West Side—and any and all points in between—in less than twenty minutes, faster than people I knew who lived farther uptown and were, technically, closer to those locations than I was. And, no matter where I was in the city, I could always orient myself back home by looking for the twin towers of the World Trade Center. I'd been used to living in the city I had grown up in, a place I knew so intuitively, I'd never had to consult a map in my life. Learning my way around Manhattan was a challenge, but I always had some sense of where I was in relation to where I lived simply by consulting the skyline. This was true even in maze-like neighborhoods like SoHo or the West Village, where the streets were named instead of numbered and would otherwise have been hopeless for a newcomer to make any sense out of.

I spent a great deal of time with Andrea and Steve, the boyfriend who was now officially her fiancé, and their circle of friends. I made one trip back to Miami, for Tony's birthday, a month after I'd moved, and Andrea introduced me to her pet-sitter, Garrett. When I'd lived in Miami and traveled, my cats had always been cared for by either my parents or by some friend who Homer already knew, one who lived close enough to pop in and out once a day. But Manhattan was a place that made quick visits inconvenient and so, despite apprehensions about turning my cats and my home over to the care of a stranger, I decided to call a professional.

Garrett came over to meet us before my trip, and I went through my customary introduction ritual with Homer, holding Garrett's hand in mine and bringing the two hands together under Homer's nose. I left him with lengthy and detailed instructions: The windows and balcony door were *always* to remain closed; food dish and water bowl had to be separated enough that Homer couldn't toss the contents of one into the other; et cetera. I couldn't help it; my habit of worrying about Homer, of fretting irrationally over his safety far more than I did over Scarlett's and Vashti's, was too deeply ingrained. I tried not to be more skittish than Garrett's typical clients—although I'm sure I was—but Garrett was an unusually patient man, and he and Homer seemed charmed with each other from the beginning. "We're going to be buddies, aren't we, Homer?" Garrett said, and Homer brought over his stuffed worm to drop at Garrett's feet—his highest stamp of approval.

I called Garrett each day that I was gone, and he left written notes on the kitchen counter every time he visited. They went something like this:

> **Day 1:** *Changed food, water, litter. Gray guy hid under the bed, white guy seemed happy to see me, played worm fetch with Homer for half an hour.*
> **Day 2:** *Changed food, water, litter. Gray guy hid under the bed. White guy wouldn't stop dipping paws in fresh water. Homer threw a can of tuna out of the kitchen cabinet so I fed it to them. Hope that was okay.*

I preserved these notes for some weeks after I returned, hanging them on my refrigerator with magnets. I felt like a parent receiving her children's first report cards, with detailed accounts of who had been a good sharer or who played well with others. Although I'd had plenty of corroboration over the years, it still felt good to realize that I wasn't the only one who found Homer irresistible.

IT HAD BEEN JANUARY when I began interviewing for jobs in New York and February when I moved, and everybody—including the HR guy at the company that hired me—told me I was crazy to move from South Beach to New York, especially in the dead of winter. "But it's warm in Miami *all the time*," they would say, as if this simple and single fact rendered all other considerations moot.

With all the changes in our life and circumstances that moving to New York brought, I think it was the cold that was the hardest adjustment for the cats. Even the smell of the gas that powered the stoves and ovens in our building, which bothered the life out of Homer those first few weeks (every home we'd had in Miami had functioned solely on electrical power), wasn't as much of a shock as the ubiquitous cold.

I remembered how, as a six-year-old child visiting New York at Thanksgiving with my parents for the first time, cold air—cold air *outside*—had been a revelation to me. I'd read books, of course, where characters lived in places like New York or Chicago or London and had to bundle up beneath coats and scarves when they went outdoors. But I'd had no physical sense of what that would feel like. Cold, in my own experience, was something that lived inside refrigerators, or that was pumped mechanically into your home through air-conditioning units. Going to Macy's with my mother, the vastness of the floor that sold winter jackets and coats—with its overpowering smell of leather; I had never smelled so much leather in one place—reduced me almost to the point of awe. So many people must live in New York! And, naturally, all of them would need heavy coats. Because it was cold here. Cold *outside*.

Scarlett, Vashti, and Homer didn't have even the theoretical knowledge of cold to prepare themselves with. The cold weather dried the air out, and their fur was always full of static electricity. Scarlett and Vashti took this in stride, but Homer found it terribly disconcerting. He would walk across the throw rug on the floor to jump into my lap, eagerly pressing his nose against mine, only to find that the contact produced a small electric shock. He would turn his face to me reproachfully, as if to say, *Hey! What'd you do that for?*

My apartment had a heater, but it was on the fritz and would periodically emit a sharp buzz followed by a resounding *CLANK! CLONK CLANK!* The heater soon became Homer's sworn enemy. No matter how soundly asleep Homer was, he leapt to attention when he heard its racket. He had become very protective of me since the break-in and would jump to stand in front of me, his back fully arched, and growl in the heater's direction. After a minute he would creep cautiously toward it, rake at it furiously with his claws a few times, and then—confident he's shown that heater a thing or two—slink over to curl warily in my lap. But within an hour, the heater would clank and clonk once again.

My building super eventually replaced the heater with one that didn't bang around quite as much but, even when it was operating at full force, my apartment was never what one might call balmy. My cats and I became very close that first winter in New York, huddling together for warmth. The smallness of my new apartment, which had caused so much initial consternation, soon came to feel like a blessing. Even Scarlett became a cuddler. This might have been good news for Homer—who, much as he disliked having less room to play in, was overjoyed that the four of us were together all the time—if only Scarlett had been gracious about sharing.

At first, in her usual peremptory fashion, she tried to keep Vashti and Homer from getting too close to me. Scarlett may have discovered the joys of near-constant snuggling with Mom, but she always hated more physical contact with the other two cats than was strictly necessary. She would bat angrily at Homer's and Vashti's heads if she was in my lap and one of them tried to curl up beside me. Homer, who was always somewhere close to me and who had clearly come to regard himself as mature enough not to have to submit to Scarlett's thralldom anymore, would slap right back at her. *You're not the boss of me!* Occasionally, they got into downright fights that I had to break up by physically separating them. But eventually Scarlett learned to respect Homer's space, albeit grudgingly. Homer was nearly five years old now and wedded enough to his habits, more so than even the most habit-centered cat, that he wasn't about to be displaced jus because Scarlett had had a come-to-Jesus moment in her philosophy of physical affection.

Vashti, however—who was neither as aggressive as Scarlett nor as persistent as Homer—found herself crowded out. I had to make a concerted point of ensuring that she got her fair share of lap-time. Still, Vashti wasn't as happy as she'd been in Miami, and I felt guilty at times, worried that she was becoming the classic neglected middle child.

It was the first snowfall that brought Vashti around. Scarlett was captivated as it blew against the windows. She threw her upper body at the glass and did everything she could to catch the white stuff in her paws through the panes. She didn't know what snow was—she didn't realize that snow was *cold*. All she knew was that little flakes of things danced tantalizingly in front of her from the other side of the window glass, begging to be caught and played with.

But Vashti had been bred for snow—with her long white fur, her luxurious plume of a tail like that of an arctic fox, and her miniature snowshoes in the form of the little tufts of white fur that grew lush between the pads of her feet. She seemed to have an inborn memory of what snow was and what it would feel like. Perhaps that was why she'd always been so fascinated with water. As the snow piled up on our balcony, Vashti stood before the balcony door and pleaded mutely with her eyes for me to let her out into it. I did a few times, and she hurled herself into the middle of the deepest drifts. Her pupils were wide and wild and the only sign of darkness in the white-on-white landscape she created as she gamboled around and all but buried herself. It was only when a large gust of wind would come along that I could coax her back inside. Vashti may have loved snow, but wind terrified her and always drove her indoors.

It was around the time of the first snowfall that Homer discovered the magical world of under-the-covers. In Miami, he'd been content to cuddle with me on top of the blankets. But he was smaller than Scarlett and Vashti, and lying with me on top of the covers didn't keep him nearly warm enough now. He would burrow as far beneath the covers as he could, purring from between my feet and generating as much warmth as a tiny space heater. Scarlett and Vashti, not always realizing he was under there, would jump up to join me and frequently landed directly on his head. Homer hadn't landed inadvertently on another cat since he was a kitten. It was now his turn to wonder why the other two cats couldn't tell where he was—how come everybody knew where he was most of the time, but sometimes it was like they didn't know he was there at all? Homer would leap to his feet indignantly beneath the blankets, squawking a complaint.

I don't know if he couldn't tell when I wasn't lying beneath blankets, or if he simply refused to accept that they weren't there, but if I happened to be lying on the couch without a blanket over me, Homer would claw in frustration at my clothes. If I wore a baggy-enough sweatshirt, he would worm his way beneath it, poking his head out of the neck of my shirt and resting it on my shoulder, the rest of his body purring with loud contentment against my chest. I'd read aloud to him from whatever book I was in the middle of, and he would nuzzle happily against my neck until he fell into such a deep sleep that even his purring stopped. All that was left was the sound of his breath whistling past my ear, and the sound of the snow falling against the windows.

Spring came eventually, as spring is apt to do, and if there's anything more gorgeous than Manhattan in springtime, I've never seen it. I had grown up in a city of flowers (*Florida* is actually Spanish for *land of flowers*), but the blooms that sprang riotously from trees and bushes and flower beds in New York City dazzled me, seeming to tumble unexpectedly in the profusion of a single day. The air grew less dry, Homer's coat lost its static electricity, and Scarlett, almost cheerfully, made room for him beside me on the couch.

Only Vashti sat longingly before the windows, her eyes scanning the clear, sundrenched view of the streets below.

What? she seemed to ask. *No more snow?*

19 • A Hole in the Sky

We wept and lifted our hands to heaven on seeing such a horrid sight, for we did not know what to do.

– HOMER, *The Odyssey*

THERE ARE EARLY-FALL DAYS in New York so staggeringly beautiful, so laden with the promise of fall beauty still to come, that to experience them is, you tell yourself, worth all the money and hassle, all the striving and frenzy, that it takes simply to exist in Manhattan. The leaves are still green and the air hasn't turned cool yet, but it isn't hot anymore, either. There's a crispness to it that siphons off the brown industrial haze that hovers over the skyline during the humid days of July and August, leaving the air as clear and crystalline as God ever intended.

It was on the morning of one such day, at around eight fifteen, when I found myself facing an empty cat food bowl, an emptier cupboard, and a dilemma. I typically fed the cats a premium dry food (Vashti had developed food allergies, and the only brands that didn't trigger them were, naturally, the most expensive) supplemented by a can of moist food made by the same manufacturers (I had also learned that the more expensive the moist food, the less likely it was to make Homer gassy). Occasionally I fed them a can of the cheapest cat food out there, because my cats loved the cheap stuff with all the ardor of a child who'd much rather eat McDonald's than her mother's healthier home-cooked meals.

But I had nothing on-hand at the moment, not even a can of tuna that could substitute as a festive, hasty meal in a pinch.

I could rush out now to the little grocery store across the street and refill their food before leaving for work. While they didn't sell the specific brand I liked, I could buy a small box of a good-enough brand that would be gentle on Vashti's sensitive system and hold us over for a day or two.

Or I could wait a few hours until lunchtime, walk over to the pet store that was closer to Broadway, buy the better food, and dart back to my apartment to feed them then. My office was only a block away from my apartment, and only three blocks from the pet store, and I had made this round trip often enough. Living so close to my office, I hated the idea of being even five minutes late to work—feeling that I had no excuse not to walk in punctually at the dot of nine every morning. So it was usually during lunch that I made these midweek pet food runs. Besides, I liked to visit my cats midday. It was about the only free luxury my life in New York offered, and the cats—particularly Homer—always treated these spontaneous midday appearances like a holiday.

In the end, it was the complete emptiness of their food bowl that convinced me. I had sometimes gone to work leaving them with only a little food, but never leaving them without anything. Vashti sat next to the bowl and squeaked at me in a beseeching, yet pointed, way. *No food at all?* she seemed to ask. *You'd really leave us with no food at all?* Sighing at my own lack of foresight for not having stocked up on supplies over the weekend (I was running dangerously low on kitty litter as well), I grabbed my purse and headed out.

The street in front of my Financial District apartment was one of the oldest in New York, and so narrow that I could cross it in fewer than five steps. The line at the grocery store's cash register was long, as it always was in the mornings when nine-to-fivers grasped for their coffee as if it were a draught of sweet life itself. But the queue moved efficiently, and barely fifteen minutes had passed before I was once again in my apartment.

I had just emptied the entire box of food into their bowl, with all three cats seated in an eager semicircle around me, when there was an enormous muffled *BOOM!* It was more felt than heard, like the vibrations caused by a speaker with the bass turned all the way up. My apartment building shook slightly, and a few kernels of food spilled from the bowl onto the floor. Scarlett and Vashti darted under the bed so fast, it was as if a chain had been yanked that jerked them under. Homer leapt to stand in front of me, all his hackles raised, his nose sniffing the air as his ears moved from side to side. He growled a warning to whatever this invisible menace was. *Stay back*, the growl said. *Stay away from us...*

"It's okay, little boy," I said stroking his back. "It was just a car backfiring. There's nothing you have to protect Mommy from."

Homer didn't like it. For no reason at all that I could discern, he didn't like it. He ran from corner to corner of the apartment, hackles and ears still at full attention, a sentry securing a perimeter. Every so often, he would come to stand in front of me, continuing his growl. Scarlett and Vashti were equally unnerved, refusing to put so much as a whisker out from under the bed. By the time I lured them out, it was a minute or two past nine o'clock. It looked as if, for the first time since I had started my job in New York, I was going to be a few minutes late after all.

I had slung my purse over my shoulder when the second *BOOM!* came, shaking our building once again. This time, the cats couldn't be comforted. My apartment was a corner unit, with windows facing north and east, and Homer leapt to the sill of the westernmost of the northern-facing windows, hissing wildly.

There was snarled traffic and endless construction work around my building all the time, and the very narrowness of the streets—surrounded like a canyon with buildings that stretched thirty, forty, fifty stories high—echoed and magnified random sounds beyond their actual volume, even all the way up where I lived on the thirty-first floor. So I truly wasn't worried about anything at that point beyond how upset the cats were. I hated to leave them in that state, but what could I do? I certainly couldn't call my boss and tell him I was taking the morning off because my cats were upset.

So I left them, Homer still hissing at the window, Vashti and Scarlett huddled up beneath the bed.

The lobby of my building was serene as I dropped three pairs of pants with the on-site dry cleaner and crossed toward the front door. Tom, my doorman, usually waved a cheerful goodbye to me, but today he was on the phone, speaking in a hushed, anxious murmur. His expression was pained, and I remember feeling a fleeting sympathy for him as I passed. Tom was a good man; I hoped that whoever he was talking to wasn't delivering bad news.

The street in front of my building was as crowded as it had been earlier, when I'd darted out to get the cat food. There were people everywhere. They stood on sidewalks, in doorways, and in the middle of the street itself. But now, the street wasn't the buzzing hive of rush-hour activity it had been less than an hour ago. These people standing here now were completely frozen. Nobody spoke. Nobody moved. It was as if wax figures from a museum had come to life, wandered out into the streets, and then simply decided to stop and resume their waxy poses where they stood. The only noise I could hear was what sounded like the sirens of a thousand fire trucks, spilling over one another and competing to be the first to blare their panic into the early-fall air.

The silence and stillness of that Manhattan street, in the heart of the Financial District, at the height of rush hour, was the first time that day when—still not knowing why—I felt a creeping fear. Everybody was looking in the same direction—due west. Of course I turned, to see what they were all looking at.

The World Trade Center was on fire.

The towers were etched against the perfect blue of the morning sky, and they were on fire. They loomed over everything, appearing to be five feet from me rather than the five blocks they actually were. Black smoke billowed up, and shards of glass and debris fluttered down, as gracefully as the fall leaves that were only a few weeks away. Then I saw what couldn't be, it couldn't possibly be—and yet it was, it *was*—a man on fire, falling from one of the highest floors. He didn't fall in the elegant spiral of the debris, but in a straight-down plummet.

My stomach contracted into a painful dry heave and I retched, suddenly grateful that I hadn't eaten breakfast.

The people around me had seen it, too, and many of them turned to clutch the arms or bury their faces in the shoulders of those standing closest to them. From the stiff, automatic way in which these gestures were received, I guessed that some of those grabbed were strangers to the people who'd grabbed them.

I didn't want to touch anybody, and I didn't want anybody to touch me. There would be an indisputable reality in human contact, like when you say to somebody, *Pinch me*, so that you know you're not dreaming. Holding myself as carefully stiff as something made from wood, I walked the block to my office.

The message light on my phone was already blinking, and the phone itself rang incessantly. My coworkers were speaking quietly, clustered in groups of two and three around the windows in our office that faced onto the World Trade Center. *A plane hit it. A small plane. But how could a pilot not see...got disoriented...an accident...a horrible accident...*

The windows from my own desk looked directly onto the World Trade Center. The black smoke still gushed upward. I saw helicopters weave through the smoke, circling...circling. Helicopters have always been the paranoiac's symbol of government omnipotence, gliding with sleek menace through movies about evil federal conspiracies or dystopic futuristic societies. Now I thought that I had never seen anything as helpless-looking as those helicopters, small hatchlings continually repulsed from their nest. *There's no way they can land*, I thought. *How will they get those people out?*

The first call I made was to my mother. I felt an absurd need to announce to somebody that I was okay—even though, obviously, I was okay. This was something that was happening to other people, to the ones in the World Trade Center. Not to me.

Once I heard my mother's voice on the phone, I felt comforted. "Don't look at it," she instructed. Obediently, I drew down the shade over my window.

My next phone call was to Tony in Miami, who was watching the story unfold on the local news. "They're saying it was terrorists," Tony said.

"Don't be ridiculous," I replied immediately—and it wasn't denial. I really meant it. Terrorists! Who could believe such an absurdity? The people putting forth this theory were of the same ilk as the ones who believed the government was hiding little green men in the deserts of New Mexico. "Of course it wasn't terrorists. It was an accident."

"Gwen, they flew two huge passenger jets into those buildings on purpose," Tony insisted. "I'm watching the footage on the news *right now*."

The PA system in my office building, the one that informed us of fire drills or elevator outages, began to spit and crackle. The Jamaican-accented voice of the security guard downstairs came on, only it didn't have the jovial resonance of the voice that greeted me every morning with a "Hello! Good morning, miss!" This voice sounded strained and awful. Our building was being evacuated, the voice said and would not reopen that day. We were to proceed calmly to the emergency stairs and exit the building as quickly as possible.

"I have to go now," I told Tony. "I'll call you later, okay?" It felt odd, I thought, to go through the polite formalities of hanging up on my friend when the voice over the PA had just told us, in a way his words hadn't, that we were all being instructed to run for our lives.

A coworker named Sharon stopped by my desk. Sharon was a few years older than I was and one of the directing partners of the company I worked for. We had collaborated on a few projects and exchanged friendly enough words in passing, but had never spent time together socially outside of the office. "You live around here, don't you?"

"Yeah," I told her. "I live a block away."

"Why don't you come with me," she said. "I was going to walk over the Brooklyn Bridge and get a room at the Brooklyn Marriott. We can have drinks and call people to come over and meet us." When I hesitated, she added, "You don't want to go home and sit alone a few blocks away from all this."

I'd had a half-formed idea that I might call Andrea or one of the handful of other friends I'd made since moving, on the chance that they, too, had been released from their offices. But going to see any of them would mean traveling all the way uptown. Getting into the subway or riding on a bus seemed unwise at the moment. The far side of the Brooklyn Bridge was actually much closer to my office than, say, Midtown Manhattan.

And I didn't want to stray too far from my cats. Without really thinking about it, I was operating on the vague assumption that the fires would rage for a while until they were finally put out, at which time the dead would be collected and the grieving—bottomless, incalculable grieving—would begin.

But I also knew that, when all that had happened, and when I was tired of being with other people and talking over this thing, this horror, I would want to return to the quiet of my apartment, and to the warm certainty of the furry bodies of my cats.

So it was a relief, when Sharon extended this invitation, to feel that somebody else was taking charge. Sharon wasn't exactly my boss, but she was one of the people I answered to and, moreover, had lived in New York her entire life. Sharon would know, better than I possibly could, what we were supposed to do.

The two of us walked the few blocks to the Brooklyn Bridge. Nobody else from the office joined us, and the thought occurred to me that Sharon's invitation hadn't been entirely casual, that she was—for reasons that couldn't be found in the very slight interaction we'd had thus far—looking out for me. Clearly, we were not the only ones who'd had the idea of leaving Manhattan; the Brooklyn Bridge was a solid wall of human flesh. It had been closed to vehicular traffic, and people were climbing up the sides of the railings to access the bridge, pulled up and over by pedestrians on the other side, rather than walking all the way down to the pedestrian entrance.

For all that there were thousands of people on that bridge, the crowd was strangely quiet. The word *terrorists* could be heard in almost every single murmured conversation, and I was now long past the point of disbelieving it. Then somebody near us said, "What if they blow up the bridge?"

It was a preposterous idea. The notion of somebody having the audacity to blow up the Brooklyn Bridge—the sheer impossibility of its disappearance from the New York skyline—was so absurd as to sound almost like the punchline to a bad joke.

Once introduced, however, it was an idea that was impossible to put from our minds. Sharon and I tried to distract ourselves by talking about the likelihood of finding a free room at the Brooklyn Marriott, and making lists of the people we would call to join us. Did it make more sense to stop for bottles of liquor on the way, or to pay the exorbitant prices that the hotel's honor bar would surely levy? Our backs were turned to the World Trade Center, and our view was of nothing except thousands of people and the sanctuary of Brooklyn before us. As long as we walked and talked like normal people, speaking of normal things, the world was still manageable.

The air was acrid with the smell of smoke. A woman walking near us limped slightly, and she complained—with a forced, aren't-we-being-brave-about-this good humor—that if she'd known she'd have to walk so much today, she would have worn more practical shoes. Sharon and I smiled sympathetically, and were on the verge of responding, when a man streaked by, shouting, *"They blew up the Pentagon! They blew up the Pentagon!"*

We heard a colossal crack and groan. The bridge trembled, a vibration radiated from the soles of our feet up to our legs. They were blowing up the bridge! *They were blowing up the Brooklyn Bridge!* People began to scream and cry and rush and push, they knocked into other people and those people fell down and the people behind them kept running over them and Sharon and I grabbed on to each other to keep our footing. I wanted to scream, too, but there was no air in my lungs. There was no air anywhere. The Brooklyn Bridge was exploding, disintegrating, and I was standing on it!

Every muscle and tendon in my body strained to be yards and yards ahead of where I stood. The only thing that held my body back was the hard barrier of my skin, which stubbornly refused to go forward. My hands and legs shook with the desperate effort my body made to jump out of my skin and rush away, away, away from all this.

A flash of vision swam before my eyes, not of my own life, but of grainy black-and-white footage from Holocaust documentaries I'd seen. It was a group of old Jewish men, lined up facing a wall. Each had his hand clasped in the hand of the man next to him, and they were praying—the prayer all Jews are supposed to say at the moment of their death. I could hear them as clearly as I heard anything around me, and then I heard my own voice—as if it were something separate and outside myself, thick and unrecognizable—reciting with them: *Sh'ma Yisrael, Adonai eloheinu, Adonai eh-chad...*

Then everybody stopped abruptly, as if we had all been connected to a central power source whose plug had just been pulled. We had realized that the bridge wasn't disintegrating, hadn't been rent in half to spill us into the East River below. As one body, we all turned our heads to look back at the city we were fleeing.

One of the towers of the World Trade Center was collapsing inward upon itself. Within seconds, there was nothing left of it but a smoky hole in the skyline where it had stood. The soke of the fire had been black, but the residue of the collapse was a shimmering beige. It hung in posed perfection, like the afterbirth of fireworks, in the brilliant blue air.

"It's okay," I said to Sharon. "It's okay. It's just the tower collapsing."

It was a ridiculous thing to say. What could be less "okay" than the collapse of a tower of the World Trade Center? And yet, at that moment, it *was* okay—not only because it meant that the Brooklyn Bridge hadn't been blown up, but also because *it made sense*. Buildings burned, and then they fell down. What was the expression? *Burned to the ground*. I'd never seen it happen before, but I'd heard that expression all my life. *It burned to the ground*, some reporter would say. *Firefighters responded to the four-alarm fire but were unable to overcome the intensity of the blaze, and the warehouse burned to the ground.* This was a thing that happened all the time and everybody knew it and it made perfect sense.

Except it didn't, of course. The thought that piled into my already overactive brain in the next millisecond was that there had been people in that building. Whatever hope had remained for rescuing those trapped in the fire was now gone. Again, reflexively, I began to pray, this time murmuring the Mourner's Kaddish. *Yitgadal v'yitkadash sh'mae raba...*

The ball of smoke held itself carefully aloft for a moment, a hooded cobra that swayed and hypnotized its victims. We watched it, mesmerized. Then it began to descend and spread. It radiated outward in an opaque cloud of soot and debris that swallowed up everything in its path for blocks around—birds and trees and people and buildings.

The building where my cats still were.

My body followed the direction my head was already pointing in, and I began to push my way through the crowd that was now, with frightened cries and more determination than ever, heading into Brooklyn. "Excuse me," I said politely. "Excuse me." Weren't you supposed to say *excuse me* to people as you pushed your way past them? They jostled against me, bumped into me hard, but that was okay. I understood. They had to go one way, and I had to go the other. If I was patient and persistent enough, I would get through. Every time someone knocked into me, I repeated, "Excuse me."

Sharon grabbed my arm. "Gwen!" she shouted "What are you doing? We have to go *this* way!" and she pointed vigorously in the direction of Brooklyn.

"Let go of me!" I began to fight a double battle against her grip and the crowd that wouldn't let me through back to Manhattan. "My cats are in there!"

"Gwen!" she shouted again. She grabbed my shoulders with both hands and shook me a bit, and I wondered, with a sort of detached and analytical interest, if she was going to slap me.

Was I hysterical? I didn't *feel* hysterical. Despite my panic and my shrieking, I felt perfectly lucid. Sharon pointed again, at the remaining tower, which listed dangerously to one side. "Gwen the other tower is going to collapse any second. *You cannot go back for your cats!* We have to keep going!"

Almost as soon as she said it, the second tower began to implode. People buried their faces in their hands, they covered their eyes, they sobbed and wailed. I felt dry-eyed and hollow as I watched a second beige ash monster merge with the first one. It had already reached the foot of the bridge, and nothing was visible of the city anymore.

"Your cats will be fine," Sharon said. "They're in your apartment, and they're safe, and they will be fine. I promise."

Broken windows, I thought. *Broken windows and a blind cat.*

"They're not going to let anybody off this bridge and back into the Financial District," Sharon continued. "The bridge is going one way, and that's the way we have to go."

Of course. I had made a stupid decision—an insanely, cataclysmically, unimaginably stupid decision—when I had first set foot onto the Brooklyn Bridge and left my cats behind. They were alone and unprotected, and it was my fault, my fault, my fault.

"We'll figure it out when get into Brooklyn." There was a note of desperation in Sharon's voice. "We'll make calls, we'll find someone in your building, *and they will be fine.*"

We turned and walked toward Brooklyn once again. This time, there was no discussion of what we would do when we reached the Brooklyn Marriott. Without saying anything to each other, that plan had been scrapped. Our only goal now was to walk until we got out of reach of the soot cloud, which fell wrathfully upon us within minutes. Soon we could barely see or breathe; we took off our shirts and tied them around our faces in an attempt to filter the air. With the part of my mind that was numb and detached, I thought how astonishing it was that one minute you were in one of the most technologically advanced cities the world had ever produced, and a minute later you were any refugee of any war zone at any time or place in history, fleeing for your life on foot.

Our skin and hair were gray from the ash by the time we reached the far side of the bridge, and still we were in the thick of the cloud. We walked for miles. The rhythm of my footsteps echoed in my head. *My cats. My cats. My cats my cats my cats.* Somewhere in Brooklyn—I didn't know where we were by now—a mechanic was standing in front of a garage, handing out surgical masks to people as they walked by. We nodded an acknowledgment to him, our throats sore with smoke and stunned into silence.

Eventually, we had walked so far that Sharon said we might as well keep going to her apartment in Bay Ridge, which was a good ten miles from where we'd started out that morning. "You'll stay at my apartment," she said. I was grateful, but it was more of an intellectual gratitude than an emotional one. I knew Sharon was doing a kind thing; where would I have gone, where would I have slept that night, if not for her? Yet I felt dissociated from all outcomes. What difference did it make where I went or where I stayed? The only thing that mattered was how I was going to get back.

I wanted to call my mother, to let her know I was all right, and I wanted to call my apartment building. But our cell phones weren't working. "My mother's office is near my apartment," Sharon said. "We can use the landline there."

It was nearly two o'clock in the afternoon, according to Sharon's watch, by the time we reached Bay Ridge. We had walked for almost five hours. We were now far enough away from Lower Manhattan to attract stares, covered as we were from head to toe in grayish beige ash. The streets were wide and clean, and the crowds were orderly. I noticed the order and the stares in a dim sort of way that didn't connect to anything inside me. Things were happening around me, and I was aware of them, but I couldn't participate in them or feel anything about them. It was like sitting in the backseat of a cab and watching the world rush by, knowing that you had no part in what was happening outside the cab's windows.

It was in that same detached way that I watched Sharon's mother grab her into a damp, tear-laden hug as we entered her office. Another woman who worked there showed me discreetly into an empty back office. "There's a bathroom, if you want to wash up," she said tentatively. I was wearing a sleeveless shirt, capris pants, and open-toed sandals, and the ash had settled into my skin until the one was indistinguishable from the other.

The first call I made was to my mother's elementary school. "Thank God, thank God," the receptionist breathed when she answered the phone and I identified myself. "Your mother's in the teacher's lounge. Some of the other teachers are sitting with her. I'll let her know you're on the phone."

There was a brief hum of hold music—which struck me as another bizarre thing; why should something as innocuous as hold music still exist?—and then my mother was on the phone, and she was crying. She cried so hard that she couldn't speak, couldn't breathe. Her sobs sounded more like howls and they were continuous, painful, as if something were being wrenched out of her body with brute force.

I hadn't shed a single tear yet that day, and I didn't want to. If I started to cry, I would break, and the most important thing now was that my core remain firmly held together. But all the tears I hadn't cried rushed up into my throat to choke me, and my voice was thick as I repeated, "Mommy, don't cry. I'm okay. I'm okay, Mommy, don't cry."

One of the other teachers took the phone from her. "Tell me where you're staying," she said quietly. "We'll let her know."

I told her I'd be staying with my friend Sharon in Brooklyn, and that I would call later with the phone number. After we hung up, I tried the front desk of my apartment building. There was no answer. I tried the apartments and cell phones of the handful of other tenants I knew in the building. Nobody was home. Nobody could be reached. The only hope I'd had left, that somebody at my building would answer and say, *Gosh, how silly you were to worry! Everything's peachy-keen here!* flickered out.

Broken windows, I thought. *Broken windows and a blind cat.*

Sharon and I walked the few additional blocks to her apartment—a homey, plant-and-sunlight-filled, two-bedroom affair. We immediately turned on the TV. Sharon had been right; not only had both towers of the World Trade Center collapsed, but all the buildings in the plaza around the Trade Center had either collapsed or were about to. Manhattan was completely shut down below 14th Street. The perimeter had been barricaded. It was being guarded by the military, and the only ones allowed in were military personnel, police officers, firefighters, and rescue workers.

There was no point in thinking about broken windows. It was a counterproductive thought. I had to believe that my building was intact. The cats would be fine. I'd left them with plenty of food and water, and this would be no more to them than if I had gone away on an overnight business trip. Because surely, I thought, I'd be able to get to them tomorrow.

We knew we should shower, or eat, or do something, but Sharon and I couldn't pull ourselves away from that TV screen. They were playing cell phone messages from people who'd been trapped in the rubble of the collapsed buildings. *Their final words*, the reporter intoned. The pain of it was insupportable, and Sharon grimly produced two bottles of vodka.

I drank as I had never drunk before. I wanted to drink until the bottle ached as much as I did, to drink until the room spun and I forgot my own name. I wanted to drink until I passed out. And, mercifully, I did.

20 • September 12, 2001

I took a wallet full of provisions with me, for my mind misgave me that I might have to deal with some who would be of great strength, and would respect neither right nor law.
– HOMER, *The Odyssey*

I SHOULD HAVE AWAKENED the next morning with a vicious hangover, but I didn't. In fact, I had never felt so clearheaded and single-minded of purpose in my life. It was as if my mind had spent its unconscious hours solving problems for me, so that by the time I woke up the process had resolved itself, and all that was left was the series of steps I would undertake.

A quick check with the news revealed several things. The first was that Lower Manhattan was still shut down, still barricaded, and still restricted to military and rescue personnel. The roads below 14th Street were closed to vehicular traffic, and the subways and buses weren't running down there—although the rest of the trains and buses in and around the city were essentially on schedule.

This meant my best shot at getting in would be on foot. I fired up Sharon's computer, consulted an online subway map, and plotted three separate routes that would get me as close to the sealed-off perimeter as public transportation would allow.

The news also informed me that there was no electricity or running water in Lower Manhattan. So if I did get to my cats, it would probably make sense for me to remove them from the apartment even if my building was intact. The four of us couldn't live indefinitely in an apartment that had no water and was accessible only by climbing thirty-one flights of stairs. I decided to call my friend Scott to see if he could put us up for a few days. Scott had recently moved from Miami to Philadelphia—only an hour and change by train outside of New York—where he lived alone in a three-bedroom townhouse. He was the kind of friend you went to in a crisis, and was also the only person I knew who had the space to accommodate all four of us. I wrote down Scott's name on the piece of paper with my subway routes, and next to his name I wrote *litter/litter box/cat food*, a reminder to myself that I should ask him to purchase these things ahead of our arrival. I would reimburse him when I got there.

Of course, it was possible that Scott wouldn't be able to receive us, at least not for a couple of days. Or maybe electricity would be restored, and it wouldn't be logical to take the cats all the way to Philly. In that case, I would need supplies—supplies I couldn't assume I would be able to get in my own neighborhood if the shops were all closed. I found a separate piece of paper and filled it with a list of the things I would need to buy. I also made a note to pull as much cash as I could out of an ATM. Cash, I had found, was always a good contingency plan in a crisis.

My last note to myself was to call the appropriate city and state agencies to see if anybody was organizing a rescue effort for pets trapped near what every news outlet was now calling

Ground Zero. There was an emergency information phone number that flashed on the bottom of the TV screen, but after several calls all I got was a busy signal. It was probably better that way, I told myself. Let the government agencies attend to people. I would take care of my cats.

Sharon was still asleep when I poked my head in to check on her. I scrawled a note and propped it up on her bathroom mirror to let her know where I was going. Then I pulled on my filthy clothes of the day before, grabbed her keys and my purse, and headed out.

The day was as clear and beautiful as the previous one had been. I expected my muscles to be stiff from all the walking I'd done yesterday, but they moved smoothly and eagerly in time with my thoughts—as if they, too, had been awaiting only daylight and consciousness to begin turning plan into action. I walked a few blocks up what appeared to be Bay Ridge's main thoroughfare until I came upon a large drugstore. There I purchased a cheap pair of jeans, two large T-shirts, underwear, a sturdy pair of inexpensive sneakers, socks, a toothbrush, deodorant, and soap. I also bought two gallons of water, a box of kitty litter, a large bag of off-brand cat food (Vashti might just have to be itchy from allergies for a few days), a flashlight and batteries, and the biggest backpack they had.

It was a job of work getting my haul back to Sharon's apartment, but I was so pleased with myself that I hardly noticed. Embarking on the earliest components of my plan put me one step closer to my cats. I felt as if they were half rescued already.

THE R TRAIN OUT of Bay Ridge was crowded that morning, but not unbearably so. Probably, I thought, a lot of people who worked in the city were off for the day. I hadn't considered it, but I realized that my own office would, perforce, have to remain closed. What felt odder than having an unexpectedly free Wednesday, however, was the idea of people who weren't taking the day off. It was impossible to imagine that in the same world that contained the smoking ruins of what had been the World Trade Center were people doing commonplace things like dressing for work, making coffee, or packing lunches for their children. Yesterday had felt disconnected and unreal. Today, it felt like something I had been born knowing would happen eventually, and it was the people going about normal, everyday things who were the ones living strange lives.

"You're crazy," Sharon had told my flatly when I unfolded my plan to her upon returning from the store. "Listen to the news—buildings are still collapsing down there."

"All the more reason to go now," I replied.

Sharon went on at some length, insisting that people weren't being allowed back in, that there was no way I'd get through. I was welcome to stay with her at least through Friday, she told me. She was itchy to get out of town—a lot of people were—and she and her mother were planning to go away for the weekend. But her spare bedroom was mine until then.

This should have been of some concern to me because, technically, I was homeless. As far as I knew, the things I'd purchased that morning might be the only possessions I had left in the world. But that was a long-term problem, the consideration of which could only make me emotional and distract me from the immediate business at hand. In the short term, I'd already put my friend Scott on alert and he was more than willing to welcome me and my three cats if, upon reaching my apartment, I decided it was necessary to remove them. Today was only Wednesday, and by Friday I would be long gone from Sharon's apartment.

Sharon had insisted I take her spare keys with me anyway, in case I returned that afternoon and she was out. "Once I get to my cats, I probably won't come back here," I warned.

Sharon shrugged. "Then you'll give the keys back next week at the office."

My backpack rested on the floor of the train at my feet, next to a shopping bag that contained the items I hadn't been able to fit into it. Everything together probably weighed about twenty pounds, but wasn't so bad to carry when most of the weight was distributed on my back.

The R train crossed over the Manhattan Bridge on its route back into the city, surfacing so quickly from subterranean darkness into sunlight that the change was startling. It was like a rewind of the walk I'd made yesterday. A wall of smoke rose from the ground to the south of the Brooklyn Bridge, and even on the train and at this distance, I could smell it. I turned away from the window.

The train deposited me at 14th Street. I had never thought of Manhattan as being a place with a particular, universal smell until the only smell of it—at least for me, there at the border of downtown—was the singed smell of the rubble at Ground Zero. I thought of Homer, of Homer's sensitive nose and his hyper-acute hearing. What must it smell and sound like to him, so much closer than I was to where fires still burned and buildings continued to collapse? Somehow it seemed as if

Vashti and Scarlett, who could see out of the windows of our apartment, would be less frightened. At least they would be able to connect something visually to what they smelled and heard—surely it would be less terrifying for them.

Or would it? I understood so much more than they did, and even I couldn't make sense of it all.

Stop it, I told myself. *This isn't helpful.*

The intersections of 14th Street were barricaded to keep vehicles from passing, but a handful of people crossed the barriers either on foot or mounted on bicycles. I had thought earlier how odd it was that the world that held the rubble of Ground Zero could also contain normal people going about normal lives. Now I realized that there were actually two worlds: the one on the northern side of the barricades—where people sipped coffee outdoors at trendy cafés, and cars and cabs propelled themselves impatiently toward shops or office buildings—and the world on the other side of the barricade, devoid of cars and navigated only by a handful of persistent pedestrians. Tightening my grip on my backpack and shopping bag, I joined them.

I walked south and east, zigzagging through the streets, the plume of smoke that had once been the World Trade Center serving as my compass. Businesses were closed and deserted, their windows papered over with flyers and posters that had materialized overnight. *Have you seen our son?* the signs implored. *We don't know where our daughter is. She works in the World Trade Center.* Smiling faces looked at me from the flyers, grinning beneath graduation caps or beaming from the safety of honeymoons and family fishing trips. *Do you know my husband? Have you heard from my sister? If you know anything, please call...please call...please call...*It was a journey through the underworld, the shades of the dead clamoring all around me.

I made it to Canal Street before I was stopped by military personnel guarding the impromptu checkpoint I would have to pass if I was to continue. The young men in army fatigues with machine guns strapped across their chests were polite, and vaguely sympathetic, and called me "ma'am," but they were completely unwilling to let me pass.

"This entire area's locked down, ma'am," they told me. "We can't let anybody through."

"But I live there," I pleaded, "and my cats are—"

"Sorry, ma'am," they said firmly. "We can't let anybody in."

A flatbed truck carrying men and women was waved through. "But you're letting those people in," I argued.

"They're journalists, ma'am."

Recognizing a lost cause when I saw one, I headed east across Canal Street. When I reached the next checkpoint, I tried once again.

"I'm a journalist" I said, without hesitation.

The young men guarding this barricade looked at me with polite skepticism, their gazes taking in my jeans, backpack, and sweat-streaked face. "May we see your press credentials, ma'am?"

"Um..." My smile faltered. "Well, you know, it's buried in my backpack and I..."

"Sorry ma'am," I was once again told. "We can't let anybody through.

"But—"

Their expressions were unyielding. "Please step away from the barricade, ma'am."

I continued onward, hoping that I might find some back street, some tiny alley that, in the haste and confusion, had been overlooked and left unbarricaded—or, barring that, a sympathetic soldier. None was forthcoming. I'd had a hazy idea, when I'd pulled cash out of the ATM that morning, that I would be willing to bribe people if I had to. But when it came down to it, I was too intimidated to make the attempt. Nor did I really want to know if any of the soldiers could be bribed. It would have been unsettling to learn that the people now protecting us were subject to petty corruptions.

It's okay, I told myself. *You left the cats enough food and water to last at least through today, and by tomorrow morning you'll be able to get back in.*

I pushed the thought of broken windows firmly from my mind. I had spent the morning walking among the images of the dead, but my cats were still alive. If they weren't, wouldn't I have known? They were alive, and they were fine, and my plan was a good one that would reunite me with them tomorrow.

They would be fine until tomorrow.

I RETURNED TO SHARON'S apartment disappointed, but not yet despondent. This was only a minor setback. I told myself that it still made sense to try to reach somebody at my building, and even if nobody was there, I'd certainly be able to get back in the next day.

"Try the ASPCA or PETA," Andrea suggested when I called her that afternoon to check in. "I'm sure they're coordinating rescue efforts for pets."

I was angry at myself for not having thought of this before Andrea did. As a Miami native, hadn't I lived through enough hurricanes to know that there were always animal rescue organizations that helped reunite owners with their pets in the wake of a disaster?

I called the ASPCA, and somebody answered on the first ring! Hope continued to mount when I explained my situation, and the woman on the other end said, "Yes. We're working with local authorities to help reunite people with their pets. Give me your information and I'll have someone call you back."

"My name is Gwen Cooper," I began, "and I—"

"Wait, you're Gwen Cooper?" the woman interrupted. "Gwen Cooper from John Street?"

In fact, I *was* Gwen Cooper from John Street. But how could this woman know that? Unless, I thought, there had been some further catastrophe, some additional disaster that had only affected *my* building, and maybe they had a list of tenants who they'd have to break the news to and—

"Your pet sitter—Garrett?—has been calling us all morning. He doesn't know if you're alive or dead and he's frantic. He told us to have you call him if you call us. He says that your contract with him gives him access to your apartment in the event of an emergency, and he'll show it to the people in your building in case they won't let him in. He has food, water, and litter, and he's going to try to ride his bicycle in. He said, *Tell her I'm not leaving my buddy down there.*"

The potted plant resting in front of Sharon's phone twinned and blurred. Always, always, people were willing to go above and beyond for Homer. My cats had always been a reminder to me of the capacity for human goodness in the world; each of them was alive because someone else had done a kind and charitable thing for something small and helpless—down to the burly mechanic I'd had all those years ago in Miami, or my mother who, on paper, didn't even like cats in the first place.

"I'll call him," I told the woman at the ASPCA. "And thank you for giving me the message."

I had to collect myself for a minute before I could call Garrett, my gratitude tumbling out in a confused jumble of sentences that only somebody as patient as he was could have unraveled. I wanted to convey something of what I felt—of what it meant to realize that my cats and I had been remembered, were being thought of by someone who I hadn't thought about since the terror of the day before.

"Of course," Garrett murmured, whenever I paused for breath. "Of *course*. I know, believe me, I understand...I'll do everything I can...I'll call you if I manage to get in..."

Garrett wasn't the only one who was thinking of Homer and me. When I checked the voice mail of my home machine, it was full. It seemed as if everybody who'd ever known us wanted to know if we were okay: old boyfriends from Miami, the friends I'd made since I moved to New York. "What's our plan to get your cats?" they would ask. "I have a bicycle...I know a rescue worker...I know somebody at the mayor's office...I can send you money...will money help? What can be done? What can *we* do? Homer's my buddy, my boy. We'll get him. We'll get him, Gwen, you'll see..."

It was still only the first day, and hope was everywhere. Somebody would get to the cats. We would be fine.

THE NEXT MORNING WAS a retread of the morning before. Once again, I tried to get into the Financial District. Once again, I was turned away. I knew of at least three different people attempting to get to Homer, Vashti, and Scarlett on foot or on bicycle, but it seemed unlikely that anybody else would be successful where I had failed.

I calculated that the food I'd left for the cats Tuesday morning would last about a day and a half. That meant that, probably right around now, their food was running out. What concerned me more, though, was water. The air in New York was far drier than it had been in Miami, and no matter how much I filled the water bowl, it would completely evaporate within twenty-four hours. I'd heard that humans couldn't live more than two or three days without water, but I didn't know how long a cat could go.

"They can always drink from the toilet if they have to, right?" Andrea said.

"No." I was anguished. "I keep the toilet lid closed so Homer won't fall in." I mentally vowed that I would always leave the toilet lid open from then on.

Thursday was the first day, since September 11th itself, when I felt true panic. I was worried for the cats' survival, but I also found the thought of what they must be going through unendurable. They had never been left alone for so long without anybody's checking on them—they had never gone so long without food or a change of the water. Their litter box hadn't been cleaned since Monday and must, I was sure, be an abomination by now. They wouldn't understand—they would think I had abandoned them to hunger and thirst, and the horrible sounds and smells coming from Ground Zero.

I don't know what my state of mind would have been if I hadn't gotten the call, late Thursday afternoon, from the ASPCA. The area had finally been deemed stable enough to allow residents with pets back in just long enough the following day to collect their pets. "President Bush is going to speak from Ground Zero tomorrow," the woman from the ASPCA warned. "So you'll need photo ID proving you live in the area."

I still had my Miami driver's license, which I hadn't bothered to change since moving to New York. I didn't drive a car anymore, and the license hadn't yet expired, so it functioned just fine for normal ID purposes. Trading it in for a New York license had seemed more like an inconvenience than anything else. But I did have a checkbook in my purse with my name and New York address listed on it, and I hoped that the two together would provide sufficient evidence that I was who I said I was and lived where I said I lived. And going in with a group of ASPCA volunteers would undoubtedly help. Maybe I could avoid an ID check altogether.

Sharon left town on Friday morning. I handed her the spare keys and tried, in the fierceness of the hug I gave her, to convey my gratitude for these last few days. "Good luck," she said into my shoulder. "Call me when you've got them."

I phoned Scott and told him to expect the four of us—definitely, for sure—that night. My situation had all the pristine clarity of a syllogism. I would have to leave New York that night, because I had no place to stay. But I wasn't going to leave New York without my cats. Therefore, I would get my cats that day.

No matter what.

THE WOMAN WHO CALLED from the ASPCA had directed me to an airplane-hangar-sized space at Chelsea Piers. Chelsea Piers was a huge entertainment/all-purpose complex on the

West Side Highway. It featured bars, restaurants, an ice-skating rink, a bowling alley, batting cages, and several facilities large enough to host trade shows. In the last few days, it had been utilized as an overflow hospital for survivors and rescue workers injured at Ground Zero. The ice-skating rink had been appropriated as a makeshift morgue.

Before going to Chelsea Piers, I had made one last effort to reach my cats on my own. I'd made it as far as the City Hall terminus of the 6 train, mere blocks from my apartment. Upon reaching the top of the stairs, however, I had been stopped by soldiers asking for my photo ID. I tried showing them my Florida driver's license in tandem with my checkbook, but had been unable to convince them to let me through. Reluctantly, I'd boarded the train once again and headed back uptown.

I found the ASPCA's area easily enough once I reached Chelsea Piers, and signed in with my name and address in the front of the room. They had divided Lower Manhattan into zones, and would bring in groups of people divided by their specific locations. The weather had turned gray and sharply cold that morning; all my own heavier clothes were in my apartment along with my cats. The woman who took my name and address, noticing that I shivered in my thin T-shirt, directed me to another enormous room, filled with boxes of donated clothing. I selected an overlarge flannel shirt and buttoned it over my T-shirt and jeans, topping it with a sturdy windbreaker. Nothing fit quite right, but at least it would keep me warm.

I returned to the waiting room and seated myself in a plastic chair, settling my backpack and shopping bag on the ground beside me. There were scores of other pet owners there, trading stories and rumors in grim, hushed voices. One man said he knew a guy who'd made it all the way to the front door of his building, only to find that the doormen had left and locked the main door to the building behind them. The man didn't have a key to that front door—and who did, when you lived in a doorman building? He'd made it all the way and, in the end, hadn't been able to get into his building after all.

I lived in a doorman building. With all the careful planning and foresight I'd attempted to employ, it had never occurred to me that, upon reaching my building, I might not be able to get through the front door. The anxiety already churning in my stomach increased threefold.

All of us were nervous; we didn't know if we'd make it to our homes, or what we'd find once we got there. We distracted ourselves as best we could, trading photos of our pets and sharing anecdotes of their courage or cowardice, their likes and dislikes, the quirks that made them real and individual to us. "This is Gus, and this is Sophie," one woman said, showing me a snapshot of two Border collie mixes. "Our kids are just crazy about them." Her fond smile wobbled. "They've never been alone this long. I don't know what our kids will do if they're not okay."

"Of *course* they will be," I assured her. "Of course they'll be fine."

I showed her pictures of my own brood. Like most people, she marveled at Vashti's beauty and laughed at tales of Scarlett's sulky hauteur. "Poor thing," she said pityingly when she came to Homer's photo. "Poor little thing. He must be terrified."

"He's the toughest little guy you've ever seen," I told her. "He once chased a burglar right out of my apartment." I related the story of the break-in, and noticed that my audience was growing. "Pets can adapt to so much more than we give them credit for. This'll be nothing for him." People around me nodded, and I prayed as I said it that I was right.

The hours rolled by in pet-owner purgatory. From time to time, one of the women or men with the ASPCA would stand in the front of the room to announce that they were heading to a specific set of blocks, and a small band of pet owners would excitedly move forward, driver's licenses held at the ready. Sometimes, they would make announcements like, "Anybody we bring to a building, who goes into that building and comes out without a pet, will be taken straight to jail." Apparently, some people were down there pretending they had pets so that the ASPCA could help them return to their apartments to retrieve laptop computers or business documents. "This is no joke, folks. We have police officers going in with us, and if you come out of your building without a pet you will go *immediately* to jail."

After two hours, I was antsy beyond endurance. I was losing confidence that they would be able to smuggle me past the checkpoints without proper ID. The crowd in the room should have been thinning out, but it didn't seem like it was. I couldn't detect a patter in the zones they were calling—if they were moving from north to south or east to west. All I knew was that they hadn't called mine. *The next zone will be mine*, I kept telling myself. *The next one will be me*. Another hour passed, however, and it never was. Finally, unable to wait any longer, and deciding that I might actually be better off on my own since I didn't have a New York ID, I decided there was nothing for me to do but try to go in myself.

I walked from Chelsea Piers until I reached Seventh Avenue, then turned south. My backpack was on my back, and I clutched the large shopping bag containing the items too large to fit into the backpack. After three days of handling, the bag was coming apart, and I had to hold it in both arms to keep everything in place. I kept going until Seventh Avenue intersected with Houston Street and became Varick Street. There was a barricaded checkpoint guarded by three police officers—two young men, and one who looked a bit older. It was the first checkpoint I'd encountered that wasn't monitored by military personnel, and I took this as a positive sign.

"ID, please," the older officer said. I pulled out my Florida driver's license along with the checkbook that bore my Manhattan address. The cop put them together and regarded them doubtfully. "We're not supposed to let anybody in without ID."

"Please," I said desperately. "I just moved here—that's why I don't have a New York license yet. You can search me. You can *strip*-search me. You can truss me up like Hannibal Lecter and roll me in on a dolly. I just want to get back to my cats. Please, sir, please, *please* let me in."

The three of them looked at each other. They were cops, not soldiers—and, unlike the soldiers, they were *from* here. This was their city. I was somebody in that city who needed help. They could tell at a glance, with all the instincts of a cop, that I wasn't a threat.

Still, orders were orders.

"Please," I said again. "They haven't had food or water in days. They'll die if I can't get back to them. They'll die without me. Please, sir—I promise I won't hurt anybody. I just want to get to my cats. Please help me. All I need is someone to help me. I've been trying to get back to them for days and days. Please, sir, please help me—*please* let me in!"

I had been prepared, as circumstances dictated, to fake-cry as a way of gaining sympathy. There was nothing I wouldn't stoop to at this point. But now I found, to my complete humiliation, that my crying wasn't fake. I was sobbing—huge, racking, genuine sobs that took all the air from my body and doubled me over. I buried my face in the shopping bag I clutched, I dragged my sleeve across my face to clear my eyes, but the tears kept coming. My cats would die because I hadn't changed my driver's license. They would die over a driver's license. It seemed like such a stupid, impossible thing, yet here was the reality of it.

The three cops stood there, looking at me a bit uncomfortably, until I had cried myself out. Finally, one of the younger ones spoke. There was a slight trace of a Hispanic accent in his voice as he said. "My wife is pretty crazy about our cats. She'd probably kill me if we didn't let the girl in."

I looked up hopefully. Was it going to happen? Had I really and finally succeeded?

"Here are pictures of my cats," I said, scrambling around in my purse for my photos. I struggled to hold them up along with the shopping bag cradled in my arms. "That's Scarlett, and that's Vashti," I pointed to each in turn, "and that's my youngest, Homer."

The three of them squinted and looked where I pointed. "The little one's interesting looking, isn't he?" said the older policeman.

"He's blind." I was pulling out all the stops now. "Anything could have happened—if a window broke, he wouldn't know now to jump out of it, and I live all the way up on the thirty-first floor. And he must be so terrified—he can't see what's going on. Can you imagine what it must sound like down there, to such a little cat who's blind?"

The older police officer heaved a deep sigh. "All right," he said. He stepped away slightly from the opening between two barricades and waved me through. "Go on."

"Oh, thank you!" I clutched his hand, pressing it between both of my own. "Thank you! Thank you!" I pivoted blindly to each of the three police officers and thanked them in turn. Then I readjusted the weight of my backpack and shopping bag, wiped the last of the tears from my cheeks, and stepped past the barricades.

"*Vaya con dios*," the younger officer said as I passed. *Go with God*.

I stuck mainly to back streets as I made my way from the West Village down to the Financial District. I was afraid that if I used the main thoroughfares, I might encounter another checkpoint, somebody else demanding ID before allowing me to continue on my way.

It was something I needn't have worried about. I walked for more than three miles, and that entire time I didn't see or hear another living soul—not a car, not a person, not a bird in a tree. It felt eerie, almost post-apocalyptic, as if I were the only living human left in Manhattan. I had never seen or even heard of a completely deserted New York City street. No matter how late the hour or how quiet a neighborhood, there was always something or someone else—a woman walking a dog, a man delivering produce to a twenty-four-hour grocery store, lights in window. You were never so far from a major thoroughfare as to be unable to hear cars whizzing by like comets in the distance.

But now there was nothing but silence. Smoke and silence.

The sky was still gray, and it seemed to grow grayer as I approached Ground Zero, the smoke intensifying until my throat stung and my eyes watered. My arms and back ached almost beyond my physical capacity to stand it. Once, I tripped over a crack in the pavement and dropped the shopping bag I carried. The sound of it hitting the ground rang out and echoed from the walls of buildings like cannon fire and I jumped, even though I knew where the sound had come from.

The silence of the streets had felt unnatural until something broke it—and then the sound was even more out of place.

Ash had settled onto everything, and grew thicker the farther south I went. The green leaves of trees and bushes and the once festive awnings of boutiques and cafés were caked a uniform gray-white. Even the mannequins inside display windows were coated so thickly that they were indistinguishable from the clothes they modeled.

After an hour or so, I reached Ground Zero itself and rejoined the world of noise and other people. I could hear the groans of trucks and men, the metallic chatter of walkie-talkies and the barking of police dogs. I had seen pictures of the rubble on TV and in newspapers, but it had still been impossible to imagine how enormous the devastation was, the acres and acres of fallen, heaped-up metal and concrete. The thing was still belching smoke and occasional flames. Tiny specks of men, their faces black with soot and drenched in sweat, dotted the ruin as they looked for survivors.

I didn't look at it for long; it felt disrespectful, somehow. And there were other places I had to be.

My anxiety grew as I turned the corner onto the block where I lived. What if, like the man I'd heard about back at the ASPCA relief center, I'd come all this way only to find that my building was locked and empty? To my utter joy and relief, however, the front door of my building was open when I reached it—and there in the lobby were Tom, the doorman, and Kevin, the building super. I'd had countless interactions with each of them, of the semi-friendly/semi-professional variety, but now I was so happy to see them, I dropped my shopping bag and threw myself into their arms. "You're here!" I cried as they each wrapped me in bear hugs. "I can't believe you're really here!"

"We never left," Kevin said. I knew Kevin had an enormous family—something like eight kids and twelve dogs and Lord-alone-knew-how-many cats—all the way up in Queens. "If we'd left, we might not have been able to get back in."

"You're so not wrong about that." I couldn't stop grinning.

"We still don't have phones, electricity, or water," Kevin said, "so I can't recommend you stay here. We're on the same power grid as the stock exchange, though, so we should be back up in a couple of days."

"And the building itself?" My voice was anxious as I asked this question. "Were any windows...?"

Kevin's face softened. He knew all about Homer—he was the one who had supervised the installation of childproof guards on my windows that kept them from opening wide enough for a small, blind cat to wriggle his way through. "No broken windows," he said gently. "Homer and your other cats should be fine."

"We were just doing a sweep for pets," Tom added, swinging his arm around to indicate the pet carriers of all sizes, each containing a dog or cat, scattered throughout the lobby. "People have been trickling back in to get them."

"Well, I'm here now." I reached into the side pocket of my backpack to pull out my flashlight. I flicked it on and off once, to make sure it was working. "Just point me in the direction of the stairwell."

"Do you need any help?" Tom regarded me with concern. "That's a lot of stuff you're carrying."

"I'll be fine," I assured him. "You guys worry about the other pets whose people haven't gotten back yet."

The stairwell of my apartment building was an interior one, windowless and entirely encased in concrete. Without any electricity, even from an emergency generator, it was completely black. The sole illumination came from the pale, round pool cast by my flashlight.

I was so eager to get back to my cats that I hated myself for having to stop and rest as I climbed up thirty-one floors. My arms, thighs, and back ached beneath the weight of the things I carried, and I was drenched in sweat. By the time I reached the thirteenth floor, I was panting so hard that I had to sit and catch my breath. My gasps echoed loudly in the cement stairwell as I unscrewed the cap of the small bottle of water Tom had pressed into my hand. I sipped from it sparingly; I didn't want to drink too deeply and end up with a cramp that would slow me down further.

After a few minutes, I continued my ascent. I had to stop again to catch my breath at the twentieth floor and at the twenty-eighth floor. My legs were starting to shake by then, but I was only three floors away—there was no point in resting any further. When the sign that said 31 swam before my eyes, I almost wept for the second time that day—this time in gratitude.

My fingers had stiffened around the shopping bag, and I fumbled with my keys as I inserted them into the lock of the door to my apartment. I had expected the smell of smoke to hit me in the face when I opened the door, and so it did, but overwhelming even that was the putrid smell of the litter box that hadn't been cleaned since Monday night. My heart tore. *Poor things*, I thought. *Having to live with that all week!*

I had been almost afraid to enter the apartment, unsure of what I might find. But a quick peek through the through the front door confirmed that everything was intact, unharmed, and exactly where I had left it Tuesday morning. The only difference was that there wasn't so much as a crumb left in the cats' food dish. The water bowl was dry as a bone.

Scarlett and Vashti were huddled together miserably on the bed, but their heads flew up as I entered. Homer was standing in front of the windows. His body was held with an alert, tense readiness, as if he'd been pacing before he'd heard the key hit the lock. His nose was in the air and his ears zipped around. *Who is that? Who's there?*

I carefully set down my bag and backpack, not wanting to frighten them further with any loud or unnecessary noise. "Kitties," I murmured hoarsely. "I'm here."

Upon hearing my voice, Homer responded with a piercing *Mew!* He covered the distance between us in two bounds and leapt at me, hurling himself at the center of my chest with a force that almost knocked me down. I sank to the floor to prevent any mishaps, and Homer burrowed his head into my chest and shoulders as hard as he could.

"Homer-Bear!" I said. At the sound of his name, Homer rubbed his whole face vigorously against my cheeks and resumed his cries of *Mew! Mew! Mew!* Beneath them I heard rich, singsong purring, the way he'd purred as a kitten when he'd realized I would be there every morning when he woke up. "I'm so sorry, little boy." The tears Homer couldn't see in my eyes were audible in my voice. "I'm so sorry it took so long."

Vashti approached almost shyly, as if she respected the intensity of Homer's joy and didn't want to intrude on it. She put her two front paws on my leg and squeaked tentatively, and I drew her into my arms as well. Only Scarlett remained aloof. She looked at me balefully through narrowed eyes, then turned her face away. *Look who finally decided to show up.* But even she relented after a moment. *I guess you* probably *came back as soon as you could.* She, too, crawled into my lap, for once not swatting impatiently at the other two as she jockeyed for position.

"I will *never* leave you alone this long again," I told them. "I will never, *never* let anything bad happen to you, and I will never leave you alone this long again." I pried Homer from my chest and held him in front of me, as if I wanted to be sure he understood what I was saying, even though he couldn't—not really.

Yet I felt sure he knew. Somehow, he always did.

"I promise," I said. "I *promise* you."

The next morning, from Philadelphia, I mailed Garrett a check for the equivalent of a full week of pet-sitting. I mailed another check to the ASPCA.

21 • None So Blind

I shall never all my days be as good a man as he was.
– HOMER, *The Odyssey*

My friends in Miami were united in their opinion that I should move back in the wake of September 11th. There was no question that life in New York became as hard as I could have anticipated back before I'd moved, when I'd posed myself worst-case hypotheticals. The stench of smoke and ruin from Ground Zero lingered for months; to this day, I associate the smell of things burning with my first autumn in New York. It bothered Homer especially, and it was months before he stopped wandering around the apartment, complaining fretfully about something he couldn't quite identify but that created a constant, low-level anxiety. The clamor of dump trucks and helicopters was constant, and this made Homer jumpy as well. The high point of Homer's day had always been the early part of the evening, when I would return from work. Now he was so ecstatic every time I reentered the apartment—even if I'd gone no farther than the grocery store across the street—that it was several minutes before I could detach him from me long enough to put down my purse and hang up my coat.

I would have considered moving to a different neighborhood, but within two months of September 11th I lost my job. My company had primarily serviced the large financial firms that had been decimated near Ground Zero and was struggling for bare survival. Good luck finding an apartment in Manhattan without a letter from an employer—even if I'd had the lump sum necessary to pay first, last, and security (plus moving expenses) at a new building.

The entire economy had tilted into recession, and it took me eight months to find another job. I was as relentless in chasing down freelance work as I'd been a few years earlier, when I was first trying to gain a foothold in the marketing industry. When I did finally find a job, it was a permanent freelance position in the online marketing department of AOL Time Warner, one where I worked a fulltime fifty hours a week but received no benefits or guarantee of long-term employment. I went one terrifying year without health insurance. There were days when, as my grandmother used to put it, I lived on mustard sandwiches without the mustard. Somehow or other, though, I always paid the vet bills and the rent.

Curiously, it was my parents who were the most supportive of my decision to remain in New York, alive though they were to the dangers that a life in Manhattan now seemed to present. They knew how important the move had been to me, how personally and professionally dead-ended I'd come to find my life in Miami. They were proud of the fact that, no matter how rough the going got, I didn't creep back home with my tail between my legs.

If I had learned one thing from Homer over the years, it was that just because you couldn't see your way out of a difficulty, that didn't mean a way out didn't exist. I'd also learned the value of persistence. The two of us—Homer and I—weren't quitters. And as the months rolled by, I found another reason for refusing to leave New York if it was at all possible to remain.

New York was the city where Laurence Lerman lived.

I FIRST MET LAURENCE a month before September 11th. He was a close friend of Andrea's fiancé, Steve—Steve's "big brother" from college fraternity days and one of the groomsmen in their upcoming wedding.

That August before September 11th was probably the most comfortable I had felt in New York since I'd moved. Work was still good, I finally felt confident in my ability navigate the streets of Manhattan on my own, and my cats seemed to have completely reconciled themselves to this major life change I had subjected us all to. Homer had formed a particularly strong attachment to the pizza deliveryman, who was at our door at least twice a month. Just that afternoon, he had presented Homer with a can of tuna when delivering my small pie with light cheese and extra sauce, which pretty much endeared him to Homer for life.

So I was in an expansive mood that night when I arrived at the party where I met Laurence—ready to add more people to my growing network of New York friends.

The occasion was the thirtieth birthday of our mutual friend Peri, held on a tar-covered rooftop under the warm skies of Manhattan in summer. I remember perfectly the first time I saw Laurence. He was standing next to Steve, and the two of them were engaged in what appeared, from a distance, to be a lively discussion. Laurence wore a white button-down shirt with the sleeves rolled up, blue jeans, a black belt, and black loafers. He gestured emphatically to Steve as he spoke, using his entire forearm, and leaned in intently. You might have thought the two of them were having an argument, except that Steve was laughing and the look on Laurence's face was one of twinkly-eyed humor. "You remember who Laurence is," Andrea said, and I dredged up some faint recollection of outrageously funny comments—or comments that Andrea had insisted were outrageously funny as she'd repeated them to me, laughing so hard she could barely breathe, before conceding that they probably lost something if Laurence wasn't telling the story himself.

Several of Laurence's close friends were there, two of whom were professional comedians and one of whom, within the next few years, would go on to become quite famous. There was certainly no shortage of humor, or funny stories, or hilarious insights that night. I can remember word for word some of the jokes and stories that other people told, but I can't remember a single word that Laurence said, not even whether he shook my hand when were introduced or merely waved at me in a friendly fashion.

But I do remember thinking that Laurence was the funniest person there—probably the funniest person I had ever met. People came and went, small conversational circles formed and re-formed, but I didn't move an inch from Laurence's vicinity all night.

It wasn't just that Laurence was funny, though; some of the funniest people you meet are performers by nature and, entertaining as they are, you get the feeling in talking to them that you're simply an audience, that the things they're saying to you are essentially the same things they've said to countless other people, and in that sense your presence makes very little difference to the flow of their thoughts.

But Laurence liked to listen at least as much as he liked to talk. He would ask you questions and make you talk about yourself, and you would begin to think, in talking to him, that you were a more entertaining person than you'd ever suspected. Laurence liked to talk fast; he was quick-witted, and the speed at which his mind and mouth worked was a thing to be marveled at. Yet he never once talked over you, never cut you off in his haste to give voice to whatever was going on in his head. You would be the sole focus of his attention when he talked to you, yet suddenly you'd look around and realize that a small crowd had gathered to listen in on your conversation. You could never exactly say that Laurence had been the center of attention of any group he was a part of. But he was always the one who had made that group interesting.

And then there was Laurence's voice, which was one of his great charms all on its own. It was a deep, rich voice with a booming resonance, as if his chest contained its own echo chamber. There was a raspy, smoky undertone to it, and when he was being funny it seemed to contain all the laughter in the world. It was a voice that could roar out at you like a lion, then suddenly drop to a murmuring intimacy that created instant in-jokes just between you and him.

Much later, Laurence would tell me about the year in his twenties when he'd lived in Sweden, where he was a DJ for Stockholm's first rock-and-roll station after the government deregulated radio. Everywhere he'd gone, even if it was just to a McDonald's for an order of fries, people would excitedly say, "You are the Laurence from the radio!" It was a telling detail in Laurence's personal history; his was a voice that, once heard, was never forgotten.

At one point, Andrea indicated Laurence's girlfriend, who sat a few yards away on the bench of a chip-and-dip-laden picnic table that had been set up on the rooftop. It was a sultry night, and I wore one of those strappy tops that bare a great deal of cleavage. I remember thinking that if I had been Laurence's girlfriend, and had observed him cracking up for hours with some cleavage-y, unattached girl nobody had ever seen before, I would have put a stop to it with a quickness.

I CAN HONESTLY SAY, however—at least so far as my own intentions went—that I was no threat to Laurence's girlfriend that evening. Simply learning that he had a girlfriend, and that they had been together for over four years, would have tamped out any thoughts I had in that direction. I never was interested in unavailable men. I always found the quality of being interested in me one of the most interesting qualities a man could possess—and you can call that egotistical if you want, but it was a quirk that had painlessly extricated me from more than a few dead-end relationships.

I was still fairly new in New York, and it would have felt almost incestuous to immediately begin dating one of my friend's fiancé's best friends. Who knew how such a relationship would turn out, and Andrea and Steve's wedding didn't need to be about my relationship dramas. Surely, in a city of eight million, I could find other options. And then there was the question of age difference. Laurence was nearly nine years older than I was—which, in the general sense of things, hardly qualified as an age difference at all, but I didn't need to consult books like *The Rules* to realize that a man approaching forty who'd never been married might be someone who wasn't too keen on the institution to begin with. The only thing I found less appealing in the abstract than a man who was unavailable was a man who, while technically available, would someday have to be talked into making a lifetime commitment.

I had never thought of myself as a person who was attracted to a set physical type. Looking back, though, I realize that most of the boyfriend's I'd had—the ones I would have called serious—more or less conformed to a particular physical template. They tended to be tall and skinny, with dark hair and eyes, large noses, and ears that stuck out farther than they probably should. These men were literary or artistic—or, at least, frustrated artistic or literary types—and we would have long, intricate discussions about books and politics. They were a bit shy and awkward, and were always surprised that somebody as outgoing as I was was also as interested in books and politics as they were.

Laurence was barrel-chested, with short, stocky legs that looked so strong, it was if they had been cast in iron. Wrestler's legs, I would have called them. His eyes were blue, and sometimes, if he wore a shirt of a particular light-blue shade, you'd swear that you'd never seen anything bluer. You couldn't say if his features were large or small because they were so elastic. Look through my own photo albums and what you'll see is a series of identical smiles aging as the years progress. I've seen hundreds of photos of Laurence, and I have yet to see any two in which he wears the same expression. I always, from the first time I met him, loved to look at his face, but for a long while the symmetry of it—the reduction of it to a simple collection of features—was too elusive for me to get a fix on. Laurence's mind and his face together moved so rapidly, I had a sense that they presented a challenge I might not be up to.

It wasn't as if I sat down and drew up this list of reasons why Laurence and I couldn't be a couple. I'm just trying to explain why Laurence, despite the strong first impression he'd made, was immediately and almost irretrievably slotted into the category of Boys Who Are Friends But Not Boyfriends. My reasons for thus categorizing him were largely unconscious. As our friendship grew and people occasionally asked why we weren't a couple—and they did—I always felt a vague surprise. It seemed so obvious that the two of us were destined to be the best of friends.

IT WAS A FRIENDSHIP that was initially slow to develop. I knew, the first night we met, that he was somebody I wanted to be close friends with—talk-every-day, see-each-other-constantly kind of friends. But that wasn't something that happened right away.

For one thing, Laurence was the kind of person who'd retained just about every friend he'd made since nursery school; arguably he didn't need another one. And then, of course, there was his girlfriend. Benign as my intentions may have been, I wasn't naïve enough to think that a close and hasty friendship with a single woman he'd met five minutes ago, as it were, might not cause some friction. You don't live with three cats without learning something about respect for territory.

Laurence and I met from time to time at group dinners or special occasions—engaging in the kind of energetic, laughter-filled conversations that always left me with a lingering regret that I didn't see more of him—but that was all. Andrea and Steve were married in May 2002, and as we posed for formal photographs Laurence told me I looked beautiful in my bridesmaid's dress, and that was the last I saw of him all night.

A few weeks later, Laurence and his girlfriend broke up. I was giving Homer his monthly nail trimming (which was always an ordeal, Homer being fiercely resistant—far more than my other cats—when it came to anybody's touching his claws) when Laurence called with the suggestion that the two of us go to some independent film he particularly wanted to see. Laurence was passionate on the subject of film—his knowledge was encyclopedic, but he wasn't a guy who did nothing more than spit out dry statistics about who had directed or written or starred in every movie ever made. Laurence had a keen eye for camera angles, narrative arcs, character development. He could find beauty in something as minor as the specific patter in which a director had chosen to shoot glass falling from a broken window. And he loved it all—even the silly stuff, the ridiculous comedies or shoot-'em-up action films that self-conscious intellectuals often eschewed. I loved that Laurence was "geeky" about something; I was geeky about things, too. And I liked that he knew so much about something that I knew very little about. I learned things from him.

Laurence was a writer and editor for a well-known film industry trade publication. Part of his job was interviewing actors and directors, many of whom were living legends who had shelves filled with every award under the sun. In listening to tape recordings of these interviews, you could tell how much they loved speaking with Laurence about film. You could hear it in their frequent laughter, or constant noting of, "Wow...that's a good question. Nobody's asked me that before." Interviews that were scheduled to last fifteen minutes typically stretched to an hour and a half or longer.

I was overjoyed when Laurence called and asked me to see a movie with him, and I phoned Andrea to tell her of this development. It wasn't until after the movie, when we were seated in a Moroccan restaurant in the East Village and Laurence asked about my family, that it occurred to me that perhaps he'd meant this to be a date? But he didn't try to kiss me, or hold my hand, or make any other overtures toward physical intimacy, and I brushed the idea from my mind.

I think I was able to do it so easily because I wanted to; I thought of Laurence as a potential friend, not as a potential boyfriend, and I was too eager to establish our friendship to allow it to disintegrate before it even began for that most banal of reasons—that we'd tried dating each other and found it didn't work.

That it wouldn't work was something I was so sure I knew, I didn't even bother asking myself the question. Neither one of us was exactly a kid anymore, and how many successful relationships did we have between us? It was a risk I wasn't willing to take. Not with Laurence.

OUR FRIENDSHIP PROGRESSED OVER the next three years, and eventually came to be as close as I ever could have wished for. We talked on the phone several times a day, every day, and saw each other at least once a week—which, given how frenetic life in New York could be, was saying something. There was nobody, not even Andrea, whom I saw or spoke with as frequently as I did Laurence. When, early in 2003 and after more than a year of freelancing, I finally landed a permanent position in the marketing department of the company that published *Rolling Stone* and *Us Weekly* magazines, it was Laurence, and not Andrea, who got the first phone call.

Laurence was probably the first person to become important in my life without meeting Homer. This was not a conscious plan on my part and had more to do with the realities of life in New York. South Beach was a small town (consisting of only one square mile) and was the kind of place where friends dropped in on you at odd hours just to hang out. Manhattan was enormous, a town that encouraged efficiency and forethought plans. It was a city where you met people at the place you would be going to, rather than meeting first at somebody's home and proceeding out. People did occasionally come by my apartment just to kill time or watch a movie, but these were friends whose apartments were smaller and less comfortable than my own. Laurence—with all the luxury of a huge living space—had the most comfortable apartment by far of anyone I knew. On those occasions when we got together to relax on a couch over a pizza or bottle of wine, it was always at his place.

Not that it was crucial for Laurence to meet Homer—it wasn't as if I planned on *marrying* him or anything.

Besides, the two of us spent most of our time together out and about. Laurence had been born in Brooklyn, raised in New Jersey, and moved to Manhattan almost as soon as he'd graduated college. He was deeply in love with all things New York and, consequently, was the one I roped into all the touristy New York things I was dying to do. We went to Ellis Island, where I found the official record of my great-grandparents' arrival in the United States, and to the Statue of Liberty. We went to the top of the Empire State Building and to the West Village dive bars and subterranean restaurants where, a hundred years earlier, some of our favorite writers had caroused and drunk themselves to death. At the Museum of

Modern Art, I was surprised to learn the depth of Laurence's knowledge of modern art—far deeper than my own. Laurence was also a theater buff and procured tickets for everything from *Henry V* at Lincoln Center to *Sock Puppet Showgirls* downtown, which was—as its name would imply—a stage adaptation of the film *Showgirls,* as acted by an all-sock-puppet cast. (Word to the wise: You haven't experienced the true glory of live theater until you've seen sock puppets pole dance.)

By now, you're probably saying, *Okay...surely this paragon of male virtue had at least a few flaws. It couldn't all have been this idyllic, could it?*

Well, it is my sad and solemn duty to inform you that Laurence Lerman was a hoarder. He lived by himself in a rent-controlled, three-bedroom apartment that he'd occupied for nearly twenty years, and it was packed to the rafters with...junk. He had stacks of newspapers, magazines, comic books, and action figures. He had the *Playbill* for every play he'd seen since moving to New York, the ticket stub from every concert he'd attended since middle school, and a matchbook from every restaurant he'd dined in over the past two decades. Once, on a lark, I weighed his matchbook collection. It weighed seventeen pounds.

"That's probably a fire hazard, you know," I told him, and it was shortly thereafter that I began referring to him as Templeton, after the pack rat in *Charlotte's Web.*

I should add that, given how much space Laurence had, the vast bulk of these things were neatly stored in closets and drawers; he wasn't one of those people you read about who lives their everyday lives amid towering piles of discarded stuff. Laurence's apartment was invariably tidy, and you wouldn't have known all that stuff was there unless he made a point of showing it to you.

Still, I was a reader and apt to think in metaphors. It struck me that Laurence wasn't leaving any room in his life—literally or figuratively—for the addition of another person.

Laurence also had a fearsome temper, one thing even the people who loved him most would never deny. It wasn't frequent, but it was deadly. His anger came from some deep, physical source, and he would seem to come at you like a bull. Laurence wasn't a person who you normally thought of as physically intimidating, and to my knowledge he'd never struck another person in his life. But I've seen people twice his size back up when Laurence was angry, instinctively fearful for their safety. His deep, booming voice, which I loved so much, became a brutal weapon when Laurence was angered. It roared at ear-shattering volume, and—if he was especially enraged—he was capable of saying very cruel things. The unfailing brilliance Laurence had in knowing exactly what questions to ask you, the questions you would be most interested in answering, let him know intuitively what things it would be most painful for you to hear—and he would say them.

I had found it easier to stand up to the burglar in my apartment than I did to stand up to Laurence when he was in a temper. I had a deep-seated dislike of loud "scenes," and my response, on the few occasions when we were really furious with each other, was to coldly withdraw. "Clearly," I would tell him in an even voice—a voice that was deliberately many decibels lower than his—"you are not capable of discussing this rationally right now." Then I would leave.

I would have said that I was merely trying to have a "productive" argument, as opposed to an illogical and unfocused one. Laurence would have said, sighing in mock dismay, that I was simply no fun to fight with. What was less fun, when you felt like shouting, than somebody who wouldn't shout back?

But when we had calmed down, we were both anxiously willing to listen to what the other one had to say. It was more painful for me to be at odds with Laurence, to feel that I had somehow compromised his good opinion of me, than it was with any other person I knew.

And to his credit, Laurence never had to be told when he had gone too far, never had to be bullied into making an apology. If Laurence was sure he was right, you'd never get him to apologize simply for the sake of making you like him again—but if he knew he was wrong, his remorse was instantaneous, and no false sense of pride kept him from expressing it. Yet he was never one to plead for forgiveness. Laurence was precisely aware—without, as far as I could tell, ever having to consciously weigh the matter—of the extent to which he was wrong and how much restitution he owed. Beyond that, you could take it or leave it.

I think it was that utter lack of affectation—that core inability to do or say anything, or to refrain from doing or saying anything, merely so you would like him, or forgive him, or think of him a certain way—that ultimately made Laurence who and what he was. It was the thing that made him not a guy, but a *man*. One of my favorite novelists, Anthony Trollope, once wrote: "The first requirement of [manliness] must be described by a negative: Manliness is not compatible with affectation."

Laurence was innately incapable of doing that which was essentially wrong or unmanly. It was the quality that all his other good qualities stemmed from—how he could be funny without ever being obnoxious; how he could talk without trying to dominate a conversation, and listen without being impatient. He was never remotely envious of the success or attainments of those around him. He would share his time, money, and possessions with lavish generosity, but nobody was ever foolish enough to make the mistake of trying to take advantage of him.

I had to think about the balance of things like this all the time. I would never be as instinctively close to getting it all right as Laurence was. And as the years of our friendship passed, it was what I came to respect and admire most about him.

I had never known anyone quite like him.

Obviously, I was in love with him. Just as obviously, I was the last one to know it. By the time we were close friends of some three years' standing, it seemed as if somebody asked me every day why the two of us weren't a couple. I always demurred when this question was asked, although not from coyness or any attempt to deny the obvious. My experience with falling in love was that you met someone, were attracted to him right away, and then, as you got to know him, figured out if that attraction was substantive or merely the delusion of a few weeks. I had never experienced love the other way around—where first you got to know somebody and then realized your interest was deeper than friendship. Having never experienced it, I didn't recognize the thing when it happened to me.

Truly, there are none so blind as those who will not see.

Then, one late-summer Sunday afternoon, as Laurence and I shared hot dogs and piña coladas at a beachy, outdoor grill at Chelsea Piers, he told me that he was dating someone, and my world fell apart.

It wasn't as if Laurence and I had passed the three years we'd spent not-dating each other also not-dating anybody else. Various boyfriends and near misses had come and gone, and I had shared with Laurence the details of all of them. Now that I thought about it, though, I realized Laurence had never discussed with me the women he'd been involved with. It wasn't that I'd assumed he'd remained celibate all this time. Truth be told, I hadn't thought about it much at all. I had taken it for granted that a man like Laurence would have a hard time finding a woman who could capture his serious interest, but that when that woman came along, he would tell me about it.

Well, now she had. And he did.

My first thought was that Laurence's and my days as friends were numbered. It was hard to imagine that any girlfriend would tolerate his close friendship with the likes of me. Then I immediately hated myself for thinking of me, rather than being happy for my friend's happiness. But as soon as the word *happiness* crossed my mind in relation to Laurence and some woman who wasn't me, my head shut down and my body went numb. I felt as if I were in shock, like somebody who's walked away from a car accident.

I tried to conceal all this from Laurence, to act as if everything were normal, but I don't think I did a good job because he kissed me on the cheek more gently than usual as he put me into a cab bound for home.

The insomnia set in that night, and it went on for weeks. Poor Homer, who slept when I slept and—so it would seem—didn't sleep if I didn't, got very little rest himself. I took to pacing the floors, and Homer dutifully followed me step-by-step in slow circles around our one-room apartment. I felt bad for depriving him of a full night's rest, but I had a lot to think about, and there was no point in wasting eight perfectly good hours sleeping.

I tried to reason myself out of my funk, to convince myself that I only thought I wanted Laurence now because he wanted somebody else. I was the worst kind of cliché and, more than that, I was selfish. I was spoiled and selfish and used to having all of Laurence's attention to myself, and it was clearly the attention—and not the man—that I was suddenly so covetous of.

But then, as the sleepless nights rolled by, I understood—in a way that was so clear, it was shocking I'd never seen it before—that I had compared every man I'd dated over the past three years with Laurence, and they'd all come up short. They were never as funny as Laurence, never as smart as Laurence, never as manly or strong of character as Laurence was.

Anybody with two eyes in her head would have seen, long before this, that the essential complaint I'd had about all these men was that...they weren't Laurence. I thought I'd been evaluating them on their own merits, but really all I'd done was reject them for committing the unpardonable sin of not being the one man I was in love with already.

Perhaps it had taken me so long to recognize that I loved him because he didn't look the way I'd always thought the man I would end up with would look—he had none of the skinny, bookish appearance of the men I customarily dated. Then I thought about Homer. Homer lived in a world where vision didn't exist, where the way things and people looked wasn't only an irrelevant consideration, it was no consideration at all.

I could wrap things up with a nice neat bow right now if I said that I learned from Homer that love is blind, that it doesn't always grow in a straight line from the way somebody looks.

But that wasn't true—looks *did* matter. No matter how much of a life I'd been able to give Homer, no matter how much happiness he'd been able to carve out for himself, the one thing I could never give him was the specific joys that vision could bring. It was the easiest thing to take for granted, how looking upon a well-loved face could lift your spirits in a way that nothing else could.

So it wasn't that I realized looks were irrelevant—it was that I realized that nothing in life made me as happy as seeing Laurence's face. Sometimes, if I was meeting Laurence somewhere, I would pick him out from a crowd while he was still yards away. When I saw his face, even at a great distance, I would laugh—not because he looked funny or was doing anything particularly humorous, but because seeing his face made me so happy that some of my happiness had to spill out in the form of laughter, or else it would make me too giddy to stand.

I had been given a gift. There was something I could see with my eyes that filled me with joy every time I saw it. Not everybody was as lucky as I was.

Still, I had no more reason for supposing now than I'd had when I met him that Laurence would ever be interested in fully committing to someone. I had even less reason for thinking that "someone" might be me. Now there was this other woman—Jeannie or Jeanette, or whatever Laurence had said her name was. For all I knew, Laurence, like me, had never thought of the two of us as anything more than friends. Or maybe he'd thought about it, I was pretty sure he'd thought about it, but that had been three years ago. How could I know what he thought about me now?

What scared me the most was the prospect of losing our friendship. I didn't know what I would do if I tried to be Laurence's girlfriend and wound up losing him altogether.

And yet, I'd barely been able to speak with him since he'd told me about the woman he was dating. I might be terrified of moving forward, but moving backward was impossible and even standing still was rapidly becoming an unrealistic option.

That was something else I'd learned from Homer—sometimes, to get the things that were good in life, you had to make a blind leap.

It was Homer, I realized, who had brought me most of the insights I'd acquired about relationships over the past few years. It was Homer who had taught me that the love of one person who believed in you—and who you believed in—could inspire you to attempt even the most improbable things. Somewhere along the way, I had decided that because Laurence and I had yet to find a lasting love with another person, we were somehow fated to be unable to do so—at least not with each other. But where was that carved in stone? If anything, Homer was living proof that dark predictions about potential happiness were nothing more than an opportunity to prove all conventional wisdom wrong. Wasn't Homer someone who was supposed to have been timid and fearful, someone who might go on to live *a* life, but who would never have an exception one? Yet who had I ever seen find as much to celebrate in the midst of the everyday than Homer?

Actually, I had found one person like that—and that person was Laurence. Like Homer, Laurence had that within him which was incorruptible, and which could find something to rejoice in among even the most grindingly mundane aspects of day-to-day life. Not only was it a quality I respected, it was something I aspired to. Perhaps that was why Laurence and Homer had become the most important fixtures in my life.

I had nothing but logical reasons why Laurence and I shouldn't try to be a couple, just like I'd had nothing but logical reasons why I couldn't possibly adopt a blind kitten—which only went to show that, sometimes, the thing you hadn't even known you were looking for could only be found in the very last place you would have expected. It was Homer who had, from the first time I saw him, begun to change the ways I evaluated my relationships. When I'd met him, and recognized his innate courage and capacity for happiness, I'd understood that when you see something so fundamentally worthwhile in somebody else, you don't look for all the reasons that might keep it out of your life. You commit to being strong enough to build your life around it, no matter what.

In doing so, you begin to become the thing you admire.

Above all things, Homer had taught me that there was great joy to be found in great risks. I had been dating since I was fifteen years old, and in that entire time I had never once made anything like a declaration of love unless and until someone else made it first. The potential reward had never seemed to be worth the risk. Laurence had begun dating somebody else, and I had less reason now for thinking that risk might lead to an eventual reward than I ever had. I think, though, that I was almost more afraid of success than failure. The prospect of picking up the phone and making a single call that would, if it went the way I hoped, change the entire course of my life was terrifying. But if you were never willing to be fearless, you would never achieve anything worth having.

Homer had shown me that, too.

So, one Sunday morning in early October, I closed my eyes and leapt. That is to say, I called Laurence to tell him how I felt.

"Listen," I said, "I have to tell you something, and it's okay if you don't feel the same way, but..." I paused, finding it difficult to know how to continue. Suddenly, I was too far in to back out, but I still had no idea where I'd land. "I think...I think I have feelings for you that are more than friendship. And I understand," I rushed on, "if you don't—"

"Yes," Laurence interrupted. "I do. I always have."

We talked for a long time—more laughing than talking, and saying little that was coherent. It was a conversation that, now that we were having it, seemed inevitable. Yet it was equally hard to believe it was really happening.

"You know," I said, "it could be really awkward if things don't work out for us. Because of Andrea and Steve, I mean."

"I've thought about that," Laurence replied gravely. "There's only one solution."

"What's that?" I asked.

"We'll have to be madly in love with each other for the rest of our lives."

Laurence and I hung up an hour or so later, having made a plan to see each other the following night right after work. I made a mental note to carefully review my wardrobe options. And I would have to call Andrea. Andrea had to know about this new and startling turn of events (although probably not so startling from her perspective) as soon as possible.

But all of a sudden, I found that I was too exhausted to think about any of that. Homer and I got into bed, and the two of us slept straight through until Monday morning.

22 • A Canticle for Vashowitz

May heaven grant you in all things your heart's desire--husband, house, and a happy, peaceful home; for there is nothing better in this world than that man and wife should be of one mind.
– HOMER, *The Odyssey*

IT HAD ALWAYS BEEN my opinion that when a couple decide to move in together, they should find a new apartment rather than having one person move into the other's home. I had developed this theory years earlier, around the time when I'd moved into—and subsequently moved out of—Jorge's house. Humans, in my experience, can be as territorial as cats, and it's best to head off any *but I've always used this closet to store [fill in the blank]* arguments before they crop up.

It was a fine principle, as such things go, but it failed to take into account that first commandment of Manhattan real estate: Thou shalt not relinquish a rent-controlled, three-bedroom/two-bathroom apartment with a balcony. Laurence paid less in rent than I did for my studio, and had more than twice the space. When we decided to move in together, it was never a question that my cats and I would move into his home.

Still, Laurence and I were a couple for a full year before I moved in, as I'd begun writing a novel about South Beach. I couldn't tell you why I had woken up one morning so completely convinced that what I truly wanted in life was to be a writer (although the four layoffs I'd endured in a two-year period had persuaded me that self-employment might be my best bet). Nor could I tell you why I persisted when everybody I knew in publishing told me that the only thing less likely than an unpublished writer's landing a book deal was an unpublished writer's landing a book deal for a novel.

But I'd learned from Homer long ago that the difference between "unlikely" and "impossible" was all the difference in the world. After many months and I don't know how many rejection letters (I stopped counting when I reached twenty), I found an agent and the whole thing became an honest-to-God professional endeavor. Since I continued to work fulltime, it took me over a year to finish a first draft of the manuscript, and during that time—wherein Laurence patiently read, critiqued, and then reread every word I wrote—we agreed that it made sense for me to finish writing before I moved.

It would be misleading, however, if I were to suggest that my South Beach novel was the only thing keeping Laurence and me from cohabitated bliss. The truth was, Laurence was not thrilled at the prospect of living with three cats.

Laurence and I had innumerable quibbles during the first year we dated, but only one knock-down, drag-out fight. "Do there have to be *three* cats?" he asked one day, about six months into our new relationship—and he couldn't have more precisely worded a question more likely to turn me cold and unyielding as a lake that had frozen over. "I don't know if I can live with three cats."

"Well, there *are* three cats," I replied. "There have always been three cats, and there will always be three cats. If you're having any *Sophie's Choice* delusions, I suggest you forget them."

It was and remains the only moment when I was halfway convinced that Laurence and I, as a couple, were a failed experiment. It wasn't learning that Laurence didn't like cats—I'd always known that Laurence didn't like cats (although, Laurence indignantly insisted, it wasn't that he "didn't like" cats; it was just that he *did* like dogs). But I felt that nobody could truly love me—could profess to care about my happiness—and even consider subjecting me to the wholly unbearable pain of...what, exactly? Deciding which of my cats I loved least and sending him or her to live with strangers? Or to a shelter? While I could understand someone's not wanting to live with three cats, it struck me as the kind of thing that—having known me well for *three full years* before we were a couple—Laurence should have thought about far earlier than this. Had I walked into Laurence's apartment and found him in bed with another woman, I couldn't have been more convinced that I had been completely—*completely*—miles wide of the mark in my assessment of his character.

Deep down, ever since the day I'd first considered adopting Homer, I'd been waiting for the moment when a promising relationship would fall through because the man in question was unwilling to live with three cats. I'd always known it would happen, and the only surprising thing was that it had taken so long.

Laurence and I fought for hours, until finally we arrived at the crux of what he really meant. "You always stay at my place," he said. "You've never once let me into your apartment. Maybe there's something so horrible about living with three cats, you don't want me to see it. Or maybe you're not ready to let me into your life."

Well, he had me there. It was true that I'd never invited Laurence into my home. Before we were dating, there had been no imperative reason to do so. Now that we were a couple, I was too anxious about our relationship to make any mistakes—and I was terrified that if the four of them met and didn't like each other, I might lose Laurence. But my clever plan of avoiding this scenario by keeping everybody separated had obviously backfired. I could understand why Laurence found it difficult to believe I was serious about spending the rest of my life with him, when I wouldn't even let him spend the night with me in my own home.

So we arranged for an overnight visit, and it couldn't have gone any worse. Scarlett had sprained her leg that morning due to an overly enthusiastic leap, and limped away from the newcomer in an even surlier fashion than usual. *He'll think I'm running a halfway house for blind and lame cats*, I thought. Vashti peed in Laurence's overnight bag. Homer had gotten used to a life without doors—the only door in my apartment was to the bathroom, and I always kept that open. When Laurence went in to use the bathroom, closing the door behind him, Homer sat at the door and wailed, crouching down to slide one front leg, all the way up to his shoulder, into the crack between the door and the floor. The visual of Homer's disembodied leg and outstretched claw reaching for him beneath the bathroom door was, as Laurence reported, "terrifying."

"Are you guys *trying* to make my life harder?" I asked them in despair after Laurence had left the next morning. "Couldn't you pull it together for *one night?*" Their only response was to descend upon me in a happy, purring heap. *Thank God that guy's gone.*

Still, I think it worked out for the best—insofar as Laurence was now convinced that I *must* love these pain-in-the-neck creatures beyond all reason if I was willing to put up with them. His philosophy after that night was that he loved me, and I loved the cats, so therefore...well, he probably couldn't *love* them, but he would try to tolerate them.

LAURENCE HADN'T LIVED WITH a pet of any kind since he'd graduated high school (his parents had had a dog). He had, however, occasionally taken care of Minou, his landlord's cat, while his landlord was out of town. Minou was closing in on twenty years of age and, as Laurence's landlord proudly insisted, had lived so long because he was too mean to die.

Minou was not a social cat. Sometimes, when staying with Laurence, he would jump onto the computer keyboard while Laurence was writing (I felt that my own novel was coauthored by Homer, so frequently was he perched on my left knee while I wrote it), but other than that Minou kept mostly to himself. Laurence would say that at times he forgot there was a cat in the apartment.

The chief difficulty in living with three cats, as Laurence was at frequent pains to explain to me once the four of us had moved in, was that there was always a cat *there*. I had come to take my cats' omnipresence for granted—nor would I have wanted it any other way; why have pets if they weren't around? It's true, though, that despite how large Laurence's apartment was—larger than any home the four of us had lived in together for quite some time—there was never a moment when Laurence and I were alone. At least one cat was always somewhere close by.

Nobody had an easy time adjusting at first, although Scarlett took the most straightforward approach. Scarlett had an idea that there were two types of living beings in the world. There was Mom—who dispensed food, love, and occasional discipline—and then there were other cats. As far as Scarlett was concerned, she was the eldest cat in the household and her authority over the cats was absolute. Laurence might be a bigger cat than most, but he was still just a cat, and since—Scarlett could only assume—it was he who had moved into *our* home, it fell upon her to clarify Laurence's limits regarding everything from where he was permitted to sit, to how close to her he was permitted to walk. That he was not permitted to touch her, or approach her directly, went without saying.

Now Scarlett's favorite method of enforcing discipline in the ranks had always been an angry swipe of her claw. If Laurence was walking down the hallway and got too close to her, she swiped at him with her claw. If she was lying in the hallway and Laurence attempted to step over her, she swiped at him with her claw. If she was sitting on the ledge of the couch behind my head and Laurence sat down next to me, inadvertently brushing against her, she swiped at him with her claw.

It would have been galling enough to Laurence that he was suddenly made to feel like an intruder in the home he'd occupied for two decades. But being slashed at by an aggressive pet is also viscerally upsetting. And it was downright scary to stumble down a pitch-black hallway in the middle of the night and feel invisible "talons," as Laurence insisted on calling them, rake the skin of your leg. Knowing how much bigger you are than the pet means nothing when you also know—as Laurence did—that you're unwilling to risk inflicting injury.

What was he going to do, I'm sure he asked himself more than once, fight her?

I did my best to intercede, but cats are notoriously hard to discipline and Scarlett was no different. It wasn't as if spanking her with a rolled-up newspaper would have any effect, the way it might with a dog. Such a course of action would only have made Scarlett more hostile and aggressive—even if I'd been willing to try it, which I wasn't.

Laurence, having grown up with a dog who *was* spanked when she was "bad," took this to mean that I wasn't trying to remedy the situation at all. This wasn't true, though. I spent a lot of time thinking about how to make life with Scarlett bearable for Laurence—and if it took longer than I would have liked to arrive at a solution, it was only because I'd never been in this particular situation before. I'd lived with Melissa and then with my parents during Scarlett's pre-cuddling days, when she was content to hide if I wasn't in the house by myself. Now Scarlett wanted to be with me all the time; she just wished everybody else would clear out and leave her alone while she did so.

The only place where Laurence could be sure of respite from Scarlett and her claws was in our bedroom; Laurence had insisted the bedroom remain a "cat-free zone." He said he didn't want cat fur on the bed, and I'm sure this was true (I, for one, had always been grateful that only Homer slept under the covers, meaning fur accumulated on top of the blankets but nowhere else), but I'm also sure that he didn't relish the idea of fighting with three cats to claim a spot next to me at night. It was a fair compromise, yet the sudden banishment of the cats from my bed, each of whom had slept in bed with me for at least part of every night of their entire lives, caused more separation anxieties on all sides than I could have foreseen.

Scarlett resented her exclusion, and made her resentment known. She would sit at the bedroom door and meow loudly as soon as I went in at night and, when it wasn't opened promptly, she would slip one paw beneath the door and rattle it almost angrily. *Open this door! Open it NOW!* I think the idea of a room with no other cats—where she could have me all to herself—was Scarlett's idea of Nirvana. Here was an opportunity to relive the glorious days of her youth, when she'd been an only child, if only someone would hurry up and let her in! No matter how many times I tried to shoo her away, or how often Laurence roared, "Enough already!" Scarlett refused to be deterred or consoled. Her incessant meows at the bedroom door were driving Laurence even crazier than her constant swipes at him.

The solution I finally devised solved both problems at once. Laurence usually stayed up several hours later than I did, and he began to feed the cats a small can of food late at night after I went to bed. In the first place, the food distracted Scarlett from crying at the bedroom door. By the time she finished eating she seemed to have forgotten that I had left her, and she would curl up on the living room rug or in one of the closets she liked, contentedly purring herself to sleep.

And once Laurence began feeding the cats, Scarlett seemed to understand that he was definitively *not* another cat, and was to be considered in the same general category that I was. In her own way, she came to respect him. I can't quite say that they bonded, but her philosophy seemed to be, *I don't like you, and you don't like me, but I will accept your food and leave you alone.* She seemed to think that Laurence should be grateful that she'd conceded this much and, as any cat owner will tell you, he really ought to have been.

Homer was, of course, as different from Scarlett as a cat could be, and had always been willing to make a friend of any new person. But for the first time in recorded history he was afraid of someone—and that someone was Laurence.

I think, in part, this was due to Laurence's loud, powerful baritone. One of the things I loved most about Laurence was his voice, but it must have sounded like the booming voice of God to Homer, whose hearing was so much more sensitive than any of the rest of ours.

Laurence was also the first person to have spent significant time with Homer without going out of his way to make friends. Everybody wanted to be friends with the "poor little" blind cat. Laurence was the only person I'd ever brought into my life who was willing to accept the cats on whatever terms they offered, but who refused to offer any terms himself. By this I mean, for example, that Laurence didn't crouch down on all fours to get to know Homer on his own level, didn't try to create games the two of them could play together or request the formal "introduction" that Homer required before he felt comfortable letting a new person pet him. Laurence didn't care whether he petted Homer or not. If Homer had wanted to be petted, Laurence would have been happy to do so, but if Homer wanted to be left alone, that was fine with Laurence, too.

This was actually a quality I appreciated in Laurence. He felt no need to prove to himself, or to me, or to anybody else, that he was a good person because he'd forged a "special" bond with my "special" cat. Laurence didn't even really think of Homer as being blind; once he saw the ease and energy with which Homer got around, he accepted it as a given that Homer was essentially the same as any other cat. Laurence, in fact, was the first and only person who ever did the one thing I always claimed I wanted everybody to do—he treated Homer, automatically, as if he were normal.

Homer, however, was at a loss to account for the behavior of a person who didn't go out of his way to befriend him. Homer thought people existed for the sole purpose of playing with him, and must have felt that a person who didn't do so could only regard him with hostility. Consequently, those first few months, he fled in terror whenever Laurence approached. It cut me to the heart to see Homer—brave, irrepressible Homer—finally fearful of something after all these years.

Perhaps the only time Homer wasn't afraid of Laurence was when Laurence was in the kitchen. Laurence and Homer shared a similar passion for sliced deli turkey, and whenever Homer heard Laurence open the refrigerator to pull out sandwich fixings, he'd race over from wherever he was in the apartment—his fear of Laurence momentarily dispelled. He would sink his claws into Laurence's pant leg and climb it like a rope ladder up to the kitchen counter, where he would burrow his entire head into the waxed paper containing the turkey, trying desperately to snag himself a morsel.

Laurence was afraid to pry Homer off his leg, and equally afraid to lift Homer from the counter or push him off, which meant Homer frequently ended up with more turkey than Laurence did. It got to the point that when Laurence wanted to make a sandwich, he would first run the faucet in the kitchen sink at full blast, use the sound to conceal the opening of the refrigerator, then sneak turkey and bread into his bathroom, close the bathroom door, and run the sink in there. It was an elaborate, and successful, way of keeping Homer out of the turkey, but it was hardly an enjoyable way to prepare a sandwich.

"This is no way to live," Laurence said once.

No, it wasn't. But Laurence was a grown man, and Homer knew the word *no*, and I saw no logical reason for all these shenanigans. "Homer is perfectly aware of what the word *no* means," I told Laurence, "and you need to get used to saying it." Then I added, "It's just as frustrating for Homer as it is for you. He doesn't understand why you're not saying *no*, but also not giving him any turkey."

It wasn't that I didn't know Homer was wrong. Of course Homer was wrong, and my not-to-be-argued-with *"No! No, Homer!"* brought him to heel on numerous occasions. But I couldn't be there all the time. Laurence and the other cats, to a certain extent, would have to work things out on their own.

Nevertheless, there were days when I felt so guilty about the whole thing that I didn't know what to do. Nobody was happy—not the cats, not Laurence, and certainly not me, the cause of everybody's unhappiness. "You and Laurence love each other," Andrea would say when I called for advice. "Yeah, it sucks that it's hard for him and the cats right now, but what are you going to do? They all just need a minute to get used to each other. Laurence would still rather live with you than without you."

Maybe. Some days, I wasn't so sure.

Alas, turkey was merely the tip of the adjustment iceberg. Homer was as "talkative" as ever—still far and away the most verbal of my cats—and, whenever he was awake, he was engaged in a running conversation with me. He still had his *Let's play!* meows, his *It sure has been a long time since I had any tuna* meows, his *Why aren't you paying attention to me?* meows. "What is with that cat?" Laurence would ask in exasperation, having rewound for the third time whatever movie he was watching because he'd missed several lines of dialogue.

Homer's silences, on the other hand, were nearly as troublesome. Sometimes, in the middle of the night, Laurence would get up to use the bathroom, stumbling with his eyes half closed down a hallway he could have navigated blindfolded, so familiar was it. Yet now, I was almost always sure to hear the hard thud of Laurence's shoulder hitting a wall, followed by a loud exclamation of *"Dammit!"* and the startled *clip-clip-clip* of Homer's paws scuttling down the hallway. Homer liked to sleep in the hall, and it never occurred to him to alert Laurence to his presence by meowing. But Homer was invisible in the dark, and Laurence constantly tripped over him late at night.

This disturbed Homer to no end. Homer didn't know the difference between a hallway flooded with daylight and a hallway in total darkness. He only knew that sometimes Laurence tripped over him and sometimes he didn't, for reasons that were mysterious and impossible to predict. Laurence's "kicks" (of course he never meant to kick Homer) and yelling could only confirm what Homer already suspected—that Laurence didn't like him. Laurence was convinced that Homer slept in the hallway, where he must have known Laurence was sure to trip over him, out of pure stubbornness. I bought a few nightlights for the hallway, which seemed to help, but the truce I effected in this way was wary at best.

Despite his shyness in Laurence's presence, however, Homer was as mischievous as he'd ever been, and Laurence's home provided him with endless adventure. Homer loved nothing more than creating chaos from order, and there was so much more for him to climb and explore here than there' been in the studio apartment we'd lived in for so long. Laurence and I found it impossible to keep Homer from scaling bookcases or the entertainment center, throwing mounds of books and DVDs onto the floor from their original homes on neatly arranged shelves. He was especially merciless when it came to Laurence's closets, whose boxes of newspapers, photographs, posters, matchboxes, letters from friends overseas, and the carefully preserved effluvia of forty years drew Homer like a siren song. Laurence had discarded a great deal of his...junk...to make room for me when I moved in. Still, a mind-boggling quantity of it remained. There was so much stuff to play with here! How had Homer ever lived a happy and complete life without having this much stuff!

He would wait until nobody was around, then use a single paw to slide open a closet door so he could pillage the boxes ruthlessly, pulling out all manner of papers and objects to chew up, bat around, or claw to shreds as his fancy dictated. I can't tell you how many times Laurence and I would come home to find a ransacked apartment that looked like a crime scene—a cyclone of old college term papers and passed notes from high school days strewn across the living room floor, in the middle of which Homer crouched, turning an innocent face to our own accusatory ones as if to say, *Hi, guys! Look what I found!*

I bought some twine that we used to tie Laurence's closet doors closed (I didn't really mind if Homer got into my own closets). We created complicated knots, which were ultimately effective in keeping Homer out. But if Laurence, say, wanted to quickly grab a magazine he'd written an article for back in 2002, he would fumble impatiently with the knots and press his lips together in a restrained silence that spoke volumes.

For all the new things he found to get into, Homer was, as he had ever been, a creature of habit. He still wanted to sit with me or on me at all times, and still insisted on sitting exclusively on my left side. If Laurence happened to sit to my left on the couch, Homer would wander around the apartment at loose ends, "complaining" at the top of his lungs. Like a blind person—who knows the difference between a can of soup and a can of peas because soup and peas are always kept in exactly the same spot—Homer's life, curious and adventurous though he was, was manageable because certain things always happened in the exact same way. Homer knew where he was supposed to be and what he was supposed to do based on where I was and what I was doing. If I was sitting on the couch, then Homer was supposed to be sitting to my left, and if he couldn't sit to my left then something was worrisomely out of sync in the world. But Laurence couldn't understand why I would insist that we get up and switch positions, leaving my left side free. Surely, in a three-bedroom apartment, there was room for everybody to sit wherever they wanted without anybody's having to jump up and change spots because, seriously, what was that cat's problem?

And as if all that weren't enough, Scarlett was not alone in her nocturnal caterwaulings at the bedroom door. Homer had no more intention of being displaced from my bed by Laurence than Scarlett did, and Homer was more insistent than she was in demanding his rights. Homer also cried at the bedroom door at night but, unlike Scarlett, also cried whenever I went into the bedroom—whether it was for an afternoon nap or a change of clothes or half an hour of undisturbed seclusion while I read a novel. As soon as I opened my eyes in the morning, I would hear the *clip-clip-clip* of Homer's footsteps down the hall, and he was crying at the door within seconds.

What was remarkable about this was that I didn't get up at the same time every morning, nor did I use an alarm clock (people as neurotic about punctuality as I am tend to awaken on time without the aid of an alarm). I might first wake up at five or six thirty a.m. on a weekday, or at nine a.m. on a weekend, or even later, but it was never Homer who woke me up. It wasn't until I was aware of being awake for a moment or two that I would hear Homer's footsteps approaching the bedroom—and I couldn't tell you how it was that he knew. Perhaps the sound of my breathing changed? It seemed unlikely that even Homer, acute as his hearing was, could hear a change in my breathing when he was sound asleep down the hall. But there was no disputing the fact that he knew. Within only a few days, my habit of waking up briefly and then drifting back off for another hour was a thing of the past. It was one thing for Homer to cry piteously at the door at night while Laurence was still awake, and quite another for Laurence to be awakened at five a.m. by a wailing cat. So I'd grab a pillow and one of the extra blankets from the closet and head for the couch where Homer could cuddle with me—ecstatic with happiness—as I dozed until I was ready to start my day.

When I had first adopted Homer, I'd toyed briefly with the idea of naming him Oedipus and calling him "Eddie" for short. Homer the poet had been blind, but Oedipus the tragic hero had lost his eyes altogether. Melissa, however, had insisted that calling an eyeless kitten Oedipus was mean (this from the person who'd thought calling him "Socket" was a swell idea), and so the idea was discarded.

Nevertheless, I now found myself with a reverse Oedipus on my hands—he'd had his mother all to himself, and now out of nowhere was this father figure who was trying to take his mother away from him. I began to despair of ever bridging the gap between the two of them.

Amazingly, it was Vashti—Vashti who was never aggressive except when she was passive-aggressive, Vashti who never used her claws or raised her voice, Vashti who always gave in and never insisted on getting her own way—who saved the day and solved all my problems. She did so by the simplest means imaginable.

She took one look at Laurence and fell deeply, hopelessly, irretrievably in love.

VASHTI HAD ALWAYS BEEN more partial to men than to women (with the exception of me, of course). She loved to be petted and crooned to and told how pretty she was, and she liked these things especially when it was a man who was dispensing the attention. But all the men who had come into our life had only had eyes for Homer, and Vashti wasn't one to push herself on anybody.

Now there was a man who, as Vashti shrewdly surmised, didn't seem interested in Homer at all. It was true that he didn't seem interested in any of the cats, but perhaps there was an opportunity here.

She didn't leap upon Laurence all at once. But if she found a moment when the other two cats weren't around—and, miraculously, now that we lived in such a large home, sometimes Vashti had us to herself—she would jump into my lap and insist, softly and sweetly, upon being petted. She didn't try to get Laurence to pet her, but as I stroked her she would look at him with a kind of melting adoration in her eyes. It was exactly the sort of gaze that, I often thought, men must daydream about someday seeing in the eyes of a beautiful woman. *See how much nicer I can be than those two?* Vashti seemed to say. *I like you sooooo much more than they ever will.*

Vashti intrigued Laurence as well. Sometimes I caught him looking at her with an expression almost identical to her own.

"She's really beautiful, isn't she?" Laurence would say. "She has a perfect little face. I don't think I've ever seen such a beautiful cat."

I don't know the specifics of how things progressed from there, or who made the first move, but one evening I came home to find Vashti nestled in Laurence's lap. He caressed her and said, "You're a pretty girl, aren't you? Aren't you a pretty, pretty girl?" He stopped his crooning as soon as he saw me, but Vashti remained in his lap for nearly an hour. Another time, I came out of the shower to find Laurence seated at the breakfast table with Vashti at his feet while he sneaked her bits of food. "Laurence!" I said. "Do you have any idea how long it took me to train them not to beg at the table?"

Laurence looked shamefaced. "But she's so pretty, and she likes me."

Ah, well—Laurence wouldn't be the first man undone by such a pretext as that.

As the months went by and Laurence became more attentive, Vashti seemed to blossom into a second kittenhood. She was full of playful high spirits in a way that she hadn't been in many a year. She would charge around the apartment—never roughly, because Vashti was quite the lady—batting furiously at anything that dangled or bringing scraps of paper over to Laurence for him to throw for her. She hadn't done that with me since she was only a few months old. She became conspicuously more fastidious in her grooming habits, unable to tolerate the teensiest speck of dirt in her long white coat. And she would squeak with outraged jealousy if she caught Laurence and me being affectionate with each other, running over to paw gently at his leg as if to say, *Hey! Did you forget that I was here?* Laurence got a huge kick out of this; he would often make an elaborate show of hugging and kissing me while

Vashti was watching, in the hope that he could provoke a demonstration of her outrage.

"I can't tell you how much I love it when you use me to make the cat jealous," I would say.

Scarlett and Homer still clearly preferred the days when they'd lived with me alone, but Vashti had never been happier. I was so thrilled for her happiness, I think it made me love Laurence a little more.

"They really all have their own personalities, don't they?" Laurence observed once. "I knew that dogs had different personalities, but I never attributed different personalities to cats. I think that's why I never really liked them until now."

I was the tiniest bit flabbergasted. It seemed incredible to me that anybody could be unaware that, *of course*, different cats would have different personalities. Like Laurence, I had grown up with dogs, but I'd always expected, when I brought each of my cats home, that none of them would be like any of the others.

But if this was the epiphany that got Laurence and the cats to warm up to each other, I was all for it.

It wasn't long before Laurence came not only to recognize the differences among the cats, but even to form a grudging respect for them. "I can understand Scarlett," he said one day. "Scarlett just wants to be left alone to do her thing, and I get that." As a man who had lived alone by choice for the better part of twenty years, of course he would.

And the first time he saw Homer catch a fly five feet in midair, he was beside himself with admiration. "Look at that cat *go!*" he exclaimed—and he was so impressed, he hurried into the kitchen for a bit of turkey to reward Homer with. "That's a cat who knows how to *move*. Have you ever noticed about him, how his walk is so much sleeker and more graceful than other cats?"

Had I *noticed?* Was he kidding?

It was Laurence who went shopping for various types of netting and wire that might make our balcony safe enough for Homer to go out onto. He'd observed the way Homer would stand longingly at the sliding glass door when Laurence and I occasionally let Scarlett and Vashti out (a years-long source of angst for me; I hated to deprive Scarlett and Vashti of time outdoors, but felt miserable that Homer had to be excluded). Sadly, there was no getting around the fact that our balcony railing was well within Homer's jumping range. "If only Homer couldn't jump so high," Laurence would say in a sympathetic tone that was, nevertheless, tinged with appreciation. "That cat can jump so *high*."

But Vashti remained first and foremost in Laurence's affections. "Hey, it's the Vashti cat!" he would cry happily whenever she entered a room—running straight over to leap into his lap and rub her little cheek daintily against his.

His favorite nickname for her—one entirely of his own invention—was "Vashowitz." She was almost always "the Vashowitz" when he referred to her—as in, "Do you think the Vashowitz would like this brand of catnip?" or "I think we need to get the Vashowitz a new scratching post. She's clawed right through the old one."

From the way he fussed and fawned over here, you would think no man had ever fallen in love with a cat before.

One day, about a year after the cats and I had moved in, Laurence brought home a bag of Pounce cat treats. He was looking for a way to make Vashti happy, I think, but all three cats got their fair share.

They must lace those Pounce treats with crack, because I had never seen anything like the three-ring circus in our apartment whenever the bag of Pounces came out. Even Scarlett sat up on her hind legs like a meerkat and begged. *Scarlett begged!* She still wouldn't let Laurence touch her, flinching away if his hand sought her head, but she went so far as to purr and rub against his ankles when he came home at night.

Laurence also learned to lightly tap the ground with his fingernail next to the Pounces he dropped for Homer, so that Homer would know where they were. Homer was soon constantly crawling all over Laurence, nosing his hands and pockets with friendly curiosity. *Hey, buddy! Got any of those Pounce treats?*

And Vashti...well, Vashti also loved the Pounces, but she had always loved Laurence for himself. That didn't change much.

LAURENCE WAS THE KIND of person who never simply handed anybody a birthday card. He always sent them by mail because, he said, it was infinitely more fun to find a birthday card unexpectedly in your mailbox than it was to see it in somebody's hand.

The first birthday I celebrated nearly a year after moving in with Laurence, I got two birthday cards in the mail. One was from Laurence himself, and bore the return address of his office. The second had a return address and handwriting I didn't recognize (I would later find out that Laurence had gotten a coworker to address it). When I opened the envelope, I saw a card with three kittens—who looked a great deal like

Scarlett had looked as a kitten—on the front. Inside the card, I read:

Happy birthday, Mommy! We love you, even though you make us live
with that horrible man.

It was signed "Scarlett, Vashti, & Homer." Scarlett's "signature" was in red ink, naturally, while Vashti's bore a small drawing of a paw print beside it. The "R" in Homer's was backward and his whole name trailed halfway off the page. Laurence would later explain that, of *course* Homer's signature wasn't perfect—the cat was *blind*, for crying out loud.

Three weeks later, Laurence asked me to marry him. I said yes.

IT WOULD BE ALMOST two years before Laurence and I were married. The novel I had written was sold for publication, and even though I was no longer working at my fulltime job, there were months of edits to be done, followed by even more months of promotion, interviews, and travel. Trying to plan a wedding in the middle of all that would have been too stressful to think about. So we waited a year, until after the book came out, before we began making arrangements. It was just short of another year from the time we started planning until the wedding day itself.

A few months before we were married, Laurence's best man, Dave, came over for lunch. Dave had known Laurence since nursery school and had, naturally, spent a great deal of time in our apartment. But he was usually here with other people.

Scarlett and Vashti were shy of any crowd larger than three or four, so the only one of the cats Dave had met was Homer.

Homer remembered Dave and greeted him in his usual friendly, high-energy fashion. *Hi there! Wanna throw the stuffed worm for me?* Scarlett was also out and, curiously, didn't run away to hide. I was across the room when I saw that Dave was going to try to pet her. I yelled, "No—don't!" but it was too late. Dave's hand was already on her head.

I prepared myself for the worst, mentally assessing whether we had any Band-Aids left in the medicine chest, when I saw something I never thought I'd live to see. Scarlett was nuzzling her head affectionately against Dave's hand. Laurence and I looked at each other, and then at Scarlett, as if she had broken out into a soliloquy from *Hamlet*.

Dave was unaware of our astonishment. He turned to Laurence and asked, "So which cat is the mean one?"

23 • Intimations of Immortality

No one was ever yet so fortunate as you have been, nor ever will be, for you have been adored by us all.

– HOMER, *The Odyssey*

SEVEN WEEKS BEFORE THE wedding, Homer stopped eating.

Within the past few months, I had taken the cats off dry food completely as it became clear Vashti's sensitive digestive system—which had only become more sensitive with age—could no longer handle it. All three cats had responded to their new moist-food-only regimen with enthusiasm—particularly Homer, who had always been fonder of "human-food" meats than the other two.

I wasn't initially alarmed that first morning when Homer, rather than muscling past the other cats to get to his food bowl the way he usually did, approached the bowl halfheartedly and sniffed it a few times before ambling off. It wasn't his typical behavior, but more than a decade of being a "cat mom" had taught me not to be an alarmist about such things. It might be that he was tired of that specific flavor. While Homer had never been a finicky cat, he was getting on in years (it was so hard to believe he was eleven already!), and I knew it wasn't unheard of for a cat to become finickier as he grew older. Or maybe he simply wasn't hungry. Where was the law that said a cat had to eat the exact same amount of food at the exact same time every day? I made a mental note to put down a different flavor in a few hours when I gave them their midday feeding, then went about reviewing proposals and price quotes from lighting designers for the wedding.

When I put down food again a little after one o'clock, this time making sure I selected a different variety from what I had given them that morning, Homer once again refused to eat. He walked into the room somewhat sluggishly, sniffed the food as he had that morning, and made digging motions around the bowl, the way he did when burying something in his litter box.

I wondered if there might be something wrong with the food. Not too long ago, there had been a major scare among pet owners when a substance toxic to cats and dogs made its way into several popular brands. It hadn't affected us directly—Vashti's allergies and colitis having long since required me to buy specialty brands—but who was to say that this batch of food hadn't been tainted by salmonella or *E. coli*? Homer's sense of smell was so much more acute than the other two's, and the way he was acting seemed to indicate that something didn't smell right to him. Perhaps he'd detected a hazard that wasn't apparent to Scarlett and Vashti.

I took all the ceramic bowls away (over Vashti's ardent squeaks of protest), emptied them out, scrubbed them vigorously, and ran them through the dishwasher twice. While they were cleaning, I dashed out to the pet store two blocks away and selected several cans of Newman's Own organic cat food. It was pricier than I would have liked (*Hey, it's for charity!* I told myself), but I couldn't remember any negative stories or health scares associated with the Newman's Own line.

The food was new and the bowls were as sterile as they were ever going to be. To be completely safe, however, I pulled out three small dishes from the set Laurence and I used ourselves, arranged the Newman's Own food on them, and put everything down for the cats.

This time, Homer didn't even bother going into the room where the food was. He sat on his haunches in the middle of the hall as the other two cats charged past him, and then, after a minute or two of apparent deliberation, shuffled like an old man in the opposite direction to curl up in the patch of sunlight on the living room rug, carefully wrapping his front paws around his face.

I was still determined not to panic, but by now I was definitely concerned. I realized that I hadn't seen Homer scamper around playfully once all day. The only things he'd done since that morning were wander up and down the hall a couple of times and sleep. His lack of energy could be explained by the fact that he hadn't eaten—I wasn't very high-energy myself when forced to skip meals—but that, of course, begged the question: Why wasn't he eating?

As a last resort, I ran out once more—this time to the bodega across the street—and purchased a box of dry food. Maybe, enthusiastic as he'd always been about it, Homer had developed a sudden revulsion to moist food altogether. I was the kind of person who could eat the same thing for breakfast every day for two years straight, and then one morning feel as if I couldn't eat that breakfast again, ever, even if it meant I wouldn't eat anything at all. It seemed entirely reasonable that homer might be experiencing a similar feeling. Since Homer hadn't eaten all day, I bought a box of Kitten Chow, thinking it might go down easier than one of the adult formulas.

I locked Scarlett and Vashti in the far bedroom, so Homer could eat in peace. Then I poured some of the dry food onto a small plate, sat next to Homer on the rug, and stroked his back. "Come on, kitty," I coaxed, "make your mother happy and eat a little something."

Rising unsteadily to his feet, Homer lowered his head and began to nibble at the dry food. He didn't eat with much enthusiasm, but he did eat. It was only as I watched him swallow his first tiny mouthful and go for a second one that I knew how worried I had been. If Homer truly couldn't stand moist food anymore, and Vashti was unable to eat any dry food, then feeding times were about to become a nightmare of complications in our home. Nevertheless, I was so thrilled to see Homer eat that this scenario struck me as more comic than cumbersome. *Cats!* I thought. *Leave it to a cat to assume my life revolves around his food preferences.* I was laughing as I said to Homer, in a mock-scolding voice, "Silly cat! You had me so scared!" I gave him a small bowl of water and, after he'd lapped at it for a moment, I took the food and water away. I didn't want him to pile too much into an empty stomach and wind up vomiting.

After I covered up the food and water and stowed them in the refrigerator, I released the other two cats and settled on the couch. Homer crept after me, moving his joints in a slow and deliberate fashion, and halfheartedly rubbed the top of his head against my chin before curling up in my lap. He purred, but his purr was feeble. "Poor thing," I said to Laurence, when he got home that night. "His tummy's been upset all day."

Homer didn't move much the rest of the night, but whenever he seemed even half awake, I rushed to the refrigerator to pull out the bowls of water and dry food. He didn't eat or drink with as much relish as I would have liked, but he consumed enough to alleviate the worst of my fears. It seemed that whatever had been troubling him was already working itself out of his system.

I went to sleep before Laurence did that night and asked him to keep an eye on Homer. When Laurence came to bed a few hours later, I sat up groggily and asked how Homer was doing. "I gave him a little more of the dry food when the other two weren't looking," Laurence said. "He seemed fine. I think he's sleeping in one of the closets now."

Sleeping in a closet? Homer never slept in closets. Scarlett and Vashti sometimes like to burrow deep into a closet and doze where nobody could find them, but Homer always wanted to sleep in the vicinity of at least one other person or cat. I felt a small pang of alarm as Laurence relayed this information, but Homer'd had a rough day. If he wanted to be alone for a while, that was understandable.

The following morning, Homer wouldn't eat anything at all—not even the dry food he'd eaten the night before. After Vashti and Scarlett had eaten, Homer left his small cave in the closet just long enough to stumble into the far bedroom. I didn't like the way he was walking. His steps were hesitant, and he bumped his head repeatedly into walls and furniture. I had never seen homer like this before. He walked as if...

As if he were blind, I thought grimly.

Homer staggered in this befuddled fashion into the bedroom, climbed slowly up the side of the bed, and balled himself up on one of the pillows. I sat down next to him and stroked his back. Homer had always—*always*—acknowledged my touch, had purred or leaned into my hand or raised his head so I could scratch beneath his chin. Now, though, he didn't stir. He didn't so much as twitch a muscle.

"Homer?" I said. No matter how deeply asleep he was, Homer would at least lazily flick one ear at the sound of his name. But this time he didn't respond at all. It was as if my Homer, the cat I'd known and loved so well for more than a decade, was trapped somewhere inside this shell of a cat who now lay beside me on the bed.

This was something beyond the vagaries of a bad day or a sour stomach. I immediately called my vet's office.

The vet was seeing other patients, and I was told that I should leave my phone number and he would call back. There was nothing for me to do in the meantime except pace the floors and wait for a return call—which I did, for the better part of the morning.

I couldn't begin to imagine what was responsible for this dramatic change in Homer's behavior. By lunchtime, when I'd called the vet again and still hadn't heard back, I decided to consult Google. I was sure there was some perfectly benign, non-alarmist way of accounting for Homer's malaise that the collective wisdom of the online community would reveal to me. So I sat in front of my computer and typed in the phrase "cat stopped eating."

Here's a tip for the cat owners out there—and I want you to take this advice very seriously, because it's important. Should your own cat one day stop eating, do yourself a favor and *do not* Google the phrase "cat stopped eating." I mean it. You will be tempted to do so, but I'm here to tell you that you really, *really* don't want to, because *oh my good God*.

The list of maladies to which this particular symptom corresponded was as long as it was terrifying: kidney failure, liver failure, stomach cancer, colon cancer, feline leukemia, pneumonia, tumors, brain tumors, a stroke that had already happened, a stroke that was about to happen, and on and on and on. The only innocuous illness—tooth infection or gum disease—was also the only one I could rule out on my own. Homer had eaten the crunchier dry food the night before when he wouldn't eat the softer moist food, plus I couldn't find any abscesses or signs of infection inside his mouth. That Homer allowed me to poke around inside his mouth without struggling impatiently was, in itself, corroboration that something more than a tooth infection was at work here.

Somewhere around page three of the Google search results, when I reached the stories of people whose cats had stopped eating one day and then fallen over dead the next, sanity and I parted company. I called the vet's office again, and this time I demanded to speak with him. "I am not hanging up the phone until I do," I informed the receptionist, my voice choked with panic. "I don't care how long I have to hold."

I was being something of a difficult client, but the veterinarian did come to the phone after only a few minutes and asked his questions patiently. I tried to answer with equal calmness and clarity. No, I hadn't noticed any bloody stool or urine. No, neither of the other cats was displaying any unusual symptoms or behavior. Yes, it had seemed to come on very suddenly—Homer had been rambunctious as a kitten only two days earlier. I knew he had eaten and drunk a little something the night before, but he definitely hadn't eaten and I wasn't sure he'd drunk today.

The last thing the vet asked was for me to pinch the skin of Homer's neck just above his shoulder blades. I administered this strange-sounding test and reported that the skin had sunk almost immediately back into its normal position, albeit not with much elasticity. "That means he's not too dehydrated yet," the vet said. "If the skin hadn't gone back down, I would have told you to bring him in now so we could get an IV fluid drip going. He should be okay for today, but I want you to bring him in first thing tomorrow morning. A cat who goes too long without eating can sustain liver damage."

Laurence returned home from work with sliced turkey, cans of tuna, smoked salmon—all of Homer's favorites. But Homer was equally indifferent to everything. The sound of the turkey being unwrapped or the can of tuna being opened didn't bring the familiar *clip-clip-clip* of footsteps down the hall. Scarlett and Vashti followed me eagerly into the third bedroom, anxious for their share of the goodies. Scarlett clambered onto the bed and eyed Homer suspiciously as she nosed after the food in my hand that Homer hadn't even lifted his head to examine. *Aren't you going to bother me?* she seemed to ask. *Is this some kind of a trick?* Homer had always pursued turkey and tuna with an aggressiveness that Scarlett found distasteful, shamelessly pushing the other cats out of the way in his excitement.

But Homer remained perfectly still. If it hadn't been for the slight rise and fall of his breathing, I wouldn't have known he was alive.

All three cats had gradually made their way back into our bed over the past year or so (Laurence was powerless to deny Vashti anything—and anywhere that Vashti went, the other two were sure to follow eventually.) But that night I slept alone with Homer in the guest bedroom—although *slept* may be the wrong word, because I was wide awake most of the time. I lay on my side and Homer nestled into my midsection as if he couldn't get warm enough, even though it was the middle of July. I rested my cheek on top of his head and wrapped my arms around him, whispering, "You'll be fine, little boy. You'll see. The doctor will make you all better tomorrow."

Homer didn't fight me early the next morning as I loaded him into his carrier, although I would have given anything if he had. He'd always been a small cat, but today he looked frighteningly skinny. I could feel the bones of his spine poking through his skin as I lifted him into the carrier. For the first time, I found myself almost grateful Homer didn't have eyes; I don't think I could have borne the look of mute suffering that surely would have been in them. "Good boy," I murmured as I zipped the carrier closed around him. I continued talking to him in a soft, reassuring voice in the cab to the vet's office. "Good kitty. Good boy."

The vet and I had a minor disagreement once we were in the exam room. He wanted me to wait in the waiting room while he examined Homer, and I had no intention of leaving. If it had been Scarlett or Vashti I might have, but Homer—ill and miserable as he clearly was—would be terrified if left alone in a strange place with strange people. He wouldn't be able to see their faces or make any sense of what was happening to him. He wouldn't understand why I had abandoned him. I couldn't leave him; if anybody was going to hold Homer down while the vet performed his tests, it would be me.

Homer had been alarmingly listless for the past two days, but he sparked briefly back to life on the exam table. He had never exactly been a good patient (what pet enjoys the vet's office?), but I'd never—not even during the break-in—heard him growl and hiss as evilly as he did that day while the vet turned him this way and that, poking with fingers and various instruments as he collected samples and felt for lumps, tears, or obstructions.

I stood at the opposite end of the exam table from the vet, my hands firmly clenched in the scruff of Homer's neck as I tried to hold him still. "Good boy," I crooned, my thumbs rubbing behind his ears. I felt that I should keep talking, that if anything would calm Homer, it was the sound of my voice. "You're my brave little boy and you're doing such a good job. Mommy is right here with you, and this will all be over soon."

The vet announced that he was going to collect a urine sample. I was wondering how he would accomplish this—it wasn't as if he could tell Homer to pee in a cup, was it?—when I noted the giant needle he was preparing and saw his movement to turn Homer onto his back. The idea, it would seem, was to insert that long needle directly into Homer's bladder.

Homer resisted being turned onto his back with all his might—and the amount of force he was able to command was startling, considering that he hadn't eaten in two days and was now closer to weighing four pounds than five. When the vet attempted to insert the needle, Homer screamed.

I don't mean that Homer yowled or yelped or growled—I mean that he screamed. It's a sound I still hear sometimes in bad dreams, a scream of pain and fear that was almost human. The vet was trying to say something to me, but I couldn't hear him. The only thing I could hear was the sound of Homer screaming. One of his front paws rose in the air and he clawed violently at me—at *me*—missing my right cheek by only a few inches.

My face must have looked as pale and horrified as I felt, because the vet said firmly, "I'm going to take him into another room and get some of our techs to help me. you should wait in the waiting room." Then, more gently, he added, "Try not to worry too much. We won't hurt him." He bundled Homer into his carrier and exited, leaving me alone.

When I was growing up, we'd had a dog named Penny, a German shepherd who was exceedingly gentle and was, we always said, my father's dog. Penny loved my father, adored him, followed him everywhere with worshipful eyes and would have lived and died only to make him happy. Late in life she'd developed hip dysplasia, as large breeds often do, and my father for two years had patiently helped lift her to her feet when she struggled to get up, had cleaned up after her when she lost control of her bowels. Then one day, as my father tried to help her stand, Penny turned around and snapped at his hand. She was immediately contrite, whimpering and licking his hand in a desperate plea for forgiveness, which was of course immediately granted.

But my father, when he told this story, always said that that's when he knew. He took her to the vet that afternoon, and Penny never came home again.

It was Penny who had flashed through my mind when I'd seen Homer's claws—after so many years of unwavering love and loyalty—slash at me. I felt a sudden helplessness. For the first time since I'd brought him home with me, there was nothing I could do for Homer. I was standing alone in that room, Homer having been taken away because there was nothing I could do to help him. Even after September 11, there had been something I could *do*, a plan of action I could follow. Homer had always needed me in ways that my other two cats, fiercely as I loved them, had not. I'd promised that I would never let anything bad happen to him, had done everything I could over the years to keep that promise, yet ultimately I had failed. Such a promise, I knew in that moment, was by its nature impossible to keep. You could love someone, you could try to protect them from everything you could think of, but you couldn't keep life from happening to them. And with that realization came the knowledge of pain, of the pain Homer was in now and the pain that would come, of hard decisions I might have to make sooner than I was prepared for.

My cats were getting old—were, by the standards of some, old already. Homer was eleven and would soon be twelve. Vashti was thirteen and Scarlett was fourteen. I was on the brink of getting married, and Laurence and I loved to talk about our future, about what we might be doing five or ten years from now. My thoughts of the future always, unconsciously, included my cats. I simply couldn't imagine my life without them. They had come to define and shape almost all of the adult life I had known. It was yesterday, or so it seemed, that they had come to me as kittens, barely old enough to be weaned from their mothers.

But they were getting old. In that moment I understood that I would marry Laurence in a few weeks and start a life with him, but very little of the life we would live together would include all three of my cats.

Soon enough, it wouldn't include any of them.

I walked out, through the waiting room and the front door of the building to the street outside. I pulled my cell phone from my purse and called Laurence at his office. I'd meant to assume a "brave-but-shaken" tone, to tell him that I didn't know anything yet, but had wanted the reassurance of speaking with him. As soon as I heard his voice on the other end of the line, though, I began to cry.

"I'm coming down there," Laurence said. I tried to pull myself together and tell him that wasn't necessary, that I would be okay. But Laurence said quietly, "Gwen, he's my cat, too."

The vet released Homer to Laurence and me half an hour later, with a promise to call within twenty-four hours when he got back the test results. "What should we do in the meantime?" Laurence asked, and the vet responded, "Try to get him to drink some water. And if he shows any interest in eating, let him eat as much as he wants of whatever he wants."

Laurence dropped us off at home and returned to his office. I sat with Homer all day; he crept out of his carrier and, exhausted from his grueling morning, fell asleep on the floor a few inches away from it. Later that afternoon, I wrapped him in an old blanket and brought him out onto the balcony so he could sleep in the sun. It had always been Homer's fondest wish to go out on that balcony, like Scarlett and Vashti sometimes did, and I'd never let him, feeling that he tended to move so quickly, it would be impossible to keep him safe.

I didn't think there was much chance he'd dart away from me today, though.

Homer seemed completely unaware of the distinction between inside and outside. He didn't even sniff the air or flicker an ear to capture the sounds and smells he'd always been so curious to explore. "*Eres mucho gato*, Homer," I murmured, sitting beside him and stroking his head. "*Eres mucho, mucho gato.*"

The phone didn't stop ringing all day. My parents called every few hours to see if there was any word from the vet, as did Laurence. Laurence must have spread the word that Homer wasn't well, because his parents and sister also called, as did many of our friends—even our friends who weren't "pet people," who'd never had pets of their own, and who I wouldn't have expected to empathize with a pet's illness. But it had always been that way with Homer; to have met him even once was to interest yourself in his welfare. As the number of callers swelled, it was clear how important it was to many—and not just to me—that this scrappy little Daredevil, this small cat who'd made a heroic and extraordinary act out of living an ordinary life, pull yet another life from the nine he'd been burning through since he was a blind, half-starved, two-week-old a hairbreadth away from an inglorious end in a shelter.

Call me, they all insisted. *Call me as soon as you hear from the vet.*

The vet never was able to determine what, precisely, had made Homer so ill. When the tests came back, the only thing he could say was that there had, indeed, been some minor damage to Homer's liver—which could have been the cause of his illness, but could also have been one of its effects. The vet asked me to keep him apprised and to bring Homer back for a follow-up visit in a week, which I did. Homer received a clean bill of health.

Homer recovered fully. By the next day he was up and around a bit, eating sparingly and halfheartedly batting around a crumpled-up ball of paper. Within three days, he had resumed his usual eating habits.

Still, nothing can turn back the clock or change the fact that Homer's not as young as he used to be. (Are any of us?) He scampers and darts as joyfully through our home as he ever did, but occasionally I notice a certain stiffness to his joints, and I've begun adding a supplement to his food that helps promote joint flexibility in senior cats. He sleeps more often and more deeply than he did of old, and if awakened unexpectedly he can be downright cranky. He still loves to doze near Scarlett and Vashti, but sometimes he hisses at them when they accidentally disturb his rest—Homer, who never hissed, except when there was danger. His coat has been as purely black as a piece of polished onyx, but now it's flecked with gray, and a single whisker grew in a conspicuous shade of silver.

Yet not even the onset of old age can defeat Homer's irrepressible high spirits. He still scraps tooth and claw for a stolen morsel of turkey when Laurence makes a sandwich. He still hasn't given up on his life's dream of successfully trouncing Scarlett—always "sneaking" up on her from the front, in plain sight. The two of them play this game with less speed, perhaps, but with equal vigor, and the look on Scarlett's face seems to say, *Aren't we getting too old for this?* He spends entire days following the path of the sun across our living room rug, purring happily in the warmth of the light he's never seen.

Most of all, what remains the same is Homer's overwhelming joy in the morning when I get out of bed and his day begins. He still spends a good ten minutes rubbing his face vigorously against mine, still purrs with as much singsong richness as he did that first morning as a kitten, when he'd realized that both of us were still here.

With age, perhaps, Homer has realized—as Laurence himself is fond of saying—that any day spent above ground with your loved ones is a good day.

24 • Reader, I Married Him

May you whom I leave behind me give happiness to your families; may heaven vouchsafe you every good grace, and may no evil thing come upon your people.

— HOMER, *The Odyssey*

LAURENCE AND I WERE married in September, in the penthouse of a funky downtown office building. It commanded sweeping views of the Manhattan skyline at night, befitting a groom as much in love with New York as Laurence was, and reflecting all the best in my own life since moving to New York with my cats nearly eight years earlier.

We decided to dispense with many of the formalities associated with weddings. Our guest list was kept scrupulously small (although there was rather a large Swedish contingency). I wore a vintage, 1940s-era cocktail dress, wide in the shoulders and narrow at the waist, rather than a formal wedding gown. There was plenty of dancing but no seating arrangements, no five-course dinner, no flower-draped aisle or even, for that matter, any aisle at all. We opted for a cocktail party—with passed hors d'oeuvres and lots of liquor—that happened to have a wedding ceremony in the middle. When the evening was about halfway through, we gathered our friends and families together, popped up a *chuppah* (the canopy under which Jewish wedding ceremonies are held), called the rabbi forward, and were married. The ring I gave to Laurence was inscribed with a passage from the Song of Songs: *Ani l'dodi v'dodi li*, which means, *I am my beloved's, and my beloved is mine*. When we kissed for the first time as husband and wife at the ceremony's conclusion, Stevie Wonder's "Signed, Sealed, Delivered" played. Andrea and Steve, who had introduced us to each other, introduced as to the crowd as Mr. and Mrs. Lerman. Then the music and dancing resumed once more.

Laurence and I liked to speculate before the wedding as to the roles we would have assigned to the cats, if it had been even remotely feasible to have the three of them in attendance. We could press Vashti, with all the glory of her natural bridal white, into service as a ring bearer. And surely we could find important jobs for Homer and Scarlett. It was pure silliness, naturally, but still...it felt odd to get married without the cats there. One way or another, they had influenced or participated in just about every momentous occasion in my life over the past fourteen years. If not for Homer, I might never have come to appreciate the value of a man like Laurence. I would have loved Laurence's warmth, humor, and quick mind no matter what, but I might never have understood that when you find someone whose essential characters is so strong as to leave no room for doubt, you've found a rock that you can build your life on.

It's become trendy, in recent years, to talk about how much longer it takes people of my generation to grow up and think of ourselves as adults. But growing up doesn't necessarily mean getting married, having children, or taking out a mortgage. Growing up means learning to be responsible for others—and embracing the great joys those responsibilities can bring. Homer taught me that building my life around someone other than myself, making myself responsible for someone else's life, is one of the most rewarding differences between being a kid and being an adult.

Being the parent of a special-needs pet means living your life constantly poised on the edge of a double-edged sword. On the one hand, you become a fierce defender of the ways in which your little one is perfectly ordinary—all the things he or she can do that are just like what everybody else does. No need for any extra attention here, thank you very much.

And yet, you never lose sight of how absolutely extraordinary that very ordinariness is, how difficult, remarkable, and rewarding that fight to be "just like everybody else" has been.

Maybe Homer isn't really any more extraordinary than other cats. But among the small circle of people whose lives he's touched, this tiny cat who nobody wanted—who nobody, with the exception of one young and idealistic veterinarian, believed could ever go on to live a good life—has been a source of minor miracles, major joy, and a concrete example of that best of all possible truths:

Nobody can tell you what your potential is.

Back before I adopted Homer I had believed, with the certainty of a child, that the way my life was then was the way it would always be—that the career, the relationships, and the life that I wanted would always be somewhere beyond my reach. Yet here I was—a published author, a bride about to be married to the single greatest man I had ever met. The one thing I knew for sure about our future was that it could be anything we wanted it to be.

Despite having forgone so many traditional wedding trappings, Laurence and I opted for a strictly traditional ceremony. The ceremony is the thing, after all, and we liked the idea of saying the same words, and having the same words said over us, that had been said by and for our grandparents and great-grandparents, and other brides and grooms for generations before us.

This meant that we didn't write our own vows. Instead, we toasted each other once the ceremony was over. I spoke of Laurence's astonishing wit and intelligence, his strength that I never believed possible I would find in anybody. "I laugh every single day," I said. "And it is miraculous to me every single day that the greatest man I've ever known loves me, too."

"Let me tell you a little something about Mrs. Lerman," Laurence said, when it was his turn to toast me. He went on to speak about brains and beauty, about passion and compassion. "Gwen is the most passionate person I've ever met, and also the most logical," he said. "She's passionate about being logical. I had no idea this was even possible."

On the theme of combining passion and logic, I knew from years of event production that no matter how free flowing and spontaneous a party felt, it needed to have a strong logistical skeleton. So I carefully scripted everything out—lighting changes, the time for the ceremony, the schedule for toasts—in an Excel spreadsheet and sent it to all the vendors and participants (including Andrea and Steve) several weeks ahead of time. I was mocked relentlessly for this, but I was firm in my belief that without a clear, organizational flow, chaos would ensue.

Even though I had orchestrated everything down to the last detail, however, there was one surprise in store for me that night. After he concluded his toast, Laurence called forward

Alex and Zachary, his eight- and five-year-old nephews, and Allison, the seven-year-old daughter of his first cousin. He retrieved three large, foam core posters from some hidden corner I hadn't noticed, and handed one to each of them. "I need some help for this part," he told them. "Can you guys help me?"

They had obviously been prepped for this beforehand. Their faces nearly split beneath their wide grins of anticipation as they each eagerly took hold of one of the posters.

"There are three 'people' who couldn't be here tonight," Laurence said. "Technically, they weren't invited. People who know me can't believe I live with three cats. But I do, and it wouldn't be a celebration of ours if they weren't included. So it gives me great pleasure to introduce to you for the first time, in a very real and legally binding sense...Vashti Cooper-Lerman!"

Allison held up her poster, and it contained an enormous photo of Vashti in midstride, looking adoringly out into the crowd as, no doubt, she had looked adoringly at the man holding the camera.

"Three things you need to know about Vashti," Laurence said. "Number one, Vashti is beautiful. Number two, Vashti knows she's beautiful. Number three, Vashti knows that *you* know she's beautiful."

People laughed, although not nearly as hard as I did.

"Next," Laurence continued, "for the first time ever—legally and officially...Scarlett Cooper-Lerman!"

Alex held up the poster of Scarlett. In her photo, Scarlett was lying on her side, her head raised as she gazed rather majestically into the middle distance.

"I've lived with this cat for three years," Laurence said, "and last week she let me touch her for the first time."

Poor Scarlett! Always fated to be misunderstood.

"And, last but not least, the star of our family, our Daredevil and truly the coolest cat in town...Homer Cooper-Lerman!"

Zachary held up a poster-sized photo of Homer sniffing inquisitively at the camera lens. "And he's blind!" Zachary announced with great pride. "He's blind but he can walk around and everything!"

The crowd chuckled appreciatively as they clapped and cheered. It was Homer's first official standing ovation.

"This is a cat who knows how to *live*," Laurence said. "He's got this huge world in that little head, and you can tell just by looking at him that every second of every day of his life is an adventure. I only wish," he concluded, "that I could see what that cat hears."

It was the first time I had heard Homer described by somebody else, the first time I wasn't the one who explained him or answered questions about him. But if anybody has asked me that night, *What do you mean he has no eyes? How does he get around? How can a cat live with no eyes?* my answer would have been different, and infinitely simpler, than the stock answers I usually gave.

I am Homer's eyes. And he is my heart. And finally, the two of us—Homer and I—had found another person whose own heart was big enough to carry us all.

HOMER
The Ninth Life of a Blind Wonder Cat

"Touches the reader's heart in a profound and lasting way."
-The Conscious Cat

GWEN COOPER
New York Times bestselling author of Homer's Odyssey

HOMER
The Ninth Life of a Blind Wonder Cat

GWEN COOPER

interrobang

Copyright © 2015 by Gwen Cooper

All rights reserved.

No portion of this book may be reproduced in any form without written permission from the publisher or author, except as permitted by U.S. copyright law.

Cover design: Gwen Cooper

For Homer's Heroes--the men and women who work in rescue, the ones who adopt rather than shop, and those who know that when you help animals, you help people too. I never knew that writing about my cat would lead me to so many outstanding humans.

And for Laurence, always.

Contents

Foreword	315
1. "Cat Lovers Don't Read Books"	320
2. The World's Cat	347
3. Strong Like Bull	372
4. The End of the Beginning	406
BONUS SNEAK PEEK!	439
Acknowledgments	455
About the Author	459

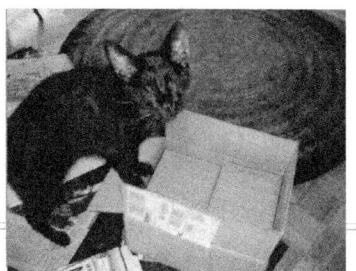

FOREWORD

I'VE BEEN WRESTLING WITH the idea of writing a sequel to *Homer's Odyssey* for nearly two years now—feeling, on the one hand, that there were certainly more Homer stories to be told; but, on the other hand, that to make something "book length" would require adding an awful lot of padding. *Homer's Odyssey* was published in 2009 and covered the first twelve years of Homer's life. Homer lived to be sixteen, and so a new book would have significantly less ground to cover.

What you are holding now is the solution I eventually reached—what I like to call a "mini-sequel," roughly one-third the length of the original. Not as long as many books, perhaps, but (I think) exactly the length it needs to be.

Length wasn't my only concern. I can't speak for other writers, but for me, to write about something is to relive it as vividly as I did the first time around. I don't know how to make a reader see and feel things that I'm not seeing and feeling myself at the moment I'm writing about them. There were many, many wonderful times with Homer during those four years after *Homer's Odyssey* came out, and you'll read those stories here. But there were also some hard times when we lost him, and I wasn't sure I could bear to go through them again.

Well, it wasn't the first time I've been wrong, and it won't be the last. One of the cruelest things about losing a loved one is the way that time makes our memories fade— until what remains isn't the substance of something, only the factual knowledge that it once existed. But, in writing this book, I've gotten to live with Homer again. I've gotten to feel his little head pushing hard into my hand as he demanded his daily pettings; to hear the distinctive *clip-clip* of his feet as he followed me down the hall; and to listen once more to the very specific melodic bird-song that ran beneath his purr. It's a sound I would instantly know from any other cat's purr, even if I were blindfolded.

The only thing that seems remarkable now is that I'd ever thought I was losing those things. And the only regret I have is that it's taken me so long to write my way back to them. I've spent the last weeks feeling Homer with me— the substance of him, a physical presence—as I haven't gotten to do in far too long.

That's the gift this book has given me. What I hope it will give to readers is more Homer, of course, more of the happy times they shared with us and loved in reading the first book, and all the comedy of seeing a little blind housecat— who, once upon a time, nobody else had wanted—take the world by storm.

I also hope that it will help bring clarity to some of the issues that we wrestled with—elder care and end-of-life issues that all animal guardians will have to face eventually. Medical treatment for animals has come a long way since I was a kid living in a family filled with rescue dogs. Often the question now isn't, *What* can *we do?* but, *What* should *we do?* How much money is too much to spend? How much aggressive medical care is justifiable, even if it's the only way to prolong a beloved cat's life?

There's no one right answer to these questions— although in this Foreword (and only in the Foreword), I'd like to float the idea of pet health insurance for anyone who knows they wouldn't be able to come up with, say, five thousand dollars in cash or credit at a moment's notice (which is probably most of us). The monthly premiums are very reasonable and, as they say, you can't put a price tag on peace of mind.

I was lucky as my cats grew older, in that whatever money I had, I'd earned by writing about *them*. I also didn't have children or a mortgage. So whether I could find the money for their care, and whether it was "prudent" to spend that money on them, weren't really questions. If the money came from them, then how could I not give it back?

Nevertheless, we ended up making very different decisions for Vashti, Scarlett, and Homer—because they were three very different cats. Vashti was easygoing and could handle whatever the doctors wanted to do, so we let them throw the whole arsenal at her. Scarlett was a surly girl and almost morbidly dignified, so we opted for a middle course—surgery for her cancer, but not chemotherapy or the removal (at the age of nearly seventeen) of her affected leg.

And Homer...well, Homer was Homer. He knew his own mind. He also knew his own strength—better, as it turned out, than even I did.

Certainly better than his doctors did.

And I have no doubt that when the kittens we adopted in 2012—whose antics, exploits, and hero-worship adoration of Homer you'll also read in these pages— become senior kitties someday, the decisions we make for them and with them will be different as well. Clayton and Fanny are as much one-of-a-kind individuals as our other cats ever were.

One last thought before moving on: Animals are luckier than humans, because animals get to live in the *now*. They do not fear death, or torment themselves with questions about what comes after. No cat has ever desperately hoped for one more year of life so she can finally see Paris, finish her memoirs, or watch her grandchildren graduate from high school. I genuinely believe that, if our animals could understand such things and talk to us about them, they wouldn't want us to spend ourselves into bankruptcy for the sake of trying to stretch fifteen years into sixteen, or even six years into twelve.

Cats know when they feel happy, when they feel comforted, and when they feel loved. None of us ever knows how much time we'll have, and you weren't put in your cat's life to guarantee him a certain minimum number of years. You were put in his life to provide him with happiness, comfort, and love. If you have given your cat (or dog, or bunny, or horse, or guinea pig) a life built on these things, then you've done your job, and you've done it perfectly. And the moment you put all those things in jeopardy is the moment you'll know you've gone too far.

It will be hard to know these things in the chaos of that moment in which they're happening, when decisions have to be made. I know that firsthand. But if you pause for a moment, take a deep breath, and listen to your cat, he will tell you.

I've spent *far* more time discussing this here than I do in the book itself. First and foremost, this is a book of stories—stories about a cat who rose from obscurity to fame, who was promoted from barely tolerated baby brother to adored "big kid," and who continues to save the lives of other animals to this day, simply because *he* lived and his story was told.

Thank you for the gift of letting me tell these stories— and for the additional, greater gift of keeping Homer alive. As long as there is you, there will be him.

Gwen Cooper
New York, NY
November 26, 2015

1 • "Cat Lovers Don't Read Books"

There is no accounting for luck; Zeus gives prosperity to rich and poor just as he chooses, so you must take what he has seen fit to send you and make the best of it
– HOMER, *The Odyssey*

FAMOUS CATS WEREN'T A *thing* like they are today, back when I first began writing the proposal and outline for *Homer's Odyssey* in 2007. There were no cat cafes. Cat videos hadn't yet taken over the internet. The "Friskies 50" list of the internet's fifty most influential cats was years away not only from execution, but from any relevance. Everybody knew about famous animated cats, like Felix, Tom, Sylvester, the Aristocats, and the perennial Hello Kitty. I remembered a movie from childhood called *That Darn Cat!* There were celebrity cats like Morris and the elegant Fancy Feast Persian, although they were "played" by a succession of different cats, more brand icons than actual felines. A fictional kitty named Sneaky Pie Brown starred in a series of cozy mystery novels. But there didn't seem to be any real-life famous cats, cats who were also members of real-life human families.

There was, however, a cat I'd read about in a recent newspaper article—a cat who'd lived in a library in small-town Iowa, and whose human caregiver had just sold a proposal for a book about his life for more than a million dollars.

My own first book, a novel about South Beach, had been published a few months earlier. Now I was trying to figure out a second book. I didn't think I could earn anything close to a million dollars for any book idea I might have, but I remember putting down the newspaper and looking across the living room at Homer—who was, at the time, visible only from the waist down, the upper half of his body buried under the sofa as he struggled to retrieve an intriguing new belled toy that had rolled away from him—and thinking, *I'll bet I could write a book about Homer. Homer's a pretty cool cat...*

Once I had the idea, I couldn't shake it loose—as if it had always been waiting there for me to unearth. Over the next few weeks, I started jotting down notes and writing out some preliminary paragraphs. I was still working full-time in an office, so I wrote in the pre-dawn hours of early morning—hours when Homer himself was the most active, sparking ideas and connections to half-forgotten memories of our earliest life together. Mornings were when Homer was likeliest to decide to use the toilet instead of the litter-box, to chase his big sisters down the hall (*Wait up, you guys!*), or to disrupt my writing with a preemptory head-bonk as he sat down smack in the middle of the computer keyboard, leaving me to wonder for the millionth time how a blind cat—just like any "normal" cat—infallibly *knew* when I was looking at a book or a newspaper or a computer screen, at anything rather than at him, and made up his mind to put an immediate end to *that*.

At the end of two months, I had enough written down to show my L.A.-based literary agent. He was decidedly under-whelmed by the whole thing. Those who've read the Afterword to the paperback edition of *Homer's Odyssey* may recall that his initial response was, "But why would anybody want to *read* this?"

"Because a lot of people like cats?" I'd been so flummoxed by his question that I heard myself phrasing my answer—a statement I knew for a fact to be true—as if it, too, were a question, the answer to which I was unsure of. "Because Homer is blind and interesting and has an inspirational life story?"

My agent was blunt. "The writing is there, but I don't think it's a good idea. I wouldn't be able to take it to editors."

I didn't just pay my agent to make deals for me—I also paid him for his career advice. He knew the publishing industry better than I did, and choosing to move forward with my blind-cat book against that advice was easier said than done.

I took to Google, trying to get a sense of how many others like me there might be out there—people who were also living with blind and "special-needs" cats. I ended up calling a woman named Alana Miller, who ran an organization called Blind Cat Rescue in North Carolina. We talked for a while about the plight of blind cats, the barriers they faced in finding adoptive homes, the way so many were summarily euthanized in open-intake shelters. We agreed—perhaps idealistically, but with utter sincerity— that if a book like this could save even one of them, it would be worth the effort of having written it.

I'd already been working with the notion of *blind leaps of faith* as being one of the central themes of this embryo book, and I decided to take one now. *Thank you so much for everything you've done for me, and for being the first person to have confidence in me as a writer,* I wrote to my agent a few days later. *But we see my proposed HOMER'S ODYSSEY project so very differently that I believe it's in our mutual best interests to part ways.*

I didn't know many other writers who could refer me to their agents, so I went back to what I had done to find my first one—sending blind query letters and emails "over the transom" (meaning without a referral from another client). But this time I didn't have to wait close to a year to hear back, as I had with the first book. Within only a few weeks, a senior agent with a prestigious New York literary agency pronounced herself intrigued by both the writing and the story as I'd outlined it, despite being a self-professed "dog person." My confidence was bolstered by this—that I wasn't just getting the, *Awwwwww...Homer's a cute kitty!* endorsement—and also by how quickly I'd found an agent this time. Surely, I told myself, this could only auger good things. The two of us spent the next four or five months working together closely on an outline, a full proposal, and two sample chapters. We went back and forth over whether those sample chapters should simply be the first two chapters—or perhaps the story of Homer chasing off the burglar? Passages about Homer catching flies in mid-air? Homer and his Kleenex guitar? Final decisions were eventually made, and it was just after Memorial Day of 2008 when we decided we were ready to share *Homer's Odyssey*—at least in its broad strokes—with others.

It may have taken months to pull the proposal together, but it took only a few weeks for the rejections to start coming in from publishers. *The writing is wonderful, and I'd love to see more from this author,* the typical rejection would begin. *But in a crowded pet-memoir marketplace, I just don't feel that Homer is interesting enough to stand out.*

"Crowded marketplace?!" I'd exclaim to my agent. The only other cat memoir at the time was the one about Dewey, the Iowa library cat, and that hadn't even come out yet.

Ironically, Homer would usually be doing something that I thought was very interesting—or, at a minimum, entertaining—whenever one of these letters would come in. I remember that when I got the first one, Homer had just "liberated" a bag full of catnip toys I'd recently stocked up on. I'd double-wrapped the toys in two plastic bags, hidden those bags inside a duffle bag, and secreted the whole thing underneath a mound of clothes in the bottom of the closet, so that I could distribute them one at a time as the old ones wore out, without the cats' pestering me to death. But Homer's unerring nose had found them anyway. He'd burrowed assiduously into that mound of clothes intended for the laundry—kicking dirty socks and underwear into a heedless pile on the floor behind him—unzipped the duffel bag with his teeth and claws, and torn through the first plastic bag. Looking for all the world like Santa Claus (Santa Claws?), Homer now pranced down the hall and into the living room with the sack of toys between his teeth, the other two cats for once following *him* eagerly as they waited for him to distribute the booty.

"Not *interesting* enough?!" Poor Laurence, then my husband-to-be, was generally the only receptacle for my indignation, which waxed hot when I'd receive one of these letters. "*The cat has no eyes!* Does he need to have no eyes and also learn how to juggle?" I'd demand. "Would that make them happy? Maybe if Homer had no eyes *and* could ask for his food in perfect sign language like Koko the gorilla."

That Homer wasn't "interesting" enough (or some variation of that) was what my agent and I heard most frequently. Also that animal lovers only wanted to read books about dogs and horses; that animal lovers didn't want to read animal books at all in "our current tech-centric environment;" that animal lovers were only receptive to picture books. One editor informed us matter-of-factly that "cat lovers don't read books." *Why do you think there aren't more cat books?* he asked with perfect *Catch-22* logic. Another said that, sure, maybe cat lovers read books, but they didn't read memoirs. A third was confident that while cat lovers might read books—and while some of those books might even be memoirs—they definitely didn't read *cat* memoirs. (I wish I could say I was making this stuff up.)

By now, I had lost my job as a marketing executive at a magazine company, which had been acquired by another magazine company and then dissolved. The crux of my job had been the analysis of market research on our readers' consumer-spending habits. The "Marketing Analysis" section I'd written for the *Homer's Odyssey* proposal had been exhaustive. I'd provided data on the percentage of cat- owning U.S. households (roughly one third—or, expressed another way, around one hundred million Americans living with at least one cat); the amount of money spent per year by those households on cat-related products and services; and, specifically, the higher-than-average propensity of a wide swath of the U .S. cat-owning population to spend their disposable income on entertainment-related purchases, including dinners out, movie tickets, *and books.*

"If there's any hard data out there," I'd say to Laurence, "supporting the thesis that 'cat lovers don't read books,' I'd be pretty darn interested in seeing it." (I'm afraid I generally used a saltier word than *darn*. Forgive me. Those were dark days.)

At this point, our wedding was only a couple of months off, and I was starting to panic. It's all well and good to get married for richer or poorer, but it still feels awful to enter your marriage without a job or prospects or any viable means of earning an income. Homer was recovering from a recent health scare, the treatment of which had not only eaten into my finances, but had taken its emotional toll on us both. As much as I tried rationally to dismiss the idea, I had the persistent feeling that Homer had gotten sick *because* I wanted to write about him—that my hubris in thinking ours a story worth sharing publicly had been met by the powers that be with a not-so-gentle rebuke. I was supposed to cherish Homer as he was, the private heart of our own home, and be grateful for that.

It was when things seemed bleakest that I got an electrifying phone call from my agent. A large publishing imprint—one of the biggest and most venerable in the industry—was interested in *Homer's Odyssey*. Not only were they interested, they wanted to meet with me in person—along with my agent, a couple of senior editors, the group publisher, and various vice presidents in publicity and marketing. Then my agent said the words that every author dreams of hearing: "They're talking about a six- figure advance."

Six figures! Between my unemployed status and upcoming wedding, money was tight. Still, in the week I had before that meeting, I went out and bought a new outfit. I got my hair professionally blown out at a fancy SoHo salon. I invested in a forty-dollar manicure and sixty-dollar pedicure at a high-end spa in the Meatpacking District, rather than relying on the eight-dollar manicures I usually got from an elderly Chinese woman in our apartment building. (I was convinced that senior-level publishing muckety-mucks would be able to tell the difference.) I spent an hour carefully applying my makeup, so it would look like I wasn't wearing any. I even sprang for a hired car service to take me to the meeting, afraid of relying on the vagaries of afternoon cab availability to get me there on time.

I was already in the car and on my way uptown when I got the call from my agent. Everything had been cancelled. The group publisher (the big boss, basically) hadn't known what the book was about until shortly before the meeting was supposed to begin. She'd never heard of anything as "creepy" as a cat without eyes, and she was appalled that anyone on her team had considered acquiring *Homer's Odyssey*. There was a rumor afloat that she'd gone so far as demoting the senior editor who'd first read the proposal and recommended it for acquisition—as an example to others never to let anything this awful cross her desk again.

"*Homer's Odyssey* now has an official body count," I told Laurence grimly that night, when he got home from work and asked how my meeting had gone.

I'm not sure which hurt worse—the brutality of that last-minute cancellation, after a week of raised hopes and what now seemed like a pathetic level of over-preparation. Or hearing poor Homer, tiny Homer who'd never done a mean thing to anyone in his life, described as "creepy."

And whose fault is that? I asked myself. Who had subjected Homer to the mockery and derision of ignorant strangers?

I had. I had done it. And even though I knew Homer had no idea that anything unkind had been said about him—or even that such a thing as unkind words existed—those words had opened a wound right in my heart. It hadn't taken much to revive fears I'd had years ago—the sense that it was my job to safeguard Homer in the disability I'd long-since stopped thinking of that way, to protect him against people who wouldn't understand him, or who would say ugly things merely because he was different.

Homer didn't know why he, along with Scarlett and Vashti, unexpectedly found tuna mixed in with their dinner that night. He didn't know why I cuddled him closer on the couch before going to bed. He merely purred with contentment, nuzzling his head into the crook of my neck as he drifted off to sleep.

Technically, this hadn't been the final word. There were still a few more editors we hadn't heard back from. It was possible that one of them might decide to give *Homer's Odyssey* a shot.

But I knew I was finished with the whole business. It was one thing to take a blind leap of faith. It was quite another to bang your head—your own and the heads of the ones you loved—repeatedly against the same brick wall, with nothing to show for it but lumps. As soon as I returned from my honeymoon, I vowed, I would send out résumés and look for a proper job.

I got married two weeks later, and drifted through my wedding day as serene as if everything had already been settled. As far as I was concerned, it had.

LAURENCE AND I WERE married on September 13, 2008, and left for our honeymoon the next evening. And while we spent the following week lolling on Bahamian beaches, enjoying those first few days of married life, the world fell apart.

We returned to find that what would eventually be called the Great Recession had kicked off in our absence. The job I'd been sure I would land, once I devoted my time to looking, now seemed a dubious proposition at best. Nobody was hiring.

So, when I got an email from my agent a week after our return, I saw things in a much different light than I had right before the wedding. An editor named Caitlin Alexander at Delacorte, a Random House imprint, wanted to acquire *Homer's Odyssey*. After a few days of back-and-forth with my agent over numbers, they made us an offer— not the million-plus dollars the book about Dewey had sold for, but enough to cover my rent and, if I was thrifty, basic living expenses for a year. Even better than the money was Caitlin herself—kind and cat-loving but also sharp, with ideas for improving my outline that were so insightful, I was excited at the prospect of working with her.

It was Homer who gave Caitlin the final seal of approval, the night she came to our apartment for dinner. "So this is *Homer*," she said, when Homer made his usual appearance at the front door to greet the new person. There was a kind of reverence in the way she said his name, a tone that previously Homer had only been used to hearing in *my* voice, and he responded to it immediately. Caitlin crouched down and placed one of her hands beneath his nose for him to sniff. But Homer was far more interested in the cat treats she'd brought and now held in the other. One paw reached up delicately to swipe them onto the floor, where he greedily gobbled them up. Once all the treats had been dispatched, Homer placed both front paws on Caitlin's knee, so he could raise himself up and sniff her more thoroughly—obviously hoping for more treats. Caitlin was enraptured, answering Laurence and me in an absent-minded way when we spoke, wholly preoccupied with watching Homer.

"Would you like a glass of wine, Caitlin?" I asked.

"Hmmm...?" Caitlin was scratching Homer beneath his chin, fascinated with watching the muscles around the place where his eyes would have been relax in pleasure. "Sure, that sounds good."

"Red or white?"

Homer had now flopped onto the floor and rolled halfway onto his back, delighted with the attention as Caitlin continued to stroke his chin and neck. "Oh... whichever. Hey, look how well he gets around!" she exclaimed, as Homer—deciding he'd received enough pettings for now, and realizing that no further treats were immediately forthcoming—walked off to find something more entertaining to do. "Look how he knows exactly where his toys are! And he doesn't bump into anything!"

Scarlett and Vashti observed all this from the sidelines with a kind of harrumph-y disdain. *What's so interesting?* they seemed to be asking themselves. *It's just* Homer, *for crying out loud. We manage not to bump into things all the time.*

Although we didn't know it at the time, this would become a sort of template for the way many encounters would play out in our home over the next year.

The paperwork for *Homer's Odyssey* was finalized in late October of 2008, and the book was scheduled for publication in late August of 2009. It seemed a long way off. But to make that publication date, I would have to write the entire book by the end of January. I buckled down, and by working fifteen-hour days I managed to have my complete first draft written and submitted by Monday, February 2.

Homer would have his first professional photo shoot later that same day.

By then, the book about Dewey the Library Cat had finally "pubbed," and it had been a big hit. Suddenly, the conventional wisdom on whether or not there was a market for cat memoirs had shifted. Between that and the success of *Marley and Me,* pet memoirs were the hot new thing. And what had begun as the small passion project of one cat-loving editor had now become worthy of the full weight of Delacorte's serious attention.

I had taken numerous photos of Homer when I'd first started working on the book proposal, in order to submit them along with the writing. They had been deemed "just darling" by Caitlin, although of course none of them were of the professional caliber required to grace the cover of a book Delacorte hoped might be one of its bigger Fall '09 titles. A professional photographer was therefore dispatched to our apartment with all due haste—and an entirely new phase in our lives began.

People who came to see us had always been interested in Homer. He was (the opinion of certain editors notwithstanding) an interesting little guy. But now began an influx of visitors who were *only* interested in Homer. My day would come eventually, further down the road, when it was time to do in-studio radio spots or phone interviews for newspapers and magazines. I was fated to become one of the luckiest "cat ladies" ever—because people *wanted* to hear me talk about my cat! At length! Sometimes for as long as an hour at a stretch!

The focus for now, however, was on turning Homer into a star. You've probably heard that stars aren't born, they're made. Well, I'm here to tell you that it's true. Behind every star is an entire team of people invisible to the public. Not just the photographers, the editors, the lighting assistants, the stylists (or, in the case of a cat, professional groomers—although they learned quickly that *our* star strongly preferred *not* to have anyone but mom trim his claws or touch his paws, thank you very much). There are also managers, publicists, "stage moms," personal assistants, gatekeepers, and lackeys whose job it is to keep the star happy and engaged, to get him out of his trailer in time for the shoot and in a suitable emotional state to work, to run and fetch whatever the star may want to eat or amuse himself with.

When it came to making Homer a star, all of those latter roles were filled by me—with an occasional assist from Laurence, who these days was working from home. (The L.A.-based entertainment magazine where he was an editor hadn't laid off staff yet, but they had sent their Manhattan-based employees to work at home, so they could liquidate their New York office—which we took to be an ominous sign.) Laurence, however, would usually clear out for the day whenever our apartment was taken over for video or photo shoots.

"Managing" Homer soon became my full-time job. It was my responsibility to set his appointments; thoroughly brush and groom him ahead of time, so that his coat would shine with a high gloss and without any pesky stray bits of fur that might dangle from his haunches and ruin a shot; to make sure he got plenty of rest before a shoot began; to keep us stocked up on the tuna, turkey, and toys required to keep him engaged, happy, and playful; to wrangle him from spot to spot as the daylight or whims of whoever was shooting him changed.

I had to pop open cans of tuna when they wanted Homer to raise his head and perk up his ears; to dip toys and crumpled pieces of paper and bits of sisal rope in the tuna oil when Homer's interest in them flagged and he'd start to trot over to me. *Why aren't you playing with any of this cool stuff, mom?* I had to gauge when it was finally time for Homer to retire to the sanctity of his cat tree for a quick, replenishing cat nap. I'd gently suggest to whoever was in charge that Homer really *could* use a bit of time to himself—at which point he or she would cry, "That's lunch, everybody!" and the cameramen, the sound crew (if it was a video shoot), the lighting techs, the groomer and stylist, the field producer, and the field producer's assistant would ask me to recommend a nearby restaurant. And would I mind terribly calling ahead for a reservation, since they'd need a large table?

It was my job to do all these things and more and then...to get out of the shot.

I used to joke that my name might as well officially be changed to Gwen "Thank You Now Please Get Out Of The Shot" Cooper. "We'd like to shoot Homer in front of the bookcase—he looks adorable with all those books behind him! Thank you so much [after I'd lured Homer to the desired spot with a cheerful, *Come on, Homer-Bear!*]... but could you move juuuuuuust a little to the left? A little more? We can still see part of your arm."

Or, "I'd like to get Homer in front of the window. He'll be majestic with the Manhattan skyline behind him. Could you get him to...yes...perfect, that's it! But your hair is so curly and it's interfering with Homer's light—could you maybe pull it back?"

Far be it for me to interfere with Homer's light!

If Homer had been a different kind of a cat—a cat like Scarlett, for example—all the "managing" in the world couldn't have made these shoots possible. But Homer had always liked attention, and the people who gave it to him. He was intriguing not just because of his blindness, but because he had real charisma.

That might sound like an odd word to apply to a cat. Charisma, though, is little more than the ability of some people (or cats) to make you feel—even if only for the span of a few minutes—as if *you* are the most fascinating thing going, the very person they'd been hoping to get to spend time with.

Homer had that ability in spades.

Every strange person who came to our home and crawled on their belly holding a camera before them—so as to shoot Homer at his own level—was one more friend for him to make, one more cheerful greeting for him to bestow, receiving a playful scratch behind his ears in return. Scarlett and Vashti ran for the hills whenever our apartment was thus inundated, but Homer could never get over how much cool *stuff* these people brought with them! Cartons and crates, lighting reflectors, boom mics, duffel bags for Homer to crawl in, around, and over. His nose and whiskers would twitch non-stop as he tried to process all the exotic new smells of equipment bags that had been on airplanes, in studios and out on location shoots, perhaps even (in the case of the crew from Animal Planet) in the homes of other cats.

Homer resting in his "trailer" between takes

The camera crews came to our home as a team of seen-it-all professionals, out on just another job—and an annoying one at that, because what could be more irritating (or less interesting) than working with a *cat*?—but they left as an adoring cult. Like my former boyfriends of old, who'd proudly proclaimed, *Homer's my buddy!*, each photographer and videographer was convinced that he or she had formed a unique and special bond with Homer over the course of the shoot, that some magical *thing* had happened between the two of them during those few hours they had together.

Homer could make you feel that way. He seemed to know precisely when they wanted him to sit still as a statue and look majestic, to chase around toys in goofy, kittenish fashion, to run or jump or flip around on his back with un-self-conscious abandon, to turn his head shyly a little to the side, as if to say, *I'm strong, but also vulnerable.* Maybe he even *did* know. Homer was a sensitive cat, one who'd always paid close attention to the people around him. He had ways of knowing things that even I couldn't account for.

Do you see this?, they'd demand. *Do you see how he's responding to me?* Click-click, the camera would go. *He's a great cat, Gwen, a really exceptional cat.* And then they'd remind me, for the umpteenth time to, please, get out of the shot.

I knew that I hovered. Part of it was my old over-protectiveness, which reared up again and was hard to suppress as I watched strangers cluster around Homer, amidst walls of gear five times his size. As for Homer himself, he was almost never nervous with all the activity going on around him. All he needed to find these unprecedented new experiences completely enjoyable was the knowledge that I was somewhere nearby. But with so much going on— with so many people and so much equipment crammed within the relatively small space of our living room—it was difficult for him to catch my scent if I wasn't standing close. Speaking to him in a reassuring voice wasn't a great option, as it tended to cause him to leave off whatever he'd been doing and head in my direction.

As soon as Homer wasn't sure I was there anymore— when the horrifying thought that I might have left him *alone* with all these strangers appeared to cross his mind—then he was capable of being as uncooperative as any irate star. The fur on his back would start to rise, he'd twist his head wildly in un-shoot-able postures, nose in the air as he tried to figure out my location. I'd rush over to pet him and smooth down his fur. *I'm not going anywhere, Homer- Bear. I'm right here with you.* Thus calmed and restored to cheerful good humor, Homer would once again return to the work at hand as if he'd been born to do it.

And I, of course, would hasten to get out of the shot.

ALL TOLD, THERE WERE only perhaps seven or eight of these shoots, stretched out over nearly as many months. But they loomed so large with their strangeness and excitement that they cast long shadows. As the count-down to *Homer's Odyssey*'s publication date began, and as the anxiety and anticipation continued to build, it was hard to feel that our lives were quite what they had been only a few months ago—although it was equally hard to say just what, exactly, they were becoming.

Some of these shoots were arranged by my publisher for their own purposes—two sessions in our home in order to get the ideal cover shot of Homer (as well as extras to be used inside the book itself), and one at an off-site photographer's studio for additional publicity shots of Homer and me together. I talked about that one in the Afterword for *Homer's Odyssey*—the near impossibility of wrangling Homer in an unfamiliar space, trying to get him to stay still long enough to have his picture taken. All Homer himself wanted to do was explore this new place and introduce himself to all the new people within it. It was so *very* hard to get him to sit still that, as I noted in the Afterword, eventually the photographer and lighting techs unhooked all the equipment from its various stands and carried it by hand, so they could follow Homer wherever he went. As long as I live, I'll never forget the sight of a team of professionals—and one hovering stage mom— following along behind a blind cat in parade-like fashion, crying, *Wait! I think he's going* this *way now!*

People magazine wanted photos of Homer for insets to accompany the full-page review of the book they planned to run. *Ladies Home Journal* was going to excerpt a portion of *Homer's Odyssey*—from the chapter describing the night Homer had chased off the burglar—in their September issue. For this shoot, along with the usual crew they also sent over to our apartment a hair-and-make-up person and wardrobe stylist for me. They wanted shots of Homer and me together to accompany the piece—shots of Homer lying on my chest, shots of Homer in my arms, shots of Homer nuzzling my ear. In the end, though, they ran a photo of just Homer by himself.

"The problem," as I would later observe to a friend, when the issue came out and I saw that I wasn't in it, "is that I didn't get out of the shot."

Animal Planet did a segment on Homer for their *Cats 101* show. The segment was only a few minutes long, but it took a grueling eight hours to get all the footage they needed. Even Homer was spent by the end of the day, when our apartment was in shambles and all he wanted was to use his litter-box without having a cameraman closely following his movements. At one point, he turned with an indignant hiss on the cameraman, who followed behind him with dogged persistence. *Do you mind? I'm trying to pee in privacy!* I will say, though, that nobody we worked with knew how to record cats more unobtrusively than the Animal Planet crew. They were even able to capture the notoriously camera-shy Vashti and Scarlett, and there was no way any of us would have made it through a day that long without their expertise.

The coverage for *USA Today* happened in three waves. The books editor—the person who decided which books *USA Today* would cover; which of their various staff and freelance reviewers would be assigned to cover them; and who also wrote the revered-within-the-industry "Book Buzz" column, which a month earlier had decreed that, "*Homer's Odyssey* will be huge," causing bookstore pre-orders to quintuple overnight—was also a cat lover. ("So much for cat lovers not reading books," I told my agent.). She wanted to do more with *Homer's Odyssey* than simply have it reviewed, and she came over to our apartment to interview me personally—although I didn't kid myself that so high-ranking a personage would have gone to all the trouble of coming to me if she hadn't wanted to meet Homer as well.

Homer seemed almost relieved when someone came to our home wanting only to sit and chat, rather than putting him through his paces. He curled up in my lap for most of the interview, drowsy and comfortable as the editor reached out from time to time to stroke his head. "He really is a loving little guy, isn't he," she observed, and Homer rewarded this by pushing his entire face into her hand, his way of demanding that she rub him harder. For once, even Scarlett and Vashti ventured out, eager to feast upon the cat treats I'd scattered around liberally as a way of ensuring that Homer would stay in the living room throughout the interview and not head off to his "trailer"—i.e. the little cave in his cat tree.

Homer, however, was more interested in the editor than in the treats, having had so many in recent weeks that he was becoming ever-so-slightly bored with them. (Ah, the ennui of stardom!)

A day later, a photographer from *USA Today* came to shoot Homer for the story—one lone photo-journalist and his camera, without all the rigging and light reflectors and duffle bags we'd become accustomed to. I was so used to being asked to…you know…get out of the shot that I was wearing work clothes, the hair I'd washed but hadn't bothered styling that morning (because who cared what *I* looked like?) pulled back in an untidy ponytail. But the books editor had instructed the photographer to shoot Homer and me together—which is why, to my everlasting shame, Homer and I were immortalized in the pages of the nation's biggest newspaper with me looking like I'd just finished moving furniture.

Homer, it goes without saying, looked sleek and shiny and impossibly perfect.

The day after *that*, a *USA Today* videographer arrived to film me reading an excerpt of *Homer's Odyssey* while Homer scampered in the background, planning to post the video to the *USA Today* website and YouTube channel once the book had been released. I'd invested in a brand-new catnip toy for the occasion, in order to ensure maximum frolicking. Homer systematically demolished that toy over the course of the hour it took us to shoot, tearing it to shreds and releasing all the catnip into a giant mound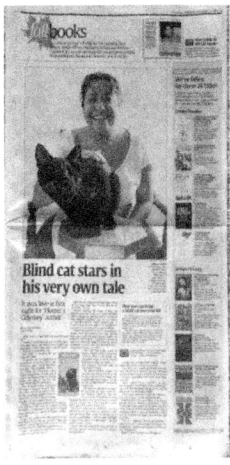
in front of him, which he then rolled and flipped around in while his entire face became encrusted with 'nip—until he looked like Al Pacino at the end of *Scarface*. The catnip made Homer talkative, and so that footage is one of the very few recordings in existence that captured the sound of Homer's own voice—and, for that reason, I treasure it to this day.

Perhaps the craziest day was when we recorded the book trailer—the promotional video commissioned by my publisher for placement on YouTube and various other websites. They'd taken over a two-bedroom suite at the Hotel Pennsylvania for the shoot, across the street from Madison Square Garden, where many a visiting rocker had stayed and partied back in the hotel's glory days.

They sent a town car to pick Homer and me up. Homer had been reluctant to get into his carrier, and it was raining as I dashed as quickly as I could from apartment building to car—although Homer did catch a few drops, which didn't improve his mood. The driver helped me load in all the gear I'd thought necessary to bring along if we were going to be shooting out of the house for an entire day—a litter-box and litter, bowls for food and water and food to go in them, a sack of catnip, a bag of Pounce treats, and a large bag of rolling-and-belled toys. I was scheduled for an early-morning arrival—before seven—and I'd requested that as few people as necessary be there when we first arrived, so that Homer would have time to acclimate to a new place before it was time for the hair-and-makeup person to go to work on me, and the groomer to go to work on him.

There was a single cameraman there to greet us when we knocked on the door of the suite. He'd beaten us to the hotel by only an hour, having just arrived on a red-eye from L.A. for the purpose of recording Homer's first hour of exploration. I set up food and water bowls for Homer in the kitchen, and placed the litter-box there as well, setting Homer in the litter-box first—as was our custom when I brought him to a new place—so that he wouldn't have to wonder where it was.

"I've never seen such big aural canals in a cat," the cameraman noted. "You can see all the way down into his ears. They're huge!"

"Homer's hearing is off the charts," I agreed, as Homer's head perked up at the sound of my saying his name, and he turned the ears we'd just been discussing in my direction.

"Are you sure he's never been here before?" The cameraman was watching as Homer—nose to the ground— began to figure out the suite and its various rooms. He didn't bump into a single thing, not a wall, not a sofa, not the cabinets in the kitchen or a lamp in the suite's living room. Homer's sensitive nose and remarkable whiskers gave him all the information he needed to navigate seamlessly— just as he'd done time after time in the many homes we'd moved in and out of, back in our earlier years of struggle and constant migration. After about a half-hour of thorough investigation, Homer happily took up play with a catnip ball, fascinated with the way it ricocheted off the bottom of the kitchen cabinets and into the living room. He chased it in and out of bedrooms, under tables, around the sofa and floor lamps, without losing track of it for even a moment.

"I can't believe he's *blind*," the cameraman marveled. "Don't take this the wrong way, but if it weren't for the fact that his eyes are gone, I'd say you were lying."

I laughed. "My husband says the same thing," I told him. "To this day, he swears that Homer's faking blindness."

It was a long day, and the suite began to fill up as the morning wore on. The next to arrive were Homer's and my respective groomers, followed by another cameraman, a lighting tech with trees and enormous reflective panels ("It's hard to get the lighting just right on a black cat," he explained—which I already knew), a sound person with boom mics, a producer, Caitlin, and my publisher's Vice President of Marketing, who had arrived to supervise the shoot personally.

But, with all the primping and preparation, with all the setting up of equipment and moving of furniture, with all the phone calls and consultations and last-minute disagreements about the shot list (which detailed the specific things they wanted to capture Homer doing), it was hours before the shoot proper—wherein I would answer questions about Homer and the book, while Homer did various adorable and active things in the background— even started.

By then, as was his preferred habit on rainy days when thunder rolled with a pleasant far-away rumble beneath the sounds of drops splashing against the windows, Homer wasn't interested in doing anything but napping. He wasn't upset. He was friendly as ever when new people came over to greet him and introduce themselves. He was simply *bored*. All the hoopla over the last few months, all the duffel bags and equipment and strangers and cat treats, all the new toys and the cameras following him to catch his every movement as he sat or ran or stretched or jumped or rolled over, had become old hat. All Homer wanted to do now was sit quietly on the couch behind my head, the way we did on rainy days when we were home alone and I read a book while Homer snoozed peacefully beside me.

Everybody's eyes were on me. But, as every cat person knows, there's only so much you can do with an uncooperative cat. I tried opening a baggie of catnip and wafting it under his nose. Nothing. I tried jangling a belled toy next to his ear. No response.

I got up and walked across the room. "Homer," I cooed. "Homer, come over to mommy."

Homer flicked one ear lazily in the direction of my voice, but didn't stir. *Nah*, he seemed to say. *Don't wanna*.

"Homer-Bear," I sing-songed. I tried rattling a bag of Pounces. "Do you want a treat, Homer? Do you want to come and get a kitty treat, baby boy?"

Homer yawned mightily and extended his front and hind legs in a long, languorous stretch. He flipped onto his back momentarily, then curled back into a ball and continued to nap.

And so, here we were. A room full of people, a crew of professionals who'd flown through the night all the way from the West Coast, my publisher's Vice President of Marketing (upon whom, I couldn't help but feel, I was making a very bad impression), all the treats and toys any cat would want—all of it here for Homer, and *only* for Homer, and Homer himself couldn't be bothered. He'd already been there. He'd already done that.

"Let me make a call," I told the room, and went to dig my cell out of my purse so I could phone Laurence at home.

"I need you," I told him as soon as he answered. "We need half a pound of that sliced deli turkey Homer likes, and a whole bunch of those little cans of tuna. Do you think you could go to the grocery store and then bring it all here?"

"Yeah, sure." Laurence sounded surprised, but willing to help. "What do you want, Chicken of the Sea?" "No, no." I was beginning to sound frantic. "Not Chicken of the Sea! He likes Bumble Bee, Laurence. *Homer likes Bumble Bee!*"

There was a pause, and then we both began to laugh. We laughed until we were practically crying. Tears ran down my face and my stomach began to ache, making it hard to breathe as I tried to suppress the laughter, aware that all the people in the other room could probably hear me.

Our lives *had* gotten a little crazy. But Homer wasn't some diva, and we weren't his flunkies. Homer was still just *Homer*—the good-natured, high-spirited little boy we fondled and fussed over at home, in private, as soon as the cameras were packed up and gone.

I'd been making myself crazy in part because— yes—I desperately wanted my book to be a success. What author doesn't want that? I knew how incredibly rare it was for a publisher to put this kind of effort and attention into a book, that this particular moment in my life was fleeting and one I needed to enjoy as it was happening, because Homer and I wouldn't be the flavor of the month forever.

But it was more than that. I was also *proud* of Homer—not just of the ease and dignity with which he'd been acquitting himself as all these unusual and unprecedented things were happening to us. I was proud of who he was. I felt entirely vindicated in all the years of faith I'd had in him. And I wanted others to see that. I wanted the whole world to see—naysayers I'd never even met and probably never would, who nevertheless I knew would think, *Why would anybody want a blind cat?* I wanted everybody to view for themselves what a blind cat—*my* blind cat—could do. The veterinarian from whom I'd adopted Homer was writing the Foreword to *Homer's Odyssey*, and I had an idea that some of the people who'd had the chance to adopt him but turned him down, all those years ago, might read this book. They might put two and two together, they might realize what they had discarded as if it were nothing. Their loss had been my infinite gain, but still I wanted them to view Homer with amazement, to read his story with envy and think, *That could have been me.*

And, although I generally didn't consider myself a vindictive person, I wanted to make that one publisher who'd called Homer "creepy" eat her words. I wanted to make her rue the day she'd turned from him in disgust. *I'll show you "creepy,"* I'd say to myself, in steely tones.

Before any of that would happen, however, there was still our immediate problem to contend with—a cat already bored with a fame he technically hadn't attained yet, and the necessity of recapturing his interest just long enough to make it through this last shoot.

"I'll be there as soon as I can with turkey and tuna," Laurence promised, when we had finished laughing.

"*Thank you*," I told him. "Oh—and make sure it's the fancy albacore. That's his favorite."

Laurence ran out to the grocery store in the rain, waited forever to find a cab—which was always tougher on soggy days like this—and sat in the heavy crosstown traffic for nearly half an hour as he crossed from Second Avenue to where we were waiting at the Hotel Pennsylvania on Seventh. Once he arrived, we had to open a slew of those little cans of tuna before the sound of cans opening and the aroma of fish filling the room intrigued Homer enough to rouse him from his slumber. Laurence went into the suite's kitchen and rattled the paper Homer's favorite turkey was wrapped in, actually going through the motions of making a sandwich until Homer rose languidly from the sofa and trotted into the kitchen to paw at Laurence's leg. *Hey—is that turkey?*

The shoot ran longer than scheduled, but in the end we got the footage of Homer we needed. I took a look at the demolished suite as I was packing up Homer and his gear to head back home. Furniture had been pushed around haphazardly. Lampshades were skewed at odd angles, positioned this way and that to better cast the light onto Homer's black fur. Cameras and lighting reflectors were lying on the floor or leaned against end tables. Nearly two-dozen small, half-opened cans of tuna were scattered on every imaginable surface, along with uneaten bits of turkey strewn across the floor, laid there to tempt Homer into various spots.

I shook my head in amazement as I took it all in, thinking, *Well, I guess we've finally arrived.* Homer had trashed his first hotel room. He was officially a star.

2 • The World's Cat

The Muse brought to the minstrel's mind a song of heroes whose great fame rang under heaven.
— HOMER, *The Odyssey*

HOMER'S ODYSSEY WAS PUBLISHED on August 25, 2009.

I had traveled to Washington, D.C. the night before to do an interview on NPR's "Diane Rehm Show" on the morning of launch, and didn't get back home again until the early evening. Homer spent the night of the book's release feasting on the lobster salad Laurence had prepared for me as a congratulatory surprise, but that I was too wound-up to eat. Scarlett and Vashti didn't care as much for lobster, but Laurence had bought them a tin of fancy canned tuna from our local gourmet shop—which Homer consumed his fair share of as well. I spent the rest of the night refreshing the book's Amazon page every hour, so I could watch as its sales rank rose. (This is something every writer does on the day her book is published, and any writer who tells you she doesn't is totally lying.) Eventually, I moved my laptop computer over to the couch, so I wouldn't have to keep jumping up to see if the numbers had changed. Homer, full of lobster and tuna, snoozed happily beside me.

With all the pre-publication craziness, I'd thought that life would calm down once the book was out. But, soon after it appeared in bookstores, there came a second, smaller wave of press rolling through our apartment in order to meet Homer—the bloggers, vloggers (those with video blogs), and internet radio hosts who hadn't required the longer lead times of magazines and newspapers, and who were thus able to wait until the book was on shelves before planning their coverage.

This second wave of press was much mellower than the first had been, requiring far less of Homer and me. Usually it would just be one person with a hand-held recording device, or perhaps one additional person to hold a video camera. Homer was able to interact with these people with nothing more than his usual level of friendly interest—although I do remember one blogger in particular for whom Homer went absolutely wild.

I had never been nearly as aware of different people's differing smells as Homer was, but this specific blogger had an especially...pungent...aroma that even I could catch from across the room. She smelled strongly of patchouli mixed with insufficiently masked body odor— which is really only worth mentioning because Homer was fascinated by this woman as he'd never been with anyone before, and as I would never see him be with anyone again. It was impossible to keep him off her, to prevent him from crawling up and around her as he tried to take in her scent from all conceivable angles, burying his head in her hair and inserting his nose deeply into more private areas.

"He's certainly a friendly little guy, isn't he?" the blogger observed, trying to angle Homer's nose unobtrusively away from her crotch.

"That he is." I was mortified. "Homer! *Homer! Come...here!*" I spoke in the guttural-voice-through-clenched-teeth tone my own mother had used to rein me in when I was small, whenever my childish high spirits had seemed in danger of causing public embarrassment.

Homer, however, was not to be deterred. "I'm *so* sorry," I apologized. "I don't know what's come over him." Homer's head was still immersed in our guest's nether regions, and finally I went over and lifted him from her, one hand under his breastbone for support while the other took the scruff of his neck in a manner meant to indicate, *I am NOT kidding around!*

But Homer wriggled out of my arms and boomeranged right back to his intrusive examination of every square inch of the blogger's body. "I can put him in the other room, if you'd like," I offered.

"No, don't worry about it!" I may have been appalled at Homer's bad behavior, but the blogger herself seemed unruffled. "But maybe we should open a window?" she added. "Your face looks a little red."

Of all the people who came and went through our home, convinced that during their time with us they'd formed a special bond with Homer unlike anybody else's, this was the one occasion when that was likeliest to be true. There were perhaps a half-dozen or so of these visitors over the course of a couple of days, and then Laurence and I hit the road. Publishers weren't as apt to finance book tours as they'd been once upon a time, but I scheduled a few readings on my own. I did one in New York, of course, where we lived. I did one in L.A. where, after nearly two decades as a film journalist, Laurence had many friends. And I scheduled one in Miami where my parents and some of my old friends still lived. Laurence had given me a necklace to celebrate the book's publication, featuring a tiny cat-shaped pendant made from small black diamonds, and I wore it for luck whenever I made a book- related appearance.

In Miami, I did an in-studio interview at the local NPR station the morning before my reading, and an article about the book and my upcoming appearance was published in the *Miami Herald* the same day. Still, I wasn't expecting much of a turnout beyond my family, my friends, and my parents' friends. Part of the reason why publishers were reluctant to underwrite book tours was because it had become increasingly difficult to get people to turn out for them, even when a book was popular and an author event had been well publicized.

So it was overwhelming to arrive at Books & Books in Coral Gables and find that nearly three hundred people had come. *Three hundred people!* The lead book reviewer for the *Sun-Sentinel*, whose work I'd been reading since I was a teenager, was the one who stepped up to the podium to introduce me, and it was one of the great nights of my life.

I don't think it really hit me until that moment that a *lot* of people were going to read Homer's story. It was one thing to see sales figures projected on a spread sheet, but an entirely different experience to see three hundred individual faces turned my way as I read from the book. There was even a cat in attendance—a tiny blind kitten named Galileo, only a few weeks old, with the two people who'd found him abandoned a few days earlier. They'd brought Galileo to the reading in the hopes that somebody there might be able to help them figure out what to do for him—and, sure enough, representatives from several local rescue groups were on-hand and able to take charge of the situation. (Galileo eventually found a forever home with a reader in Ft. Lauderdale.)

I also realized something else that night that I'd never thought about before—the deep chord that *Homer's Odyssey* would strike in the animal-rescue community. Homer represented any number of cats who rescuers would cry themselves to sleep at night thinking about— cats who were sweet and friendly and loving, cats these rescuers worked with every day, and who they knew would make a wonderful companion to anyone lucky enough to adopt them. But cats (and dogs) who, nevertheless, were consistently passed over for adoption because they were blind, or deaf, or needed extra care for ongoing medical issues, or simply because they had aged out of kitten-hood and were now "too old."

I wasn't the only one who stood vindicated by the publication of Homer's story. And, despite having cared for him for more than twelve years, I wasn't even close to being the one who'd put in the most time and effort— who'd fought the most battles or broken her heart the most often—trying to prove that a special-needs animal was just as capable of loving and being loved as any other, and just as deserving of a chance.

Eight days after *Homer's Odyssey* was published, I received two phone calls—one from Caitlin, and one from the in-house publicist my publisher had assigned to promote *Homer's Odyssey*—both with the same exciting news. After only one week on sale, *Homer's Odyssey* would debut at #14 on the following week's *New York Times* Bestseller List.

Laurence and I celebrated with champagne that night, while Homer, Vashti, and Scarlett were treated to new catnip toys and Homer's beloved deli turkey. When the *New York Times* Book Review in which Homer would be named was finally published, I saw that *Homer's Odyssey* had been called out for special attention in the "Inside the List" feature that ran alongside it. "*Homer's Odyssey* makes its first appearance on the list in 2,720 years," the writer humorously observed, before adding, "Oh, wait! Gwen Cooper's book is actually the story of a tiny blind wonder cat..."

THE NEXT FEW MONTHS were a whirlwind. Although I hadn't been sent on an official book tour, I was invited to speak at shelters and at shelter fundraisers around the country, to advocate for the cause of special-needs animals and of rescue in general.

I hated leaving my three cats as often as I did, traveling more now than I had at any previous time in my life. But, then, I was now firmly self-employed, so when I was home I got to be *home*. My cats and I had never had so many uninterrupted hours in the day together as we did during the times when I wasn't on the road. Homer would greet me with pure delight when I returned from a trip—happy I was back, of course, and also eager to make a thorough investigation of my suitcase and my person.

Every engagement I traveled to included a tour through the shelter where I'd be speaking, along with plenty of cuddling opportunities with the cats that shelter cared for. No matter how thoroughly I showered before getting on a plane, the shoes I wore home and the bag containing clothing I'd worn while away reeked, from Homer's perspective, of other cats. It could take hours for Homer to get through as exhaustive an inspection as he liked, until finally it was time to dump my suitcase contents into the laundry and get them ready for the next trip.

Best of all were the gifts I brought back for the cats. Everywhere I went, people sent me home with gifts for Homer, and I was touched by how many remembered to include Scarlett and Vashti as well—hand-crocheted balls stuffed with catnip, little satin-enclosed catnip pillows with each of the cats' names embroidered on them, hand-knitted and hand-sewn kitty blankets, colorful new bowls for food and water, bags of treats, and noisy playthings, like crinkle balls, by the sack.

Of course it was really Homer, and Homer's story, that everybody was interested in. People wanted to hear live accounts of the tales they'd read in the book, to know how Homer was adjusting to his newfound fame. But Homer couldn't travel or deliver speeches himself, so I went as his proxy. I also did interviews with, and wrote articles for, animal-centric magazines and websites, encouraging the adoption of special-needs animals like Homer. As few "famous cats" as there were at the time, there had never (to my knowledge) been a famous special-needs cat, and so Homer became something of a "poster kitty" for the cause of adopting animals once thought unadoptable. I would eventually hear from people who wrote to say that Homer had inspired them to take a chance on a blind—or otherwise disabled—cat. I can honestly say that I've received no fewer than two hundred of these emails over the past few years, and they're always the greatest letters I get.

I traveled to parts of the country I'd never seen in person before—the Deep South, Texas, the Heartland, the Pacific Northwest, the Rust Belt. I traveled from Minnesota to New Mexico, to Arizona during a heat wave so intense that I could literally feel my *eyeballs* grow warm when I stepped outside.

The landscapes would change dramatically each time a plane I was on would land, as would the regional accents, the style of dress, and the local cuisine.

Yet certain things remained constant. I met people of all ages, sizes, religions, and ethnic backgrounds—people who likely would have disagreed vehemently with their counterparts in other regions on everything from politics to place settings (because one would surely consume Alabama hominy grits very differently than Seattle sushi). But the one thing everyone I met agreed about—passionately— was the cause of animal rescue. I can't tell you how many people I've heard, over the last six years, say how much better they think animals are than people. But, personally, I think it's that animals bring out the very best in people— until you can't help but realize how ultimately insignificant the rest of the differences are.

At the Nine Lives Foundation in CA

Despite my hectic travel schedule of those few months—and despite the fact that those crazy days of video and promotional shoots were essentially over—"managing" Homer was still my full-time job. I had to answer his fan mail, oversee his social media presence, regretfully inform those who wrote to say that they would be vacationing in New York—and could they possibly drop by our place to meet Homer in person?—that, unfortunately, Homer wasn't available for personal appearances. "As if Homer were another New York tourist attraction, like the Statue of Liberty," I would say to Laurence.

And *somebody* had to write the thank-you notes for the many gifts Homer received in the mail—as various and plentiful as the gifts I brought home with me from trips. Scarlett and Vashti got their fair share of the bounty, and may, I think, have enjoyed it even more than Homer did. All the soft kitty blankets—that were just her size!—were a profound joy to Scarlett, who'd always loved anything plush and luxurious. To have something soft and warm to claim for her very own, small enough for her to guard from encroachment by the annoying other cats she was forced to live with, was a gift from above. And Vashti loved catnip even more than Homer did. People sent us catnip they'd grown themselves, on hobby farms or in backyard gardens, and the purity of this home-grown 'nip seemed to make Homer, and especially Vashti, super relaxed and flippy.

For his part, Homer was most enamored of the boxes these gifts came in. He enjoyed them all so much that I couldn't bear to take any away from him—until our living room looked as if we were moving. It was at this point that Laurence tactfully suggested that it might be time to throw at least a few of them away.

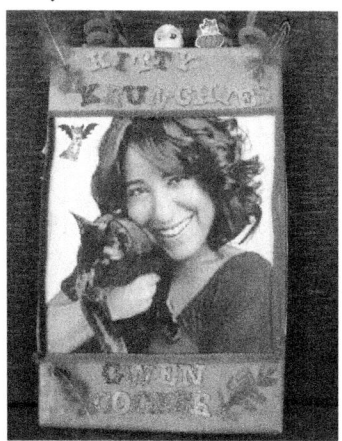

As it turned out, there were also quite a few younger readers of *Homer's Odyssey*—elementary and middle- school children who were already passionate about animals, and for whom the message that *different doesn't mean bad* carried more relevance even than it did for adults. One evening, long after the book had been published, a sixth- grade girl came to our apartment with her father, to meet and photograph Homer for an article about him she was writing for *Time For*

Kids (*Time* magazine's children's imprint). She took such a grave, shy pleasure in his presence—and Homer was so very gentle with her in his rubbing and head- bonks—that I had to smile at seeing them together.

But well before then I'd been hearing from children of about her age who were writing book reports about Homer and wanted me to answer questions they had about the book, or to know what kids like them could do for other special- needs animals. Sometimes they emailed so they could send me pictures of drawings they'd made of Homer, or of Homer-themed arts-and-crafts projects they'd created for school.

It wasn't just in the U.S. and Canada where Homer was gaining a following. Foreign rights to *Homer's Odyssey* had sold in nearly twenty countries before the book was even published, and some of those translations began to appear right around the time the U.S. edition did. I always got a kick out of the foreign editions, the different artwork of their covers, all the various iterations of Homer that differed so greatly from country to country that it was hard to believe they were all publishing the same book.

Artwork from the Korean edition

Some countries—like Brazil, France, Russia, and China—used the literal translation of "Homer's Odyssey" as the title for their editions. Others took more of a creative license. In Italy it was *Omero Gatto Nero*, in Germany *Homer und Ich*. In Finland, the book was called *Homer – Kissan Uskomaton Elama*, which meant, *Homer – A Cat's Incredible Life*.

The Dutch went with a straightforward *Wonderkat!*, and in Hungary it was simply *Homér*—the book's cover a stark block of solid red, with Homer's name in huge white letters, and in the middle of the cover a very small silhouetted profile of a black cat with a curled tail.

The Japanese title translated roughly into *I See Happy Love*. I'm still unsure as to what the Korean title meant, although I adored the artwork they included. At the end of the book were several pages of prints depicting vividly hued watercolor paintings, like something from a book of fairy tales. One of them showed a girl who I think was supposed to be me—although she looked like *Alice in Wonderland*—being borne aloft into a starry night by a tuxedoed, flower-bearing, eyeless black cat, trailing a little gray tabby and an even smaller white kitty in the air behind her. A smiling man (Laurence?) waved them all off from a bedroom window.

Homer soon began to receive cards and letters and gifts from the other countries where his story had been published. Somewhere along the line, I realized, he had become not merely *my* cat, but the world's cat.

And yet, he was still just our happy little boy. He had been with me for so long—and while I couldn't say that I took him for granted, he had become as essential, yet also as everyday, as the beating of my own heart.

I would look at Homer sometimes—as he chased a bedeviled Scarlett down the hall, or jumped onto my desk and did his best to keep me from typing, or rolled onto his back to groom the chocolate-and-black fur of his belly—and I would marvel. It was an impossible, an incomprehensible, thing to try to fathom, that so many people all across the globe knew him. Knew him and loved him.

Naturally, Homer had his own Facebook page. It was just a regular personal page at first, but when he reached his 5000-friend limit, I started a "fan" page for him—although I never thought of it that way. Only about a thousand of Homer's Facebook friends followed us to this new page—and even though it grew incrementally, adding perhaps two hundred new followers each month, it still felt like a small, intimate community.

It was Homer's page, and so I wrote there in Homer's voice—not his actual voice, obviously, but the way Homer had always sounded in my own head. I'll admit that I'd never been much for personal photographs, but now we were snapping photos of Homer, Scarlett, and Vashti constantly. I tried to mine our everyday lives for the kinds of things I thought people who'd read the book, and now wanted to keep up with Homer on a day-to-day basis, might find entertaining. *Oh boy! Turkey for dinner!*, I'd write, above a snapshot of Homer doing his best to steal a bit of food from Laurence's plate. Or, **My* little bag of catnip! MINE!* along with a photo of Homer crouched protectively over one of the small bags of home-grown 'nip a friend had sent from her Tennessee farm.

I had a hard time explaining to my mother, when she asked what my workdays now consisted of, that I spent a significant portion of my time pretending to be my cat online.

"But people *do* know that it's really you posting these things, right?" she asked.

"No, mom," I deadpanned. "People think that Homer is climbing onto the keyboard of my computer and typing these things himself."

It was a difficult thing to explain to a parent— although it felt perfectly natural and right to me. People would laugh at "Homer's" daily dispatches, and I was just as apt to laugh and sympathize with the comments and photos they posted themselves. Our regular readers would comment amusingly on my posts detailing Homer's doings, and they would also post pictures and updates about their own cats. I knew more cats on a first-name basis during this time than I ever had before. It might not be strictly accurate to say that I "knew" them—seeing as I'd never actually met them. But, then again, I knew them in the same way our readers knew Homer, through the stories their humans told, the concerns they shared, and the insights they offered when one or another of us would ask questions about preferred litter brands or appropriate diets for aging cats.

This all sounds about as "cat lady" as it gets—so I'll also add that, on occasion, our little community was able to do some real good. Every once in a while a shelter would write to me about an impossible-to-place blind cat and, inevitably, among Homer's community, we would find the perfect home for him. An acquaintance of mine living in Queens discovered two neglected cats in the basement of her apartment building. The building super had put them down there a year earlier, when they were only kittens, for the purpose of keeping the building rat-free. He'd barely thought about them since, and now my friend wanted to find a *real* home for them—one from which they could see the sunlight they'd never once experienced in their lives.

*Homer will never be able to see sunshine, but these two cats can...*my post about them began. Within only a few days, we had half a dozen firm offers of forever homes in the New York area alone. Geoffrey Jennings from Rainy Day Books in Kansas City—a passionate cat lover—offered a trove of autographed, first-edition, collectible books to go along with the cats to their new home. Five days later, all of us in Homer's community were rewarded with a picture of the two cats basking in the sunlight streaming through the bay window of a Brooklyn brownstone. The woman who adopted the cats named them Ellis, after Ellis Island, and Morgan, after the Morgan Library in Manhattan's East Thirties, because the cats had come to her with a library of their own.

We also chipped in small donations, in Homer's community, and were able to raise maybe a thousand dollars or so when natural disasters struck in various parts of the world—the kinds of tragedies that so often affected animals as well as humans, yet during which animals tended to be forgotten. My philosophy was that when you helped animals, you helped people, too—always remembering that the ASPCA, when they'd organized a rescue effort for pets in the wake of 9/11, had also helped people like me in the process. We collected food and other essentials and sent them to where they would do the most good.

Mostly, though, we simply enjoyed each other's company.

Not that everything was all positivity and sunshine. I soon learned that whereas novels are works of fiction, memoirs are true—and while (having written one of each) I'd always been aware of this technical distinction, what I hadn't thought about is that when readers don't like the "character" in your memoir, the person they actually dislike is you, yourself.

I heard from people who thought I was a heartless monster for having thought about my cats on 9/11, a day when so many human lives were lost; I heard from people who thought that I'd married a man who wasn't worthy of Homer; I heard from people who accused me of having adopted Homer twelve years earlier just so I'd someday be able to write a book about him. And I received one very long, very earnest email from an anonymous woman who was convinced that Homer had fallen ill in the months before my wedding because Laurence was slowly poisoning him with a household cleaning agent—in order to get rid of the competition, as it were, for my affections. Calling Laurence a "charismatic and sophisticated alpha male," she warned that he was likely to reveal his true, abusive nature at any moment, and advised me in the strongest possible terms to hire a private investigator to follow him—presumably so as to catch him in the act of being unfaithful.

"Follow me *where?*" Laurence seemed perplexed when I shared this email with him—albeit tickled at having been described as a *charismatic alpha male*. "You and I both work from home."

"I don't know," I replied. "But I'm going to start marking the levels on the Windex bottle—so don't get any ideas."

Poor Laurence! If only this letter-writer could have seen the grace with which—on the occasions when he joined me on one of my trips—Laurence accepted being referred to as "Mr. Cooper." (His last name is Lerman.)

But these were only a handful of negatives floating in an overwhelmingly positive sea. I had the daily joy of hearing every day from other animal lovers, from rescuers and people who were every bit as crazy about their own cats as I was about mine.

Homer's social-media community would continue to grow over the next couple of years. There was a big jump, after the paperback was published in 2010, when Homer's Facebook following expanded from two thousand to five thousand people within only a few months. But a lot of people seemed to "like" the page and then forget about it—so even when the numbers would appear to indicate otherwise, our core crew stayed more or less the same size. And, to tell the truth, at the time I liked it that way. Homer didn't have the kind of huge following that seemed likely to sell many books.

Then again, I'd never really seen Homer's Facebook page as a place to sell copies of *Homer's Odyssey*. It seemed probable that the only reason someone would follow the page was because they'd read the book already.

And, by then, Homer had gotten to be such a pro at posing for pictures, it seemed a shame to let his talents go to waste.

HOMER'S ONLINE COMMUNITY WAS always enjoyable, a place where I could post ongoing tales of Homer's amusing antics, a sounding board off of which I could bounce ideas for blog posts or new books as they came to me. But I'll always be truly grateful for the way our internet friends rallied around our family over the next two years, when first Vashti and then Scarlett fell to age-related illnesses.

Ultimately, this is Homer's story. I won't take you too far with me down the paths of confusion and sorrow that Laurence and I traveled during that time—paths well- trodden already by anyone who's loved an animal.

Suffice it to say that between the time when Vashti was diagnosed with chronic renal failure in late 2009, and the time when we lost her in August of 2010, there were many months during which she lived—a life that could only be sustained by a strenuous schedule of home treatment, which seemed overwhelming and impossible for me to undertake when her doctor first explained it. I was positive that I would fail Vashti in ways I couldn't imagine yet.

But, no matter how anxious or bewildered I felt, Homer's community was an unquenchable source of strength and insight.

By far the hardest part of Vashti's new care regimen was administering her every-other-day subcutaneous fluid injections, meant to help her body compensate for her failing kidneys. Vashti was a sweet girl who would tolerate just about anything we did to her, but it was easy to see how much she hated those injections—which weren't simply a shot, but a slow drip that had to be administered over the course of several long minutes. The subQ injections were the only thing Vashti really fought us on (and, bless her heart, she didn't fight hard—she merely struggled). Laurence had to hold her down while I inserted the tiny needle into the back of her neck, and sometimes she squirmed enough that the needle inadvertently hit a tender spot. Her tiny squeaks of pain whenever that happened left me ready to throw in the towel.

Many in Homer's community were old hands at the subQ routine. A few of them suggested a brilliant fix for us—heating the bag containing the solution in a pot of warm water until it came to Vashti's body temperature. This way, Vashti's experience would feel less like being immersed in a cold shower from inside her own body, and more like the pleasant relief of a warm bath.

Vashti and me, 2010

It was astonishing how immediate the difference was. After our first attempt with this new method, Vashti began to *like* her fluid injections. She would practically bounce with happiness by the time they were over, ready for a recently instituted ritual known as *Vashti's cuddle time.* "It's cuddle time!" Laurence or I would exclaim when the subQ was finished, and we'd climb into bed with Vashti eagerly following.

Alone in the bedroom with us—the door closed to keep the other cats out—she would enjoy one uninterrupted hour of exclusive time with both her humans, crawling first onto my chest and purring into my face for a few minutes as I stroked her back, before walking over to Laurence and doing the same with him. She'd spend the whole hour migrating back and forth between us while the warm fluids we'd just injected spread throughout her body, and when the sixty minutes were up she'd rejoin Scarlett and Homer, cheerful as ever.

It's hard watching an animal you love grow frailer— but Vashti was beautiful right up until the end. She did lose quite a bit of weight, but with her thick, lustrous coat of white fur it was nearly impossible to see, unless you knew her very well. And that fur never lost its silky luster. I have a picture of the two of us taken just days before the end, and in it Vashti literally glows, as if spot-lit from an unseen source.

The eternal feminine was what Laurence said of Vashti on her last day. It was something Lee Strasberg had said about Marilyn Monroe at her funeral, a way of describing the timeless, imperishable quality of her beauty—a beauty so overpowering, yet also so vulnerable, that it could reach right out and squeeze your heart until it ached.

Camille on her deathbed had nothing on our Vashti.

The paperback edition of *Homer's Odyssey* came out less than a month after we lost her. This time around, my publisher did spring for a small book tour—and, even though it wasn't near any of the four cities they'd originally planned to send me to, I insisted that the first stop be at Blind Cat Rescue & Sanctuary in North Carolina.

I'd seen pictures of many other blind cats since Homer's story was first published, but I still hadn't met many in the flesh. It was a moving experience to walk through Blind Cat Rescue, to enter room after room full of cats—cats who were young and old; white, gray, tabby, and calico; cats who were large and cats who were small; some who had long silky fur like Vashti's, and some who had practically no fur at all—but who all, nevertheless, looked like Homer. They raised questioning noses into the air just like Homer did, turned their heads from side to side like sonar dishes as they tried to "see" with their ears. And, even without eyes, their faces still managed to convey the joy they'd found in their life with each other, and with their human caregivers.

Vashti may only have been a supporting player in *Homer's Odyssey*. But in our lives—our *real* lives—she'd always had one of three starring roles. Reading from Homer's book now, choosing a passage that included Vashti and Scarlett as well as Homer, and having just seen so many other "unadoptable" cats like Homer who'd nevertheless found happiness in loving arms, was the first time I felt truly whole since Vashti had left us.

THERE WAS DECIDEDLY LESS *Homer* on Homer's Facebook page while all this was going on, but those core few who'd been with us from the beginning never complained or abandoned us. And they remained with us still in February of 2011, when Scarlett developed a sarcoma high on her left hind leg, the result of the rabies vaccination she'd gotten years earlier in Miami. (The specific formula that caused this sarcoma in some cats has been discontinued, by the way; you should always vaccinate your cats against rabies.)

In some ways, it was harder with Scarlett as her illness progressed than it had been with Vashti—not because it was so much worse or made her suffer more. But Scarlett had always been such a surly, feisty, irascible girl. She'd been born irritated with everybody and everything—even in her youth, she'd been the mean old lady who yells, *Get off my lawn, you kids!*

Our other cats bothered her. Laurence's mere existence—his insistence on living with us, despite her having made it perfectly clear that she'd prefer he left—was an ongoing annoyance. Guests in our home had obviously been sent by the devil himself, just so they could coo at her and make other friendly, insulting gestures until she was forced—in a state of high dudgeon—to *harrumph* her way into the seclusion of a bedroom. There were only two things in the world that Scarlett truly enjoyed— one of them was food, and the other was me. Anybody else, human or feline, was quickly reminded with a sharp *rowr!* and disciplinary smack of her paw to maintain their distance, leaving her to enjoy her wide berth of personal space in dignified peace.

Scarlett mellowed a great deal, however, during those last months—and I'll admit that it made me sad to see her become more accepting and tolerant as her health failed. I do think, though, that this change was partly because Homer was so considerate of her. He slept nearer to her than he'd ever dared before. But he no longer chased her, no longer tried to insert himself into her games of "chase the paper ball," no longer bothered her in any way. He stayed closer to Scarlett than he had in earlier years, but his closeness was far less intrusive.

We'd hoped that surgery to remove her tumor would solve the problem—and, when it didn't, we had difficult decisions to make. There were many in Homer's community who advocated for removing Scarlett's leg altogether. But Scarlett was nearly seventeen, and arthritic, and she'd always been so poised and self-possessed that forcing her, at this point in her life, to adjust to getting around on only three legs seemed almost cruel. The same was true of chemotherapy. Others among our online friends had made different decisions for their own cats under similar circumstances. But everybody understood that Scarlett was Scarlett, and that there was no one-size-fits-all solution to these kinds of problems.

Scarlett had become so quiet and tractable by the time we knew it was over, in December of 2011, that it was almost as if she wasn't there anymore. She was the first cat I'd ever lived with, and there was a special pain in her loss. When I brought her to the vet for the last time, I couldn't even give my name to the receptionist without bursting into tears.

But Scarlett had one last gift for me. She'd been so silent and immobile in her carrier that I wasn't even sure she was still awake. But when the doctor very gently inserted the needle into her neck, Scarlett's eyes—which had been glazed and unfocused for the past day—quickly sharpened and narrowed. I knew by now that a needle so small, injected into the relatively insensitive scruff of her neck, wouldn't hurt her. But Scarlett still had enough of her personal dignity left to resent that a stranger had dared touch her at all. With her typical churlish *rowr!* of old, she reached up out of her cloth, blanket-lined carrier to take an annoyed swipe at the vet's hand. *Get off my lawn, you kids!*

It was so quintessentially *Scarlett* that I couldn't help but chuckle through my tears. *There's my surly girl!* For that brief moment, she wasn't the ailing, compliant Scarlett of the last few months. She was once again the crusty curmudgeon I'd loved so well for so long.

I would always say after that, in describing her final moments, that Scarlett had gotten to die as she'd lived— really, *really* pissed off.

HOMER TRULY GRIEVED WHEN we lost Scarlett, and Homer's community grieved with us. After about three days, when it became clear that she wasn't coming back, Homer seemed to age overnight. His customary run slowed to a walk, and his walk took on the stiff, wide-legged gait of an old man. He was no longer interested in chasing crumpled balls of paper across the living room, or in demanding bits of turkey from Laurence's sandwiches. Even a fresh sprinkling of home-grown catnip on the rug would leave him apathetic.

It was heartbreaking to see the transformation— made painfully ironic by the certainty I felt that Scarlett herself would have been perfectly content to be the last cat standing.

As far as Scarlett was concerned, the best days of her life had been the earliest ones, when she was an only cat.

But Homer had always thought about his relationship with Scarlett very differently than Scarlett did. In Homer's mind, Scarlett was the (unwitting) supporting player in a thousand stalk-and-pounce adventure tales Homer liked to tell himself. She was his foil, his muse, his great nemesis, and he was never happier than when he'd finally succeeded in irritating her to the point that she would swat at him, nip at his neck, and then chase him down the hall before turning around to let him chase her back into the bedroom. While she hadn't been especially playful during her last months, she'd still been *there*—a comforting presence and warm scent, familiar for as long as he could remember, against which Homer could curl up and doze contentedly.

But it wasn't just the loss of Scarlett herself. Equally hard on Homer, I think, was the fact that he was now alone whenever Laurence and I were out. We had the luxury of spending far more time with Homer than most cat parents could with their own, simply because we worked from our apartment—but, still, we couldn't be home *all* the time. A trip to the vet, while unpleasant for all concerned (Homer's deep-seated hatred of the vet's office having only grown more intense with time), revealed that—physically, at least—he was in fine health.

What Homer needed more than anything was a new friend.

I thought that an older, more seasoned adult cat might make an ideal companion for Homer. Accordingly, I pulled first one owner-surrendered cat—and, when she and Homer didn't "click," another—from the euthanization lists at a New York open-intake shelter. My plan was to foster these cats and, if things worked out, to let them become "foster failures"—permanent members of our family.

There's always a period of adjustment when two adult cats get to know each other. Even in understanding this, however, things seemed particularly rough between Homer and first one, then the other, of the new cats we tried introducing him to. Poor Homer was utterly incapable of picking up on the visual body language of a wary cat. He had no way of seeing the arched back, the puffed tail, the backward steps of a cat who was unsure if Homer's approach was friendly or hostile. Scarlett and Vashti had known him since he was a kitten, and had grown accustomed to his seemingly odd ways. But to the cats we brought home now, Homer's eyeless black face must have appeared completely expressionless. He would approach them for a friendly, *how ya doin'?* mutual sniff, and was met with nothing but aggressive rebuffs.

Truth be told, I probably could have made it work with at least one of the cats if I'd really put the time in. But I didn't have the heart to subject Homer to any more stress after the loss of his two best friends. So I worked with a couple of the no-kill shelters I'd developed relationships with, and eventually we were able to find forever homes for both our fosters. (I still get pictures of them from their happy adoptive humans, and it always makes me smile.)

And that was how, early in 2012, we ended up adopting two little black kittens—litter-mates named Clayton and Fanny. Clayton had a damaged hind leg that we knew from the beginning would most likely have to come off sooner or later. (As it turned out—sooner.)

I'll tell their story in full later on. For now, it's enough to know that, even by kitten standards, Clayton and Fanny were ridiculously cheerful and high-spirited. There's probably nothing more irresistible than a kitten who adores you—and our kittens adored their new big brother immediately, right from the start. They were so playful, so eager to please, so ready to worship Homer in an abject, shameless way, that Homer would have had to be much more hard-hearted than he was to resist their charms. Homer couldn't see the goofy way Clayton would excitedly bunny-hop beside him on his three good legs, but I think Homer could sense it—and before long he was running, leaping, and chasing after toys, over the furniture and off the walls of our home, with all his old zest.

Ultimately, Homer recovered because he wasn't made for grief. It wasn't just that he was too innately happy—he was also too strong. Homer's strength was a force of nature, his will to live indomitable, as we would soon come to learn. All he needed in order to heal was a reminder that the world was still full of joy—that joy itself had been, and always would be, the very substance of his life.

I, of course, had known this about Homer all along. I'd written an entire book about it.

Playing the role of big brother was a new adventure for Homer. And new adventures were what Homer had always lived for.

3 • Strong Like Bull
There is a time for many words, and there is also a time for sleep.
— HOMER, *The Odyssey*

IT WAS A COLD, gray afternoon In early December, and I was pulling our freshly cleaned winter bedding from the laundry basket, planning to swap it for the lighter sheets and blanket currently dressing our bed. Homer and the kittens (who had, by now, grown into full-fledged cats) were sitting in a semi-circle on the floor at the foot of the bed. "Helping" me change the linens was always a popular activity among our three. Homer would perform the vital job of attacking each corner of the bed as the fitted sheet went over it. Fanny pitched in by diving under the top sheet and creating a lump I couldn't work around until I'd pushed her onto the floor. And Clayton, not as good a jumper as the other two, would dig in his front claws and haul himself up onto the bed—dragging blanket and sheets halfway to the floor—and hop around after the other two until I said, in an exasperated voice, "That's *enough!*" at which point he would flop down and look at me with deep reproach for having spoiled the game.

It was unquestionably a frustrating way to make the bed, but I couldn't help but smile now as I saw Homer's face turned up to mine in anticipation of one of our oldest and most cherished rituals. Homer was fifteen years old, and more apt than he'd used to be to choose naps over play. Where once he'd been the "poster kitty" for special-needs animals, he was now more of an elder statesman. His one gray whisker had become six, and the ebony sheen of his head was flecked with gray as well.

Fanny and Clayton had helped him recover the *joie de vivre* he'd lost after Scarlett's passing a year earlier. Still, I was bringing out the heavier blankets sooner than I normally would—usually I'd wait for the first snow—because I thought Homer might appreciate the additional warmth and softness a bit earlier this year.

I'd just gotten the old sheets off and dumped the new fitted sheet onto the middle of the bed, when I noticed that Homer, resting on his haunches, wobbled a bit before falling over to one side. He quickly righted himself, but fell over to the side again. Then he tried to stand, but his legs wouldn't support him. He went down in a small heap and curled all four paws beneath his body.

At first I wasn't even sure that I'd seen what I thought I saw. Maybe Homer was just lying down, and I had only imagined that something seemed "off." But then I saw how Homer struggled to hold his head up, like a kitten fighting to stay awake while falling asleep on his feet, and I knew that something was very wrong.

"Laurence!" In two long strides I was in the hallway and buried halfway to my chest in the hall closet as I struggled to free one of the cat carriers from its storage place. Clayton and Fanny had followed eagerly (*She opened the closet! Closets are awesome!*) and I shooed them away impatiently. "*Laurence!*" I called again, and found that Laurence had already abandoned his home office next to our bedroom and was standing beside me.

"What happened?" he asked.

"There's something wrong with Homer. He just... fell over." I spoke calmly, not wanting to alarm Homer, who was always so attuned to the sound of my voice. "We have to get him to the animal hospital."

Laurence regarded me for a fraction of a second. It was only when I saw his face tighten with concern that I knew what my own looked like, despite the forced evenness of my tone. "Let's go," was all he said, and went to round up keys, coats, and cell phones.

Getting Homer into his carrier was usually an onerous task. Once upon a time, a trip in the carrier had meant a move to a new home and new territories for Homer to explore. But we'd lived here with Laurence for just over seven years now—nearly half of Homer's life. These days, the carrier meant only one thing: the vet.

There was nothing in the world Homer loathed and feared as much as the vet's office. He'd never exactly been a *good* patient, but the problem had gotten exponentially worse over the years. The last time we'd gone, in January, I'd had to cradle Homer in my arms in order for the vet to get close enough to draw a blood sample. When the needle went in, Homer had panicked and bitten my hand so hard that I'd had to go the emergency room later for a tetanus shot. He'd seemed immediately remorseful upon hearing my yelp of pain, struggling to get his front paws onto my shoulder so he could nuzzle my neck, the way he had that very first day we'd met, all those years ago. When the vet had tried to approach him again, he'd hissed at her wildly over my shoulder, like a thing possessed. *Leave me alone!* he seemed to say. *Look what you made me do to my human!*

We hadn't been back since.

Homer didn't struggle at all now. He was still breathing, and he appeared to be awake. But whether he was on the floor or in his carrier seemed to be a matter of equal indifference to him.

Seeing his utter lack of resistance made the knots in my stomach tighten. I held him for a moment, pressing my cheek to the top of his head before gently lowering him in. "You're going to be fine," I assured him in a soft voice. "You'll be just fine."

It was the lunch hour—always a difficult time to catch a cab in front of our Midtown apartment—so Laurence walked a couple of blocks up while I huddled Homer in his carrier as close under my coat as I could, trying to keep him warm. With my cell phone cradled between my shoulder and my ear, I let the receptionist at the vet's office know that Homer and I were on our way in with an emergency. As I hung up, I saw the blessed sight of Laurence in the back of a cab pulling up to us.

Homer didn't budge or call out once during the entire ten-minute ride—also very unlike him—and I found myself unable to stop unzipping the top of the carrier just far enough to slip my hand in, to stroke Homer's head and side and make sure he was still breathing. The traffic on First Avenue was too heavy for our cabbie to cross, forcing him to drop us across the street from the animal hospital's entrance. I left Laurence to pay him and, like the true New Yorker I'd long-since become, darted into the street against the light, breaking into a run so none of the oncoming cars would have to slow to avoid me. I was slightly out of breath by the time I reached the receptionist's desk and placed Homer in his carrier on top of it.

Reina, the woman behind the desk, knew me well. I'd been there at least once a month during the two years when Vashti and Scarlett were sick, and more recently when Clayton had to have his hind leg removed. Laurence and I liked to say that we'd probably financed a Cooper-Lerman Memorial Wing of the animal hospital, given our outrageous expenses there over the past few years. It was a joke, of course, but I don't think I'd ever felt less like laughing than I did in that moment, finding myself yet again in that familiar waiting room.

"What happened?" Reina asked, making sympathetic clucking sounds at Homer through the mesh sides of the carrier.

"I don't know. He just kind of fell over," I told her.

Reina pressed a button on her phone that summoned a vet tech through the swinging door that led to the exam rooms in the back. She took the carrier from Reina but turned to stop me when I tried to follow. "You'll have to wait out here," she said kindly, but firmly.

"But I have to go with him." My voice was calm. *Just two reasonable people having a reasonable disagreement.* "He's blind, and he's terrified of the vet's office. I don't think you'll be able to handle him without me."

She peered at Homer, silent and stone-still in his carrier. He'd always been a little guy, but now he looked positively frail. "I think we'll manage." She smiled reassuringly. "We have to bring him to the tech area for tests," she explained, "and there are other animals back there. That's why we need you to wait out here."

I turned to Reina, who was also our pet-sitter when we traveled and knew Homer better than anyone else at the clinic, hoping for a reprieve. "He'll be fine, *mami*." Behind her, the vet tech had already disappeared with Homer back through the swinging door. "He's so out of it, he probably won't even know what's going on."

I took the seat Laurence had saved for me in the cozy, wood-paneled waiting area—made welcoming with posters of puppies and kittens, flyers for pet-sitters, and copies of *Best Friends* magazine—and tried to imagine what went on when a nearly unconscious cat was brought into a veterinary emergency room. My sole knowledge of what happened when someone was rushed unconscious to the hospital came from television and movies. Would they plop Homer onto a gurney and wheel him speedily into another room while a doctor called for CCs of this and tests for that? Would nurses cluster around trying to get blood pressure and pulse readings? I was heartsick, miserable at the thought of Homer—tiny Homer, weakened and terrified—being subjected to unknown probes and prods and lord-only-knew-what-else without me there to comfort him.

But, as it turned out, I was luckier than I realized. I wouldn't have to wonder for long.

The tech area, where Homer had been taken, was all the way in the back of the building, and the waiting area was in the front. Separating them was a long corridor with exam rooms branching off from it. We were probably a good hundred feet away from Homer, with two closed doors (one at either end of the corridor) between us. Nevertheless, within a few minutes I heard what was going on.

Everybody heard what was going on.

Over the years, I've probably heard the full range of sounds that the average housecat is capable of making—the meows, burbles, and coos; the purring and deep-throated whines; the shrill, unforgettable screams of a cat who's enraged or terrified. Homer himself had always had an especially rich vocal repertoire, with a series of highly distinct mews, yips, and growls meant to indicate things like, *I can't find you; I'm hungry; I'm coming over to be petted now;* and *This is irritating me.*

What I heard now wasn't any of those. It hardly even sounded like noises a cat should be capable of making—and, at first, I didn't think it *was* a cat. I didn't even think that the sound came from any natural source. For a second, I thought that maybe a nearby construction worker had started up a chainsaw. But, after the briefest of pauses for breath, it became clear that these were animal noises—the sound of some enraged wild beast fending off hunters or defending its territory. The vicious, furious snarls rose in volume to fill the entire waiting room, so deep now, so sustained, so impossibly loud, that they could only be described as roars.

It was lunchtime, the busiest time of day at the animal clinic, and the waiting room was packed. There were huge dogs and tiny ones at the ends of leashes, cats and rabbits in carriers, two cages containing a parrot and a parakeet. Every animal was accompanied by a human, and it was something of a miracle that Laurence had managed to score us two seats at all.

As the roars from the back of the hospital continued and grew in both volume and anger, the comfortable hum of conversation and scuffling animals in the waiting room fell silent. Reina, from her station behind the receptionist's desk, put the call she was taking on hold and turned to stare in open-mouthed wonder at the door leading to the back. For a breathless moment, the entire animal hospital was dead silent except for the enraged clamor rising from the back. Then a hushed murmuring rose in the waiting room, as if everybody was instinctively wary of elevating their voices above a whisper. *What the...? What's going on back there? What is that?* One woman, in an undertone, said something that ended with...*a panther?* The man she was with muttered darkly about the kind of idiot who thought it was okay to keep exotic pets in a New York apartment.

Two large dogs had begun to whimper and cringed behind the legs of their owners, while a smaller dog issued a low rumble, the hackles raised on the back of his neck. From the dark recesses of carriers, I heard hisses and growls. The parakeet twittered and fluttered frantically around his cage. I thought of my younger sister, who'd always shrieked so loudly and continuously when receiving childhood shots that every other kid in the pediatrician's waiting room would break into terrified sobs.

"What do you think it is?" Laurence whispered.

I threw him a wry, sideways look.

"You think that's *Homer?*" Laurence appeared dubious. But then his glance took in my face, which felt so hot that I knew it had to be fiery red. His expression changed from incredulity to awe. "Damn," he muttered.

I was already standing when the door to the back swung open, and I nearly walked right into the vet tech who'd initially brought Homer to the back of the hospital. She'd been so calm and confident when we'd first come in, but now she was profoundly flustered. Her face looked as red as mine had felt a moment ago, and I could see that her hands were trembling. "They need you back there," she blurted. Pointing down the hallway, she added, "The last exam room on the left." Once she'd made sure I was going the right way, she ducked into a small side room, quickly closing the door behind her.

I felt a bit like a character in a scary movie as I headed in the direction the vet tech had indicated—some not-very-bright girl inexplicably walking toward the room containing the terrifying monster, rather than away from it. I'd known that the sounds I'd heard in the waiting room would only grow louder as I approached their source, but it was still unnerving to hear *how much* louder they became.

The tableau that greeted me when I reached Homer's exam room might have been comical under different circumstances. Standing in a semicircle—facing the high metal exam table bolted to the wall, but at a judicious distance from it—were three women. One was the doctor, who must have been new to the practice, because I'd never seen her before. The other two were clearly assistants. They'd donned long, thickly padded gloves that stretched from the tips of their fingers all the way up to their shoulders, like the ones that falconers wear. They'd also knotted bandanas behind their ears and pulled them up protectively over their faces. Their foreheads above the bandanas were a vivid pink and beaded with sweat. Their bodies were poised with a tense wariness, leaning slightly forward at the shoulders while their feet were half-turned in the opposite direction, ready to carry them back to a safer distance if the need arose.

Seeing Homer—all four pounds of him, crouched defensively on the exam table—took me back instantly, all the way to that summer night more than twelve years earlier, when a Homer I hadn't recognized had chased a large male intruder right out of our Miami apartment. If he'd looked helpless and fragile a half-hour ago, when I'd first brought him in to the clinic, he now more closely resembled the panther the woman in the waiting room had thought she'd heard. The hind part of his body was elevated and his chest was lowered until it almost touched the table beneath him. His head was raised with his mouth wide open, lips pulled back in a cruel rictus that bared all his teeth. His head and ears moved evenly from side to side as he listened for a cue as to where the next assault might come from, one paw raised with claws at full extension, ready to lash out as soon as someone came within striking distance.

One of the assistants was holding a yellowish hand towel in front of her, the way a lion tamer might hold a chair between himself and the roaring lion before him. As I entered, the assistant—still maintaining a safe distance between herself and Homer—gingerly tossed it over his head. Homer immediately erupted into a fresh round of anguished, deafening roars, thrashing angrily as his claws attempted to escape the towel and find his tormentors.

I knew that putting a towel over the head of a distressed cat was standard procedure, that it usually *calmed* them, and that the hot bolt of rage that stabbed from my chest to my belly was therefore unwarranted. Everybody in that room wanted only to help Homer. Still, it took a wrenching effort of will to make my voice sound as serene as it needed to, for Homer's sake.

"Okay, so Homer is blind." I said *Homer* in the gentle, sing-song cadence I used at home when I was particularly happy with him. The wild thrashing beneath the towel stilled. "Putting a cloth over his head isn't going to quiet him the way it does other cats. You're just making him more upset."

The assistant who'd thrown the towel now leaned forward and, grabbing the corner closest to her and farthest from Homer's claws, quickly pulled it off while simultaneously taking a large step back. The Homer thus revealed, puffed up to several times his normal size, bore little resemblance to the Homer I knew. Nevertheless, his ears had pricked up and turned toward my voice. Once freed from the towel, his nose followed, rising inquisitively in an attempt to discern whether there was a familiar scent to match the familiar cadence.

"You're a good boy, Homer." I approached him slowly, my hands raised in front of me in an instinctive gesture of non-threatening compliance that was, of course, wasted on a blind cat. Cautiously, I put one hand directly beneath his nose.

Homer immediately pressed his whole face into my cupped palm, and I used the other hand to rub gently behind his ears. As frightening as it had been to see Homer in his rage, my heart nearly broke now to see him morph back into his normal self—just a scared little cat, terrified out of his wits at being separated from the human he trusted.

"You're a good boy, Homer, a good, good boy," I repeated soothingly, and Homer's fur sank as his entire body seemed to relax.

If I'd levitated into the air right in front of them, the vet and her assistants couldn't have appeared more gobsmacked as Homer transformed from snarling beast to docile housecat in my hands. "I'm sorry," the vet said. "With the way he was brought in, we didn't know he'd put up such a fight."

I told you so! I told you so! a voice in my brain shrieked. But I only laughed ruefully and said, "I understand. It *is* hard to believe that such a little guy can make such a big ruckus."

"He's so *teeny!*" one of the assistants exclaimed almost indignantly, as if she'd been trying to restrain herself but couldn't hold it in any longer—couldn't quite fathom how one small cat, and a sick one at that, had been able to cause three grown women who handled animals *for a living* to fear legitimately for their physical safety.

"Maybe you should spend a few minutes alone with him," the vet said now. "It looks like we'll have to sedate him before we can examine him. That might go easier if he's a little calmer before I try to inject him."

"That's a good idea," I said. "Is it okay if I sit on the floor?"

At her nod, I sat down cross-legged about a foot from the exam table. "Come here, Homer-Bear," I said, and Homer leapt a touch awkwardly from the table to the ground. In the crouched, creeping way of an animal that suspects it's being hunted, he made his way over to where I sat and crawled into my lap. The three women, still shaking their heads in amazement, filed silently out of the room.

Homer and I sat there for long minutes as I continued to stroke him. He didn't purr, and he didn't fall asleep, but he did fall into a calm, quiet reverie. *My poor boy,* I thought. *My poor, poor boy.* At this point, I felt well beyond guilty and heartily sorry that I'd brought Homer in at all, knowing how very traumatic the vet always was for him—although what choice had I had? Eventually, the vet returned and knelt over us just long enough to jab a needle into the back of Homer's neck. Homer instantly hissed and reared up, trying to catch her with his front claws. But the sedative kicked in pretty quickly, and Homer fell unconscious back into my lap.

"We can take it from here," the vet said, lifting Homer and bundling him back into his carrier. "We'll draw blood and run some tests. I'll let you know when he's ready to leave."

Laurence and I had to wait another half hour before we were able to bring a still-sedated Homer back home. I was given some instructions on how to care for him and things to watch for until the sedative wore off. "Do you know what caused him to fall over like that this afternoon?" I asked. After all the drama of the preceding hour, the thing that had brought us there in the first place seemed almost like an afterthought, like something that had happened years ago to somebody else.

"We'll know more when the bloodwork comes back tomorrow," the vet told me. "We'll call you as soon as we have it. The important thing now is for him to get some rest."

Homer slept for the rest of the afternoon. He didn't stir into consciousness again until early evening, when he woke just long enough to eat his dinner before staggering back into the bedroom and collapsing in the little nest I'd made for him on the floor from old t-shirts and sweaters.

I moved his litter-box into our bedroom and kept him in there with us overnight, away from the curious noses of Clayton and Fanny, who couldn't figure out why their big brother smelled so different (like the vet's office, although they didn't know it), and why he didn't wake and acknowledge them, even when they touched his head and face with tentative little paws. At some point in the middle of the night, Homer made an unsuccessful attempt to jump onto the bed but fell over backwards, the sedative having still not worn off entirely. I didn't want him on the bed—which, being a king-size, was rather high off the ground—because I wasn't sure he'd be able to jump off without hurting himself if he needed his litter-box. But I also didn't want him to have to sleep by himself. I ended up moving my pillows and a blanket down to the floor, so I could curl up next to him.

Homer, December 2012

The next morning, Homer was almost miraculously back to his old self. He ate a big breakfast and greeted Clayton and Fanny in his usual imperious way. A couple of hours later we were playing one of his favorite games, wherein I would wriggle my finger under the bed covers and Homer (who could once again get on and off the bed just fine) would pounce on them. I was delighted to see him cocking his head to one side in familiar fashion as he listened for the slight noises that would pinpoint where, exactly, my fingers were.

He was still doing well enough when noon came around that Laurence and I went out to grab a quick lunch at a sandwich place next to our apartment building. We'd just placed our orders when my cell phone rang with a call from the animal hospital. The vet who called wasn't the one who had seen Homer yesterday, but she assured me that she'd thoroughly read both Homer's test results and his medical file.

"How's he doing today?" she asked.

"He seems okay, actually." I'd risen and was walking through the restaurant, so we could continue the call outside where I wouldn't disturb the diners around me. "He was even playing this morning."

She sounded surprised. "He was *playing*?"

I think I mistook her surprise for reproach—as if she were implying that I was a dangerous lunatic for running an invalid cat like Homer around—and I quickly backtracked. "It wasn't *strenuous* play. He was in a playful mood, is what I meant."

"No, that's good!" She seemed to file this tidbit away for future reference before continuing. "So I've looked over the bloodwork and Homer's file, and I wanted to go over the results with you."

She started with the numbers that fell within the normal range and therefore looked good, and that was the shortest part of our conversation. The problem, it quickly became clear, was Homer's liver. I didn't have to understand all the ins and outs or medical jargon to know immediately how serious the problem was. Doing some rapid calculations, I realized that Homer's liver values (the enzymes that were supposed to be found in the liver itself, not in his bloodstream) were about fifteen hundred percent higher than what was normal in a cat. *Fifteen hundred percent!* "If his fur wasn't so black, you'd probably have noticed a while ago that his ears are yellow, and how jaundiced he is," the vet told me, and I cursed myself for having been so stupid—so unforgivably stupid and unobservant. "I sounded surprised when you said Homer was playing this morning, because frankly a cat with numbers like these shouldn't even be able to walk." She didn't say it aloud, but I knew what she was thinking: *He shouldn't even be alive.*

My mind instantly rejected that thought. Numbers or no numbers, anybody with two eyes in their head could see that Homer was still *Homer*. He ate, he played, he cuddled in my lap. Maybe on paper he shouldn't be alive, but in the real world he was still walking around the same as ever—and where there was life, there was hope. So I took a deep breath to steady myself and asked, "Where do we go from here?"

"I'd like you to bring Homer in this afternoon," the vet said, "and plan on leaving him here for a few days— maybe a week." She launched into her recommended course of treatment, an aggressive one that would involve hooking Homer up round-the-clock to various drips and medications, which would drain harmful fluids out and introduce healthier ones in, and give his liver a fighting chance to recover.

I didn't even know I'd started to cry until I became aware of a pain on my cheeks, and realized that the icy December wind had frozen the tears to my face. *My god,* was all I could think. *My god, how can I do this to him? How can I bring him back to that place and leave him there all alone?*

"Let me talk to the doctor who saw Homer yesterday," the vet concluded. "I'll call you back so we can make a plan."

Laurence was waiting at our table when I re-entered the restaurant, and I saw that our food had arrived in my absence. I couldn't touch mine, however, and as I relayed to Laurence the substance of my conversation with the vet, my tears began to flow in earnest. He reached across the table to cover my hand with his and tried to say something comforting. I suddenly became aware that we were in a very public place, and that the other patrons closest to us were beginning to take an interest in our table. "I'm sorry," I said, and my voice sounded like I was choking. "I have to go back outside. People will think you're breaking up with me." I got up and left him for a second time, crouching once I'd reached the sidewalk again and putting my head between my legs as I tried to pull myself together.

I was still outside, grateful for the cold air I inhaled in greedy gulps in the hopes it would clear my thoughts, when the vet called back. "I spoke with the doctor who saw Homer yesterday," she told me. "We talked a bit and..." She hesitated, as if searching for the right words. "We're not sure that Homer would benefit from a hospital environment."

For a moment, I was hopeful. "You mean you think I can treat him at home?"

Her voice softened. "Look, the doctor you saw yesterday told me what happened. We can't get near Homer without sedating him, and we can't keep a cat fully sedated for days at a time. And we can't sedate a cat at *all* with bloodwork like Homer's. If we'd known how bad his numbers were, we wouldn't have sedated him yesterday."

"So you're saying you can't treat him without sedating him, but you can't sedate him until you've been able to treat him."

"That's about it," the vet agreed. "The thing is, even the really mean cats, when they have numbers like these, are usually so sick and weak that we can do whatever we need to with them. I don't know how much longer Homer's strength can last—it's a miracle that it's lasted this long— but as long as it does, there's really nothing to be gained by you bringing him back here."

She was, as I would later recount at innumerable shelter readings whenever I told this story, saying to me in the nicest possible way, *Please don't ever bring your demon cat back to our animal hospital again.* I couldn't argue. I was no more anxious to bring Homer back than they were to have him.

"Is there anything I can do for him by myself?"

"I'm going to write you a couple of prescriptions," she said. "Some medication to support his liver and other functions. There's a pharmacy uptown that can compound it with something yummy-tasting like chicken or tuna. That way you can just squirt it into his mouth or mix it with his food, instead of trying to pill him. It's a two-week course of treatment."

My voice cracked when I spoke again, dreading the answer even before I asked the question. "What do we do for him when the two weeks are up?"

"I'm sorry," she said, and the sorrow in her voice was genuine. "But Homer's numbers are incompatible with life."

It was an awful phrase, *incompatible with life*—at once so brutal yet efficiently descriptive that it told the whole story. So it seemed almost superfluous when she went on to add:
"I don't think he has more than two weeks left."

As a kIndness to my fellow sensitive readers (and I'm assuming that applies to most of you reading this), I'll risk ruining the suspense and tell you up front that we did *not* lose Homer within the next two weeks. Nor did we lose him within four weeks, or even four months. Homer, as it turned out, had more fight left in him than even those of us who knew him best (and had seen him at his worst) thought he was capable of. In the end, he would stay with us for the better part of the next year.

But, at the time, we still had to go through it all and make our decisions without knowing outcomes. Looking back now, I realize that I didn't really have any decisions to make. Homer had made them already. All I could do was let things take whatever course they were going to take. But I didn't know this then—or perhaps it's more honest to say that it was a knowledge I resisted.

It was hard to believe that Homer's condition could really be as dire as the vet had said. I scanned his ears anxiously when Laurence and I got home from the restaurant, and indeed, when I looked at them closely, the insides had a definite yellow cast beneath the black of his fur. But Homer quickly grew impatient with his ear exam. He was far more interested in the bag I'd brought home containing my uneaten sandwich. After downing a generous helping of sliced turkey—which pretty much depleted my sandwich entirely, and it was astonishing to watch Homer put away a quantity of food that would have more than filled *me* up—Homer trotted over to his bed on the desk beside my computer, waiting patiently for me to sit down after lunch as I usually did, and spend the afternoon typing away with him by my side. It was as if yesterday hadn't happened.

I spent the next two weeks on a sort of doomsday watch. Every time Homer ate a meal with gusto (which was pretty much every meal), I counted it as a triumph. Every time I watched him chase a crinkle ball around, every time he cuddled up to have me spoon him on the couch, I thought, *Is this it? Is this the last time?* Every time he was slower to awaken from a nap than I thought he should be, I wondered if he was going to wake up at all.

I watched and I wondered—and I agonized. What was I to do for him? When Vashti had been diagnosed with chronic renal failure (and hyperthyroidism, and high blood pressure, and anemia), I'd forced pills down her throat once a day, and given her shots twice a day, and administered subcutaneous fluid injections every other day. I'd taken her to the vet for monthly check-ups and twice she'd had to stay there overnight. Scarlett had had surgery for her cancer, and I'd had to give her insulin shots twice a day for her diabetes. Certainly none of it could be described as *fun*— and the two of them had struggled and fled and clawed and even hissed on occasion enough for me to know how much they disliked all the poking and prodding and pilling—but all that had been a few unpleasant minutes out of our days, which the two of them seemed to forget completely as soon as it was over. And the reward for those unpleasant few minutes was the additional time we had together that we wouldn't have had otherwise.

But Homer wasn't like Vashti and Scarlett. For the past few years, he wouldn't even let me trim his claws anymore. I had known even before Homer got sick—back when I was going through everything I went through with my two girls—that I wouldn't be able to do the same for him. Regular vet visits would be difficult enough, probably even impossible. As much as Homer loved and trusted me, I knew he'd never let me pill him regularly, or stick needles in him. The best-case scenario was that I'd win those battles (maybe!) but end up injured and bloodied for my efforts, and Homer would come to fear my scent and the sound of my voice as much as he'd ever feared the vet's office. Homer would never understand why I was doing all these terrible things to him. What would be the point of extending his life only to rob him of all the security and love and trust he'd built that life on?

There would be no point, I had assured myself, back when Homer was healthy and these were only abstract thoughts.

But now the abstract had become concrete, and the sand beneath my feet had shifted. I couldn't just do nothing, could I? I mean, maybe I couldn't do *anything*—but I certainly couldn't do *nothing*. The collective wisdom of Homer's Facebook community recommended milk thistle, which I began liberally sprinkling into his drinking water. Perhaps it helped. But it certainly didn't seem like the kind of heroic measures I should be taking on his behalf. How could a few drops of milk thistle be sufficient when I was willing to do anything—literally, *anything*—that could be done for Homer, if only he would let me help him?

I remember one day when it was especially bad with me, when the certainty that I was losing Homer and could do nothing to stop it was the only certainty I had in the world, and it sat in my chest so heavily I could hardly breathe. I was at my computer, and Homer was sitting on his haunches on the desk next to me, leaning the entire weight of his body heavily against my left shoulder, as he did when he sensed that I needed comfort. I went to his Facebook page and, unlike my usual habit of posting funny pictures and amusing little stories, typed a single sentence. *How will I live without this cat?* I quickly deleted it, embarrassed at having posted such a stark (and melodramatic) cry of pain on a Facebook page for anybody to see. But it had been seen already, and my phone rang a few minutes later.

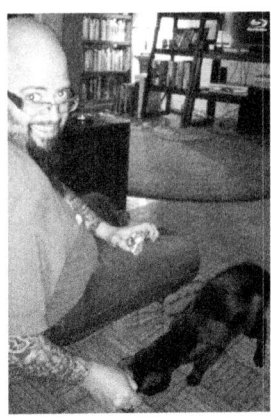

Homer with Jackson Galaxy, 2013

Some months earlier, out on the "cat circuit," I'd struck up a friendship with Jackson Galaxy—Animal Planet's famous and infamous "Cat Daddy"—and, as it turned out, he was every bit as compassionate in real life as one would expect from his show. He'd called now to see how Homer and I were doing, and I laid out my dilemma for him, sparing no details in describing Homer's recent visit to the animal hospital. I concluded by asking him the same question I'd been asking myself non-stop for days: Didn't I have to do something more for Homer—try some new doctor, some kind of medical treatment, *something* more than what I was doing?

Jackson listened until I'd talked myself out. "Homer is sending you a very clear message," he said when I'd finished. "And that message is *DO. NOT. WANT. I do not want this!* It's not fair to ignore a cat when he's talking to you that loudly and clearly."

"But how can I just do *nothing* for him?"

"Treating Homer with respect and dignity isn't nothing," Jackson told me. "Seeing him through this last phase of his life—however long that might be—with mindfulness and love isn't nothing." He paused for a moment, as if collecting his thoughts. "You have to be selfless now," he finally said. "You made an unspoken deal with Homer the day you adopted him. In loving him, you promised you'd always take care of him. Taking care of someone means putting them before you. And that means you, in this moment, don't matter. Your sadness doesn't matter. You'll have plenty of time for that when he leaves. In this moment, you're a parent with only one job. You have to listen to Homer, because the only promise to keep is not to wait until it's his worst day. Let him leave knowing love, not fear, not pain, not the flipside of love. Do you really want, *now*, to rob him of all that love and confidence he's had in such abundance his whole life?"

"No." My voice was husky. "No, I really don't."

"Just because doctors *can* do something doesn't mean they should. Just because you did certain things for your other cats doesn't mean you should do them for *this* cat. Every cat is different. You should follow Homer's lead."

"But Homer doesn't understand the choice he's making. He doesn't know what I know." I truly did want to let it go, to accept the reality of what was happening and make my peace with it. But the struggle had been too hard for me to give it up all at once.

"He knows what *he* knows. Maybe that's enough," Jackson concluded. "And Homer might end up surprising you. Cats usually do."

JACKSON'S WORDS PROVED TO be prophetic. Days became weeks became months, and still Homer was with us. Still the same Homer more or less, although he did eventually slow a bit, like a clock just beginning to wind down.

The worst thing a cat can do for his liver is to stop eating—but, paradoxically, cats with liver disease are usually reluctant eaters at best. The challenge is to keep them eating, at least enough to give their liver something to do other than eat itself.

Homer, however, had always been a cat who defied expectations, and he ate voraciously. To say that Homer became a non-stop eating machine would be an understatement—and trying to describe what it was like to watch a four-pound cat eat his body weight every day is one of the rare times when words have failed me. It started with the medication the vet had prescribed, which apparently was every bit as yummy as promised when mixed with his regular food. When the two weeks' worth of medication ran out, I made it my mission to keep the food party going. At first I started out with some kitten-hood favorites, long- since abandoned on health grounds—although my new philosophy was, *As long as he's eating and he's happy.* Kitten Chow once again became a permanent fixture in our cupboard, and Homer attacked it with so much zeal that it almost seemed as if eating the food he'd eaten when he was younger made him feel like a young cat again. Gooey cans of

Friskie's and Fancy Feast also found their way into Homer's food bowl.

But it was Laurence who really rose to the occasion. What was, for me, a medical imperative became a genuine source of pleasure for Laurence, and finding new and exciting foods to tempt Homer with was his passion. That Homer was eating at all was less surprising than *how much* he was eating, consuming more than enough food in the typical day to satisfy a grown man.

Laurence brought Homer imported European canned tunas, sliced turkey by the pound, hamburgers, prime rib, shredded roast beef, pork-fried rice, spare ribs, pizza cheese, Gerber's baby food, and lobster dipped in butter. (The only thing Homer was particular about was his lobster—which was heaven on earth when dipped in butter, but unworthy of his interest when it was not.) He brought home salmon salad and whitefish salad from our favorite bagel place, and a stinky cheese from Murray's in the West Village that was so very stinky—even when stowed in the refrigerator—we'd had to ditch it a day later, even though the aroma had Homer clawing at the refrigerator door as if his very life depended on getting in.

Homer and Laurence, 2013

Laurence's imagination ranged from the high to the low, and he also brought home mysterious "potted meats" found in fifty-cent cans at our local bodega, which Homer gobbled down as enthusiastically as if it were caviar (which Homer also grew to love during that final year). Cans of Vienna Sausages—again from our bodega—mashed with a fork and served *au jus* were a particular treat. Chinese chicken on the bone from the take-out place across the street was a big hit, although not nearly as tempting as a fried chicken breast from Popeye's, the smell of which drove Homer absolutely wild with delight. Homer could polish off an entire Popeye's breast in the space of half an hour, although perhaps Homer's greatest culinary accomplishment was the time he finished an entire mutton chop—literally bigger than he was!—that Laurence brought home from the legendary Keen's Steakhouse. (In fairness, I should add that it did take him two days to eat his way through the whole thing.) The image of little Homer, sitting in front of that giant mutton chop like a tiny Henry VIII about to dig into a palace banquet, is one I'll always be grateful to have in my memory.

Perhaps the only truly perplexing food that Homer developed a taste for was carrot cake. I'd brought home a slice without frosting from a health-food place, saving it as an after-dinner treat for myself. But a couple of hours later I found Homer on the kitchen counter, clawing off the plastic it was wrapped in and gobbling the cake down greedily. I was on the verge of stopping him—carrot cake striking me as an odd and potentially unhealthy choice for a cat. But then I thought, *why not?* and carried the rest to his bowl, for him to finish at his leisure.

It was clear to us that Homer was waging a tremendous battle, one that required an almost incomprehensible amount of fuel to keep it going. It seems to me now, looking back, that forgoing aggressive medical care turned out to be the right decision, if only because Homer would have fought it, and me, every step of the way. He almost certainly couldn't have battled on two fronts with nearly as much success as he battled now on just the one.

But even with all his strength—and I'll admit that I was a bit awed, this late in Homer's life, to realize fully just how tremendous that strength actually was—the battle was taking its toll. He napped far more than he used to, and lost weight until he was barely more than skin and bones. Running my hand down his back, I could feel every vertebra in his spine. His coat, once so lustrous and sleek, began to look oily. But as long as Homer still played and ate, as long as he still cuddled and purred and chased Fanny and Clayton around, I told myself that I would let him fight for his life on his own terms, without taking anything away from him.

Our bedroom became Homer's bedroom, and he slept with me every night. Whether because he was confused, or too tired to make the effort of jumping from the bed and walking to his litter-box (which I'd moved permanently into our bedroom), the bed became his nighttime litter-box during those last few months. Honesty compels me to add that those nighttime poops were...something—although who among us hasn't cleaned up that and worse while caring for an ailing cat? And, given both the size and nature of Homer's new daily diet, what else could be expected?

Laurence moved temporarily into the guest bedroom, and I put a rubber sheet over our mattress. Stripping off all the sheets and blankets, I made a little nest for Homer from some of my old t-shirts and sweaters. As for myself, I slept wrapped up, cocoon-style, in a comforter. Homer and I were still able to cuddle, and it made clean-ups much easier.

I realize that, in the retelling, this sounds like an odd and cumbersome way to live—although it's amazing how quickly the unusual becomes routine when it's the landscape of your everyday life. I never thought of it as an imposition at all. I *wanted* to be there for all this—not just the playtimes and the cuddling, but the late-night cleanings and nursing Homer through bouts of upset stomach and every last messy, inconvenient bit of it. Once upon a time, I had saved Homer's life. And then, years later, he had saved mine. I can honestly say that I never loved Homer more than any of the other animals I've been lucky enough to live with. But Homer and I were bound to each other in a way that was nothing like anything I had experienced before—and I knew that I would never have anything in my life quite like this again. I couldn't have felt more tied to Homer if he'd literally been flesh of my flesh, bone of my bone.

When spring came, I resumed my schedule of shelter readings and fundraising appearances. Because I worked from home and spent, in the typical day, twenty-one hours or more within ten feet of Homer, it should have been easier to leave him once or twice a month for an afternoon trip upstate or a twenty-four-hour overnight to speak at a shelter farther away. Paradoxically, though, the more time I spent with Homer, the harder it was to go away from him. Still, talking about him at these events was a source of deep, deep pleasure.

People always asked about Homer during the Q&A sessions after I'd finished reading. Was he still alive? Was he in good health? I would tell the story of that last visit to the vet's office, how Homer—tiny Homer, sick as he was!— had overpowered the staff and thrown the entire animal hospital into disarray. I told them of the dire predictions that Homer wouldn't last out the month, wouldn't live to see the New Year. But here it was, the following summer, and Homer was still with us! A little slower, perhaps, and a little skinnier, but eating like a champ and enjoying his life. People would shake their heads in astonishment.

How was such a thing possible? How could such a little cat have so much fight in him? It became a standard part of these talks, of telling this story, for me to clench my right hand into a fist and strike the left side of my chest—just over my heart. In my best approximation of a Russian accent, I would proudly declare:

"Because my cat is strong like bull."

HOMER *WAS* STRONG LIKE a bull—and he'd fought hard and far longer than any bull in a ring ever had. But it was a fight we'd always known couldn't go on forever.

The end came one late-August afternoon, nearly four years to the day since *Homer's Odyssey* had first been published. Laurence and I had gone out to run a few errands. When I walked back in through our front door, the first thing I saw was Homer hanging from the side of the couch, his front legs splayed out to full extension as he dangled from two claws—one in each front paw—that had become snagged in the fabric as he'd tried to pull himself up. Too exhausted to try very hard to free himself, he simply dangled, waiting mutely for me to find him and help.

I'd noticed that Homer had slowed down even more in the past few days, that he'd gone from being tired to being *tired*, not stirring from his spot on the couch unless it was time for him to eat or follow me into the bedroom for the night. I'd also noticed that Clayton had seemed to be sticking to him more closely. Clayton was always fascinated by Homer and loved nothing more than to follow him around, even if Homer was ignoring him. But a sleeping Homer had never held much interest for Clayton, and when Homer settled down for a nap, Clayton would usually hop off to find something else to do. For the past week, though, whenever Homer curled up on the couch to sleep, Clayton would lie down on the floor directly in front of him—not moving, not bothering Homer in any way. He'd just watch him intently without taking his eyes off him.

I hadn't thought much about it at the time, and I'd tried not to think at all about Homer's increased weariness. On the face of it, there wasn't even a connection between those two things. But it all came together in my mind now in a single, blurred rush.

"Oh, *Homer.*" I threw down my purse and ran to the couch. "Oh, my poor boy. My poor, poor boy." I gently released the two claws and sank to the floor, cradling him in my arms, my cheek pressed to the top of his head. "I'm sorry, Homer-Bear. I'm so sorry I wasn't here. I'm so sorry, little boy." I swayed back and forth, kissing his brow, as he lay inertly in my arms. "I'm so sorry, Homer-Bear. I love you so much." I placed him on the ground, on his own legs. He feebly took a few steps, then laid down, clearly spent from the effort.

Clayton and Homer, August 2013

I went outside on our balcony then. Pulling the sliding door firmly closed behind me, I began to sob—great, gasping heaves that seemed to start at my knees before being wrenched upward and out through my mouth. I cried for having been gone when Homer needed me, and I felt the pain of that, his pain, as a physical pain in my own body. I cried for all the times I knew I would cry about it again, that image of Homer hanging from the couch. Countless times at unexpected moments, down through all the remaining years of my life. I cried for what I already knew in my heart even though I hadn't yet told it to myself in words. I cried for the blind kitten nobody had wanted, who'd come at a time in my life when I wasn't sure that anybody did, or ever would, want me. I cried for the last tangible link to those years of youth and uncertainty and discovery—a time that, even though it had since evolved into things infinitely better, was a vanished country now, one I could never return to. I cried for other things that would never come back, the greetings at the front door when I came home; the funny, sonar-like, sweeping turns of a little black head; the rattlesnake vibrating of an ecstatic tail (*Hooray! We're both here! We're together!*) that had been the first thing I'd seen every morning for sixteen years.

I cried for all of it, although the only articulate word in my head was, *Never.* It was suddenly the only word I knew. *Never. Never. Never.*

I had gone outside because I didn't want Homer to hear me cry like that, or Laurence for that matter. For their sakes, but also for my own. That first convulsion of grief was an animal thing, and instinctively I'd crawled away to hide my wound, to be alone with it. There was no one to hear me now but the buildings across the courtyard from ours. Their walls caught the sounds of my cries and sent them back to me, until the entire courtyard wailed in a Greek chorus of woe. *Alas! Alas!* I hung my head and arms over the balcony railing, pressing my hands over my eyes, and howled my loss to the empty courtyard below.

But I didn't allow myself to stay outside for more than a minute or two. I knew what had to be done, and I didn't want to give myself time to second-guess, to argue that maybe tomorrow would be better, that there might still be plenty of good days ahead. I had vowed that day when I'd spoken to Jackson, in preparation for just this moment, that I wouldn't wait until worse came to the absolute worst. I wouldn't wait until Homer wasn't Homer anymore before I let him go.

Months earlier, we'd found a vet who would be able to come to us at home when the time came. I had no intention of subjecting Homer to the animal hospital again, of making him spend the last moments of his life in the only place in the world of which he'd been starkly terrified. I spent the few hours before her arrival cuddling Homer in my lap and stroking his head in our old way. Laurence went out and got him a Popeye's chicken breast, which he mixed up with some turkey in Homer's bowl. Homer managed to make it from my lap as far as the bowl, but he was too tired to eat standing up and so ate reclining, like the Roman aristocrats of old. He did eat, though. He may not have cleaned his bowl, but he did eat.

The vet, when she came, was as kind as she'd sounded when I'd first spoken with her. She sat in the living room talking to Laurence and me about nothing in particular, until her presence among us stopped feeling awkward and ominous, and I was almost comfortable. Homer was lying in his spot at the end of the couch, close to her chair, and she affectionately stroked his head while she talked. He lay passively under her touch, although at one point he turned his head to press it into her hand.

Eventually, I picked Homer up and carried him into the bedroom, and the vet followed.

In the end, Homer died in his own home, in his own bed, in the arms of the person who'd loved him most. The vet left and quietly closed the bedroom door behind her after she'd given him the shot. I cradled Homer in my lap as I watched the muscles around the place where his eyes would have been relax into sleep for the last time. "*Eras mucho gato,*" I whispered into his ear. *Thou wert plenty of cat.*

It was, in its way, one of the most beautiful moments of my life. It was so beautiful that I couldn't even cry.

When Vashti died, we scattered her ashes at Fort Tryon Park, far, far uptown in Washington Heights. It was a beautiful, hilly park with acres of wide lawns and lush flowerbeds, and it commanded stunning views of the Hudson River and the Palisades beyond. Vashti had always loved water, and I had wanted to give her a whole river of it, a place from which she could watch the water sparkle and dance before it was carried out to sea. Scarlett had never shared Vashti's love of water and grass, but we had brought her ashes there too, so that she could be with Vashti.

And so, a week later, when we received Homer's ashes, we carried them all the way up to Fort Tryon Park, to the same lawn beneath the same oak tree where we'd released Scarlett and Vashti. My original three—Homer and his first, fastest friends—would be together again. The views were as sun-dappled and peaceful as I remembered. I hoped, I wanted to believe, that Homer at last was able to see them, to see all the beautiful things in this world that he never had, even though he'd seemed to be born knowing them already.

There was hardly anybody else at the park that day, and Laurence and I were alone in our little spot. I kissed the wooden box holding Homer's ashes before I opened it. As if awaiting its cue, a breeze blew up and carried them away from us, into the sunlight and out toward the river.

I wish I could say that I had a stirring eulogy for the occasion, something as heroic and fine as Homer himself had been. Something befitting the send-off of a cat who had touched so many lives, who had become the symbol of something so much bigger than himself, but who had never stopped being my own, my much-loved, dear little guy.

But I had expended so many words on Homer already—tens of thousands of them. My words were all used up. I could only think of someone else's. A scrap of an E.E. Cummings poem I'd first read back in my college creative-writing days, when I couldn't possibly have foreseen the little black cat who would find me someday and become the author of all my good fortune.

"I carry your heart with me," I said to the air and the ashes and the water flowing below us. "I carry it in my heart."

The breeze waned, and Homer's ashes, which had risen high above our heads, began to fall into the waiting grass. Laurence and I took each other's hands, and then we turned to go.

4 • The End of the Beginning

**Do not go about with your cheeks all covered with tears;
it is not right that you should grieve so incessantly.**
— HOMER, *The Odyssey*

I WAITED NEARLY A week before I let Homer's online community know about his passing, needing time to mourn privately before I could do so publicly. I had known that the response would be overwhelming, although I didn't know then how overwhelming it would be. The news about Homer grew and spread and then grew more, changing our lives and Homer's legacy in ways we could never have imagined.

But before I write about any of that, the time has come, as promised, to write about Clayton and Fanny— how we adopted them, what they brought to our family, and what they came to mean to us. The last chapter of Homer's story is very much their story, too.

When I set out to find a kitten to adopt as a companion for Homer, it was the first time I'd adopted a cat with a specific list of "qualifications" in mind. Actually, it was the first time I'd deliberately set out to adopt a cat at all.

Homer, Vashti, and Scarlett had all come into my life through a fortuitous combination of luck and circumstances and—while not generally a superstitious person—I'd believed in the karmic destiny of that, the sense that the cats I had been meant to love had found me, rather than vice versa. This was true even of the two older cats we'd tried out previously with Homer. And while things hadn't worked out permanently with our fosters, at least I'd been able to save them from certain death and help them find loving forever homes. Maybe that also was fate at work.

Now, however, we were looking for a kitten—not just waiting for one, but *looking*, because what Homer desperately needed after losing Scarlett was someone aside from Laurence and me to keep him company. The kitten ideally would still be very young—no older than two or three months, say—so that he or she would accept Homer's unusual face and particular ways without knowing that "normal" adult cats looked or acted any differently. I felt that we were uniquely suited to give a home to a kitten who had special needs. And, I soon realized, if we were going to adopt *one* young kitten, we should probably adopt *two*. Kittens were high energy, and a kitten with no one to play with besides Homer might drive him to distraction.

I entered my search parameters on Petfinder.com, and after a few clicks found myself looking at a picture of two kittens named Peeta and Katniss. They were a bonded pair of litter-mates with a foster network called Forever Friends—located deep in South Jersey, only an hour-and- a-half away by train—who hoped to adopt the two of them out together.

Both kittens were entirely black, although Katniss had a little locket of white fur just above her breastbone. Peeta had a deformed hind leg, more of a half- leg, really, which would likely have to come off at some point when he was older than the ten weeks he currently was. It didn't reach more than halfway to the ground and was of no use in propelling him forward when he walked, but he nonetheless uselessly spun and spun the half-leg as he moved, wasting energy and risking injury.

Clayton and Fanny, April 2012

I knew as soon as I saw them that these were our kittens. The sun hadn't even come up yet when I filled out the online application, and I waited in a keyed-up state of anticipation for the hours to roll by until it was late enough for a (ahem) sane person to begin their workday and review the form I'd submitted. I received a call from Forever Friends before noon, and we talked for a while about Peeta and Katniss, their personalities, Peeta's special needs. I gave them a list of references, and a week later I stood on the platform of New Jersey Transit's Trenton station, waiting to meet the volunteer from Forever Friends who would deliver our newest family members.

Laurence and I had enjoyed the *Hunger Games* movies well enough, but ultimately wanted to name the kittens ourselves. Laurence chose Clayton for the boy, after the famous one-legged tap dancer Clayton "Peg Leg" Bates. I chose Fanny for the girl, simply because I thought it was a sweet, old-fashioned name, and in her pictures Katniss looked like a very sweet little girl.

WHEN FANNY AND CLAYTON came to us, it had been fifteen years since I'd lived with a kitten—and I'd never lived with litter-mates at all. I was charmed to see what a matched set they were, how they groomed each other lovingly and slept curled up in each other's bodies. Their faces had enough subtle differences to be distinguishable, yet the family resemblance was obvious. They had identical large, golden eyes, and a habit of sitting next to each other with their heads tilted at identical angles, regarding Laurence and me with identical wide-eyed, solemn gazes. It was adorable, yet at times could take on an almost eerie, *Children of the Corn* quality.

The most enduring early image I have of the two of them comes from the evening of their fourth day with us. We'd set them up in our guest bedroom at first, wanting to give them a chance to acclimate, to feel safe in their new space and to get used to things smelling like Homer, while also giving Homer a chance to get used to things—like the t-shirts I let them sleep on and then wore around the house—smelling like them.

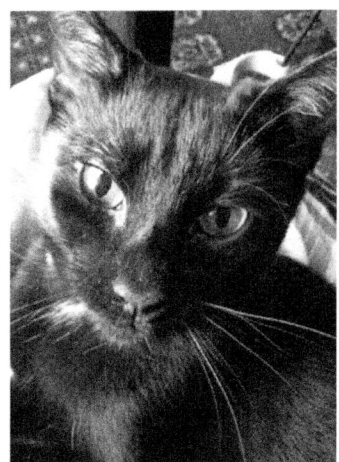

Fanny, July 2012

On the fourth day, I opened the door to the guest room and let them out into the rest of the apartment for the first time. Clayton, as if shot from a cannon, immediately took off in a quick bunny-hop on his three good legs, down the long hallway and into the living room.

Fanny, however, stood anxiously in the doorway to the guest room, crying for her brother to come back. Every few minutes, Clayton would hop back down the hall to where Fanny stood, touching his nose to hers in a reassuring way. *Come on! There's lots of cool stuff out here!* But he was too eager to see his new home to remain with her for long, and soon enough he'd scamper away again.

Much of what we came to learn about their personalities was reflected in those few minutes. Fanny was a fawn-like creature—timid at first, easily spooked, but essentially composed of such pure sweetness and affection that it was like having Vashti with us again. It should be noted, however, that in terms of appearance, Fanny was Vashti's exact inverse. Where Vashti had been a puffy white fluff-ball, Fanny's black, short-haired body grew long and slender as it took on the contours of adulthood. But she was, in her precisely opposite way, every inch the beauty Vashti had been. I liked to say that Fanny's face looked as if it had been drawn by Disney Princess animators, perfectly heart- shaped with high cheekbones, a slightly pointed chin, and tip-tilted almond eyes. "You're so pretty," Laurence would croon to her when he thought I couldn't hear. "You're a pretty,

pretty girl." And, like Vashti before her, Fanny would lean her head into Laurence's hand and gaze up at him adoringly. Perhaps because Fanny was so Vashti-like in so many of her ways, she and Laurence seemed to understand each other right from the start.

Fanny seemed to understand Homer immediately, too. She was intensely interested in him once she'd made it out of the guest room, but she always approached him gently and respectfully. She would wait until he'd finished cautiously sniffing her and seemed comfortable before attempting to touch her own nose softly to his. If Homer batted a crumpled ball of paper around the living room floor, she would bat it back to him but not otherwise try to intrude on his game until he'd come over and explicitly invited her to play. If Homer curled up on the couch, Fanny would also lie on the couch close enough to make Homer aware that he wasn't alone, but not so close as to make him feel crowded.

I don't think she understood that Homer was blind, per se, but she seemed to intuit that he was happiest when he could hear her coming. We'd bought belled breakaway collars for the kittens for just this reason. But Fanny always greeted Homer with a trilling coo, as an additional assurance that her approach was both imminent and friendly. As weeks passed and Homer began to revert to his former playful ways—to once again seek out mischief and fun and food as eagerly as he'd used to—it became clear that this was, at least in part, because Fanny was a balm on the wound that Scarlett's loss had left on Homer's spirit.

Clayton, on the other hand, was an intrepid little soul, ready of an instant to bound fearlessly and inquisitively at anything or anyone that crossed his path. Clayton darted down the hallway the day we opened the guest-room door for him, and he never stopped darting, never stopped exploring, never stopped trying to insert himself into everything going on around him. If I'd thought that Homer lacked even a concept of vision because he himself was unable to see, then Clayton seemed to lack even the idea that anyone might not like him, simply because he himself was utterly incapable of disliking anybody or anything.

I'll admit that Clayton was a puzzle to me for a long time. To say that cats are highly opinionated creatures is almost as reflexively obvious as saying that they have fur and whiskers. Even the most agreeable cat will have strong likes and dislikes. Fanny, for example, adored little toy mice and anything with feathers, but wasn't much interested in any other toys. She was passionate about cat foods made from lamb, duck, or tuna, but couldn't abide anything containing salmon or beef. As good-natured as Homer was, he had hated being picked up, loathed being turned on his back, and would instantly recoil if you laid so much as a finger on his belly.

But Clayton liked everything. Literally *everything*. He liked crinkle balls and feathered toys and little fake mice and the plastic rings from water jugs and matchbooks and eyeglass cases and takeout menus and anything else small or portable enough for him to carry off in his mouth. He would eat anything you put in front of him. Dry or moist, regardless of flavor or texture—he ate everything and ate it all with equal gusto. You could pick him up, flip him over, rub his tummy, handle him however you liked, and he would nuzzle your hand and ask for more. One afternoon he sat in a chair with Laurence's visiting ten-year-old nephew, who (only for not knowing any better) spent nearly half an hour rubbing Clayton's fur the wrong way, while Clayton closed his eyes in a drowsy half-sleep, entirely unruffled.

Clayton liked everybody who came to our home and bunny-hopped out to greet them as fast as his three legs could carry him. He had a thick, club-like tail that swung out like a rudder at skewed angles behind him as he ran, most likely to compensate for some of the balance he lacked. When he wasn't running, however, his tail seemed stuck permanently in a happy, upward thrust, guaranteeing anyone who approached a friendly—a downright enthusiastic—reception.

Clayton even liked the vet. *He liked the vet!* A little cut at the bottom of his bad leg became infected and wouldn't heal, requiring the removal of that leg months ahead of our original schedule. There were a number of vet visits leading up to the surgery—and then the surgery itself—and Clayton not only didn't struggle or complain, he actually seemed to *enjoy* himself. When the vet pried back Clayton's lips to examine his gums and teeth, Clayton purred ecstatically. When the doctor stuck a needle into him to draw blood, Clayton butted his forehead playfully into the crook of the doctor's elbow. When he poked gingerly at the bottom of Clayton's infected half-leg—which, surely, must have been at least a little painful—Clayton flipped onto his back and bonked his whole head affectionately against the doctor while licking his hand. I couldn't help but feel somewhat vindicated at entering the same animal hospital where Homer had always caused such a ruckus with a *good* patient for a change.

But still...I wondered about things.

Fanny, as she grew, began to develop an adult cat's more complex vocal patterns—perhaps not as varied as Homer's, but deeper and more mature sounding than when she'd been only a few weeks old. Clayton, however, still had a very young kitten's undifferentiated, high-pitched squeak. His *meow* didn't even have an "ow" at the end. "*MEEEEEEEEeeee,*" he would say, starting out loud but trailing off as his breath ran out. "*MEEEEEEEeeee,*" he said when I walked in the door, and, "*MEEEEEEEeeee,*" he said when he wanted his food, and, "*MEEEEEEEeeee,*" running to greet some new person, and, "*MEEEEEEEeeee,*" when struggling for a plaything that was out of his reach. I joked that when the doctors had removed his bad leg, they'd taken away his "ow."

"There isn't any sign of...neurological damage, is there?" I asked the vet during one visit, just before Clayton's surgery. "Any developmental delays?"

He seemed baffled. "What do you mean? Like brain damage?"

"No," I said hastily. "Never mind. Just forget it."

Of course, Clayton was our veterinary practice's favorite cat, and whenever we came in there was a veritable welcoming committee waiting for us at the door. What a dream for a veterinarian—who presumably liked cats, yet only encountered cats who feared him—to finally find a cat who seemed positively thrilled in his presence. And what a dream for Clayton—who happily scamper-hopped around the exam table from the doctor to the vet tech and back again, demanding cuddles with a head-bonk and a high-pitched *MEEEEEEEeeee*, hardly seeming aware of the needles, the rectal thermometer, or any of the other indignities to which he was subjected.

Perhaps the only thing Clayton didn't like was not having anyone around for him to like. It wasn't so much that he feared or disliked being alone. He simply never needed to be. Even Homer—much as he generally preferred to be with me—would *sometimes* head off to an empty bedroom or open closet. Fanny, sweet as she was and as much as she clearly loved us already, needed at least a few hours a day by herself, and would always prefer to be hidden away in some quiet spot when we had people over.

But Clayton never wanted to be alone, or even out of plain sight. Clayton didn't nap on top of chairs or under beds or buried among piles of clothing or tucked away in a corner of the closet. He'd sprawl out smack-dab in the middle of the floor of whatever room we were in, where you couldn't walk from one end of the room to the other without stepping over him. A question that, to this day, has literally never once been asked in our home is, *Where's Clayton? I haven't seen Clayton in a while.*

As I said, I loved Clayton right from the start—but he puzzled me. Part of the bond that we form with the animals we love comes from that sense that they know us, and that we know them, better than anybody else does or could. I never had—and never would—understand anybody down to the very bottom of their soul the way that I did Homer. I knew every like and dislike, every joy and fear, that Homer had, and had felt the first glimmers of that deep knowledge in those very earliest moments when we'd first met.

But what did I know about Clayton that any stranger couldn't have figured out within five minutes? What ultimately makes all of us different from each other— different and unique—are the things we like and the things we don't. Clayton liked everything and disliked nothing— or, if he did, he kept it to himself—which made him a bit inscrutable.

But if there was one thing that Clayton definitively liked more than anything else—one thing that could raise his usual level of happiness to outright ecstasy—that thing was Homer. Small as Homer was, he still towered over Clayton when we first adopted him—and Clayton clearly thought that Homer was the most fascinating thing in the whole world.

Clayton wasn't much interested in Homer when Homer was sleeping. But if Homer was awake and in motion then Clayton was right beside him. When Homer walked to his food bowl or the litter-box or down the hall, Clayton bunny-hopped along at his side. The pushiness of this—the lack of any respect for polite boundaries—irritated Homer at first. Every few steps, Homer would pause to whack Clayton in the face with one paw.

I don't know that Clayton *liked* being hit in the face by Homer, but it didn't seem to faze him, either. He'd crinkle his little brow a bit, but he never flinched or stepped back or raised his own small paw in a gesture of self-defense. He'd hop next to Homer or around him in circles, and every few feet Homer would pause to smack him in the face—and, like a Slinky, Clayton's head and neck would compress for a moment, then instantly spring back up.

Homer and Clayton together reminded me of Spike the Bulldog and Chester the Terrier from the old Looney Tunes cartoons. Spike would stride impressively down the sidewalk with little Chester scampering around him, peppering him with an endless stream of eager questions. *What are you doing, Spike? What are doing today? Where are you going, Spike? Huh? Can I come with you, Spike? Can I?* And every so often, without breaking stride, Spike would whack Chester in the face with a laconic, *Ehhh... shut up.*

That was Homer and Clayton to a T.

It pained me to see Homer bothered in any way, after the rough few months he'd had. But, ultimately, being irritated with Clayton was better than being sad about Scarlett. Homer began running and jumping again, at first to avoid Clayton, and then simply for the pleasure of it, as he'd used to do. If

Fanny charmed and soothed him, then Clayton brought him out of his shell.

Scarlett and Vashti had never been as playful as Homer would have liked, and with them he'd never been able to assume a role more authoritative than that of mildly annoying little brother. Now Homer was the big brother, accompanied by two kittens who loved to play as much as he did and then some. He had reasons to get up from his spot on the couch, other than feeding times or his daily shift from the sofa to my lap. Clayton and Fanny were perfectly content to be minions and let Homer be the boss, and it was a role that Homer clearly relished.

Even if I hadn't been able to love them for their own sakes (and I was crazy about them—they were, as I would frequently say to Laurence, "made of adorable"), I would have loved Fanny and Clayton for bringing Homer back to me—*my* Homer, the Homer I knew and loved best, the Homer who'd always greeted each new day as something to celebrate. Homer was *Homer* again.

And I honestly believe that Homer wouldn't have found the strength he needed to fight his illness for as long as he did if not for these two ridiculously happy little ragamuffins, who moved into our home and claimed our lives for themselves.

HOMER HAD SOMETHING LIKE fifteen thousand followers on Twitter, but it was on Facebook and my blog where his real community lived. By now, there were nearly thirteen thousand people who'd "liked" Homer's Facebook page, but the number of people who actually followed us there on a day-to-day basis was still very small. They were the people for whom I posted pictures of Clayton and Fanny as they grew, and who had sincerely mourned with us when we'd lost our girls. Homer's community gave us the permission and space we needed to embrace our grief fully and recover at our own pace, without having to encounter a single person who rolled their eyes and wondered rather impatiently why we couldn't get over it already—why we were so sad when it was "just a cat."

I had known that the grief would be deeper, the sense of loss more profound, when we lost Homer. It was Homer's community, after all. But I had thought—naively, I now realize—that it would be more or less a slightly larger version of the same thing. Thinking this—that the one or two hundred comments and emails of condolence we had received after losing Vashti and Scarlett might be as many as four or five hundred now—I had waited four days after Homer's passing, enough time to put on a "game face," before posting the announcement to social media. It was August 25th—as fate would have it (although I didn't register this at the time), exactly four years to the day since *Homer's Odyssey* had first been published in 2009.

Publishing Homer's story had changed my life, but that change had been a slow one—because book publishing is a slow business. I'd spent nearly a year writing the proposal and outline for *Homer's Odyssey*, another year finding a publisher and then writing the book itself, and it had been six months after *that* before the book had first appeared in hardcover. Even all the craziness of Homer's photo and video shoots had played out over a period of months, turning our lives topsy-turvy for perhaps one day every two or three weeks, and then leaving us to enjoy relative normalcy the rest of the time.

Nothing at all in my previous experience had prepared me for what it felt like to have my whole life change in a day.

The Facebook post announcing Homer's death was shared more than three thousand times, and received more than eight thousand comments, within only the first few hours. People began posting pictures and stories of their own special-needs rescue animals to Homer's page—animals they said they had been inspired to adopt by Homer's example.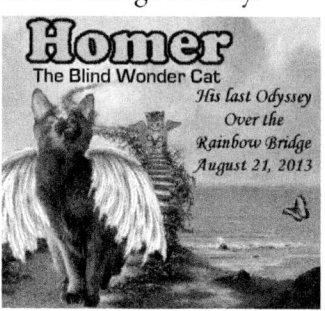

An online memorial for Homer, August 2013

Most of them were cats—cats large and small, fluffy and hairless, former street cats, backyard cats, cats who had been considered "undesirable" by their breeders. Cats who were blind or deaf or both, or who were missing limbs or paralyzed from the waist down. "Wobbly" cats suffering from cerebellar hypoplasia, and cats who were positive for FIV or FeLV. There were also many special-needs dogs, a handful of rescued bunnies and horses, and one albino gecko with poor depth perception. (I swear I'm not making that up.)

I shared these pictures and stories with Homer's community as they came in, thinking them the most fitting tribute Homer could possibly have received. But for every one story and picture I shared, three or four more would appear in the "Visitor Posts" column along the side of the page, until I could no longer keep up. And people posted other things, too. They found older pictures of Homer that I'd posted online years earlier, and they shared them again on Homer's page now. Sometimes they Photoshopped these pictures, to give Homer angels' wings, to show him at the Rainbow Bridge, to frame him with solemn black borders that announced the years of his birth and his death. Each photo and post moved me deeply—until a few days later, when the numbers were so large that I was simply bewildered. I hadn't known there were so many. I'd had no idea.

Facebook's algorithms clearly interpreted this influx of new activity on our page as "good," and began sending more and more and then even *more* traffic our way. It had taken nearly four years for Homer's page to accumulate those thirteen thousand "likes," to reach a point where content from the page reached perhaps five thousand people in a week. I had thought those numbers were pretty big. But, within a week of Homer's death, his page had acquired an additional fourteen thousand followers and reached more than two million people. Hour by hour, day by day, Laurence and I watched those numbers go up, thinking every day that surely—*surely*—today was the day when it would all begin to level off.

And every day we thought that, we were wrong.

When you lose a member of your human family, there's usually one day when you reach out to all the people who need to be called or notified, and then that part is done. But social media doesn't work that way. For all the thousands of people who'd seen my Facebook post within hours of its going up, there were many thousands more who didn't first see it in their news feeds for another day, or several days, or a couple of weeks. Every day there were people who were only now first seeing their friend's re-Tweet of somebody else's Twitter post that had gone up days ago. Every day somebody visited my website—not even knowing there was any specific news about Homer—and, reading my blog post for the first time, then forwarded it to half a dozen other people they knew, who themselves forwarded the link to a dozen more. Every day, somebody saw for the first time the share, re-tweet, or re-post of another blogger's tribute to Homer.

Sometimes the news was divorced from social media altogether—a rumor that people heard word-of-mouth, and they wrote to me for confirmation. At least twenty or thirty times in the typical day, I would receive emails from people wanting to know if what they'd heard was true, if Homer was really gone, and if so, when and how had it happened? For me, every day was the first day all over again.

I felt like a skipping record, forced to keep repeating the same notes over and over because my needle was stuck in a groove and couldn't get un-stuck.

Laurence has never said so, but I suspect that I wasn't exactly the world's greatest wife during this time. I know now that Fanny, and especially Clayton, felt a difference in me, too. I petted and played with them as much as I ever had, but something essential within me was becoming numbed.

The emails began pouring in immediately after I posted that first announcement, and within a few days they were followed by sympathy cards in the mail—first in a trickle, then in a gush, like something out of *Miracle on 34th Street*. We received hundreds—literally hundreds—of sympathy cards and letters, and hundreds more cards from shelters and rescue groups, informing us of donations that had been made in Homer's name. Along with the cards and letters, people sent us their own home-made versions of Homer—stuffed macramé Homers, ceramic Homers, Homers blown from black glass, a water-color painting of Homer from Brazil, a Homer necklace pendant carved out of an old vinyl record from San Francisco, a hand-painted sculpture depicting a super-hero-caped Homer in front of the Twin Towers from Iowa, a soft-sculpture Homer purse that came all the way from Japan, a framed

Homer needlepointed in black Egyptian silk and surrounded by gold thread from Los Angeles, and even an extravagantly framed oil portrait of Homer from "Hank For Senate's" humans in Virginia.

Soon the media inquiries followed. I ended up asking a book publicist I'd worked with once to write up a press release containing the essential facts and some boilerplate quotes from me, so that inquiring press could have something to work with without my having to tell the same story dozens of times. A few months later, *The New York Times Magazine* would run Homer's obituary online as part of December's annual "The Lives They Lived" feature, which rounded up notable deaths from the preceding year.

By then, enough time had passed for me to be proud and even a little amused, to wryly observe to Laurence that we certainly shouldn't expect the same kind of coverage when our time came.

But, at the time these things were happening, all I could think when dealing with press was that I was afraid of repeating the same things too often and sounding like a robot, yet also afraid of deviating from my stock answers and sounding like a moron.

I know how I sound in writing all this. *How* awful *it must have been for you, to receive the heartfelt love and sympathy of so many people!* It wasn't awful at all, of course. It was astounding, amazing, miraculous enough to convince even the most hard-hearted cynic of the generosity and infinite kindness people were capable of.

Every time somebody wrote to say that they felt as if Homer had been their own cat—that they'd cried upon hearing the news as if they'd lost one of their own—my own heart throbbed in sympathy. I knew—I *knew*—exactly how that felt.

When I saw all the donations that had been made in Homer's name and thought of the lives that would be saved because of them, my heart swelled with gratitude. When I received all the beautiful things people made and sent to us, I was thankful until I thought my heart would burst with it.

And that was the problem—there was too much to feel and not enough me to feel it all. My life already felt strange and unlike my own life simply because Homer was no longer in it. But now, when I woke up, I would spend a good couple of hours walking around in a daze, not knowing how to pick up the thread of the day, where I should start, who I should call, which emails and inquiries and Facebook posts I was supposed to respond to.

Once my days had flowed along a natural, effortless rhythm that I didn't have to think about. Now I spent a half-hour each morning trying to decide when to take a shower. Did it make more sense to do a little work, then shower, and then get back to work again? Or would it be more logical and efficient to shower immediately, before I did anything else? Half the time I ended up not showering at all. Better to avoid the question altogether, I'd sagely conclude, rather than come up with the wrong answer.

I eventually realized that Laurence had seamlessly taken over most of the essential tasks that kept our lives running. It was Laurence who now fed Clayton and Fanny on their regular schedule. He also cleaned their litter-box, trimmed their claws, and fished their toys out from under the couch. Laurence prepared our meals and made sure I ate, kept us stocked with toilet paper and trash bags and toothpaste, wrote out checks for bills and made sure they were mailed on time.

All the gratitude, all the love, all the sorrow for the pain of others that I felt, overloaded me until all I felt was overwhelmed—overwhelmed and anxious, slipping further behind each day on all the thank-yous and acknowledgments I owed people, which continued to accumulate in new batches by the hour.

Somewhere, underneath this giant mound of *stuff* that had amassed atop me, was my grief for Homer. I had written about it, blogged about it, emailed Homer's mourners about it. But sometime in the midst of all that, at some point after we'd scattered his ashes and there was no physical, tangible task left for me to do, I'd lost my ability to feel it.

What I needed was to cry. I hadn't cried at all since that first wild convulsion of loss on the afternoon of the night when Homer had gone to sleep for the last time. Now I needed to shed the gentler tears of letting go. I had to get back to my grief in order to heal from it and move on.

But I couldn't. I couldn't find it. I didn't remember ever having felt as tired as I did now. I was too exhausted even to look.

MY OWN LIFE HAD been turned inside out, but as far as I could tell Clayton and Fanny were as happy as they'd ever been. They still ate big meals and napped together in sunbeams, still chased crinkle balls and the laser pointer's ever-elusive red dot with the same joyous abandon. When I piled all the sympathy cards and letters we'd received into the middle of the living room rug—hoping to create some semblance of order from them—Clayton would dive right into the middle of the pile, burrowing into and under it as if he were a child in a ball tank.

It was a few weeks later, in late September, when I noticed one evening that Clayton was having trouble with his litter-box, hopping in and out of it more frequently than was usual. When I checked, however, he didn't seem to be producing anything. I assumed that he was a little blocked, and I added some olive oil to his moist food for an evening meal. He gobbled the whole thing down with his typical enthusiasm, which I found reassuring.

Later that night, however, it was a different story. Clayton was in and out of his litter-box every few minutes now, his pupils hugely dilated. When he wasn't in the litter-box, he paced back and forth across the living room in an odd fashion, crouching first in one random spot, then another.

I had been planning to take him to his regular vet the next morning if the problem persisted. But he seemed so *very* uncomfortable—and was acting in so very unusual a way—that I didn't want to make him wait another eight hours for relief. If it had been Homer, who'd hated the vet with a furious passion, I might have taken a more wait-and-see attitude. But Clayton didn't mind doctors, and even though it was 11:00 and our animal clinic was closed for the night, I thought, *Better safe than sorry.* So, bundling him into his carrier, and waiting for Laurence to grab a jacket so he could accompany us as far as the sidewalk and see us safely into a cab, I headed for the 24-hour emergency animal hospital on West Fifteenth Street.

The last time I'd been in a cab ferrying a cat to an emergency room had been with Homer, and that had clearly been a life-or-death situation. It didn't feel like that this time, though. I still believed the problem was constipation—albeit clearly a severe case—because, in my range of experience with cat maladies, I hadn't yet encountered anything else that seemed to match these symptoms. Vashti's CRF had caused her to be constipated from time to time, and Clayton's behavior now wasn't completely dissimilar to what hers had been then.

Vashti's physical inverse, Fanny, may have been sleek and slender, but Clayton was mushy in the middle. He was a bit of a food hound, and had a habit—one we couldn't break—of finishing his own meals and then tackling Fanny's. Fanny was always obliging enough to allow him to do so. She was a healthy weight, according to her doctor, and even when I'd secretly put down some extra food for her when Clayton wasn't looking, she didn't seem particularly interested. So I assumed now that Clayton had eaten too much of something that didn't agree with him, and my heart ached with sympathy for his obvious discomfort. I reached my hand through the top of his cloth carrier to stroke his head reassuringly. *Poor kitty*, I crooned. *Poor Clayton.* But I also murmured, with a kind of rough affection, *Maybe now you'll learn your lesson, and let poor Fanny eat her meals in peace.*

The emergency animal hospital on West Fifteenth was the polar opposite of our regular clinic—a cavernous, fluorescent-lit waiting area studded with row after row of hard-backed chairs. It was close to midnight, and the only other person in the enormous space was a man with a huge German Shepherd, who'd just finished being sick all over the spotless linoleum floor. Another man in a blue orderly's uniform hurried over with a mop and push-bucket, while the man with the dog patted his flank in a soothing way, helping him into an exam room in the back. The woman at the check-in desk took Clayton's name, the reason for our visit, and my credit card information with brisk efficiency. We didn't have to wait more than a few minutes before a doctor approached and summoned us into an exam room of our own.

Clayton didn't struggle as the vet lifted him from his carrier, but he did mewl in a pained, pathetic way when her hands first went under his belly for support, then gently probed his lower abdomen. I couldn't re-

Clayton, 2013

member ever hearing Clayton make a sound that wasn't *happy*. And, for the first time, I felt the stirrings of fear in my own belly.

"Have you noticed any blood in his urine?" she asked.

"No." The question startled me. *His urine?* "You don't think it's constipation?"

She removed the little blanket lining Clayton's carrier and spread it onto the exam table, so that Clayton could lie down more comfortably. "I think he has something called feline idiopathic cystitis," she said. "It's a blockage of the urinary tract. It's life-threatening if we don't catch it in time, although," she hastily assured me, "it's highly treatable when we do. We call it 'idiopathic' because we don't really know what causes the condition. Generally we think it's brought on by stress. Have there been any significant changes in your home recently?"

At first, the combination of the words *stress* and *Clayton* in the same sentence struck me as so absurd that it was almost comical. Was any cat ever *less* prone to stress than Clayton was?

But then, unbidden, a memory came back to me. When the vet had come to us on Homer's last day, she'd wrapped him in a blanket when it was over, leaving only his face revealed. She'd then placed his body tenderly in a bag she'd brought with her—a roomy leather bag with handles.

The bag containing Homer had remained opened and unzipped on the floor while I signed papers and made arrangements for the cremation. And Clayton had climbed into it. I'd thought it merely the natural curiosity of any cat to explore an open bag left on the floor. But, when we'd tried to lift him out, Clayton had clung to the blanket around Homer, whining anxiously as we'd fought to pull him away.

Grief has a way of making us selfish. As many people as had mourned for Homer—and as sincere and deep as I'd known that mourning to be—I'd been sure that nobody's loss could equal my own. Homer had been *my* cat, his loss had been *my* loss—and there was no one, I thought, who could truly know how I felt.

Clayton lay on the exam table between the doctor and me, the gold of his eyes dulled from their usual bright alertness. But when I placed my hand down on the table next to him, he laid one small, black paw over it and looked up into my face.

I had been wrong. There *had* been another who'd known how I felt. Someone else had felt his happily ordered world run off course, had lost his hero and very best friend, not understanding *why* that friend was gone and couldn't come back to play with him anymore.

He just hadn't known how to tell me.

My voice was gritty when I spoke. "Our oldest cat..." The words stuck, and I realized that, for all the blogs and emails and Facebook posts, I hadn't actually said it aloud to anyone. Not once. Not in all this time.

I cleared my throat and tried again. "Our oldest cat died a few weeks ago. Clayton was very attached to him." I felt the relief of saying it—just saying it as a commonplace statement, to a person who didn't know Homer or that I was "Homer's mom," who would greet the idea with nothing more than ordinary, professional sympathy—pass through me. It felt like having a rusty gate you'd been pushing and pushing against finally begin to swing open, just a crack.

"I'm so sorry," the vet said. "That could certainly do it."

"But Clayton will..." I cleared my throat a second time. "He will be okay, right? I did get him here in time?" *Not again*, I thought. *Please not again, not now, not so soon...*

"I think he'll be fine," she replied. "He'll have to stay with us for two or three days so we can clear the blockage and get everything flowing the way it should. Let me take him back now and get him started. You can wait up front for the receptionist to bring the papers you'll need to sign."

Clayton was away for three days. I'd always gone to visit our other cats when they'd had overnight hospital stays. When Clayton had his leg removed, I'd seen him at least once a day. He'd had to stay for two weeks then, so he could be crated while his stitches healed. It was impossible to imagine otherwise how we would have kept a rambunctious kitten stable enough not to risk the stitches—or how we would have kept Fanny, who groomed him daily, from going after them herself. Keeping Clayton crated at home—in full view of the rest of us interacting with each other, but not with him—had seemed unnecessarily torturous.

But I'd gone to see him every afternoon and brought him treats. And the doctor and other staff members had taken him periodically into an empty exam room for brief bouts of closely supervised play. He'd seemed nothing but happy when I'd visited him then, surrounded by toys that he batted around playfully when he was in his cage, and by adoring humans during the brief times he was allowed out of it.

This time, however, the hospital asked that I not come and visit. It was important that Clayton remain hooked up to tubes and catheters around the clock, and unhooking him long enough for a visit from me was, I was told, an undesirable option. I called three times each day to check on him, and at a minimum I knew that Clayton was still the easy patient, as compliant with staff as he'd always been. The day when I finally went to bring him home, a tech handed over his carrier and informed me, "Clayton is the most adorablest cat ever." Which told me that his usual sunny charm must have returned during those three days, at least in part.

I was given a sheet with after-care instructions, a case of a new prescription food, and a bill so steep that I almost reeled. (An emergency animal hospital in Manhattan possibly being the most expensive option for veterinary care anywhere on the planet.) It was worth it, though, as I saw Clayton's soft carrier pop like popcorn when he heard my voice, and realized that I had come back for him.

Clayton was overjoyed to be released from that carrier once we got home—although taken aback by Fanny's hostile reception. He may have *looked* like the Clayton she knew, but he *smelled* like something else altogether, and Fanny backed up and hissed at him angrily whenever he approached. I quickly brought Clayton into our bedroom, which I'd set up ahead of time with a new litter-box, his favorite toys and blankets, and a bowl for his new food. If stress had caused his illness, I didn't want his recovery set back by the additional stress of rejection. Within a few days, I knew, Clayton would smell like himself again, and he and Fanny could fall back into their established patterns of close companionship.

Laurence came in every so often to check on us, and Clayton scampered over to bonk his head joyously against Laurence's hand as he bent down to scratch behind Clayton's ears. *Look! I'm back! I'm finally home!* But otherwise Clayton and I were alone together for the rest of the night. He bunny-hopped frenetically around the bedroom for a long time, thrilled to be released from the confinement of the hospital, delighted to reacquaint himself with his favorite toys, which he chased with dizzying speed over and under the bed, from one end of the room to the other. Every few minutes he'd jump into his litter-box, releasing a few small dribbles each time, which would have alarmed me if his doctor hadn't told me to expect this for a day or two.

It was late by the time he'd finally exhausted himself. Switching off the bedside lamp, I crawled beneath the covers and readied myself for sleep. I'd set up a soft pile of blankets and pillows on the floor for Clayton, as he'd never really been a cuddler or expressed much interest in sharing our bed. As friendly as he could be, Clayton wasn't a lap cat. If I sat on the floor, he'd hop around me in counter-clockwise circles, bumping his head affectionately against my shoulder or back as he went, pausing on occasion to rest in my lap for the briefest of seconds before leaping up and resuming his bunny-hop circles.

I'd never expected that any of our cats would cuddle on demand—Scarlett would certainly have disabused me of any such notion a long time ago. Still, one of the things I missed most about Homer was no longer having a furry little body to curl up with. I missed that feeling of peace that comes only when a small animal trusts you enough to fall asleep in your arms.

So it surprised me, as I got under the blankets, when Clayton climbed onto the bed after me. And then he did something he'd never done before. Hopping across the bed to where I lay, he nosed the covers aside and stretched his body across mine, one hind leg tucked beneath my right arm, while his front paws sprawled out to touch my left. His chest was directly over my chest, his heart aligned with my own. My arms rose from the bed to embrace him, and Clayton nuzzled his nose into my neck, purring gently against my left ear.

It was then—at last, at long last—that my tears began to flow. Not the harsh animal sobs of the day I'd lost Homer, but something infinitely softer than that, an easing, a warm, fluid salt. Clayton's weight was heavy on my chest, and yet it felt lighter than it had in weeks, as if it were emptying out as the tears ran down my cheeks. They mingled with Clayton's black fur as he brought his head to mine and, with exquisite patience, licked the tears from my skin with his raspy tongue, as the soft thrum of his purrs rumbled against my ear.

Baby boy, I whispered. *My little baby boy.*

I wept for Clayton, for having nearly lost him. I wept for the relief of holding him again now, safe and healthy and returned to us.

And I shed the tears I'd needed to shed for so long— for Homer, so that I could finally let him go.

Homer may have been the blind one, but I'd been the one who couldn't see. I had tended to dismiss Clayton's simplicity—the ease with which he found joy in absolutely everything around him—as simple-mindedness. I had thought it incompatible with depth of feeling. Sometimes (it shamed me to admit), I'd wondered if, perhaps, Clayton wasn't very *smart*.

But Clayton knew things that I didn't know—things, I realized, that Homer had known also. Perhaps that was why Clayton had clung so fast to Homer from his first day in our family, refusing to leave Homer's side even for a moment, not even at the end.

Clayton was always happy because happiness was an essential pre-condition of his life. Everybody wants happiness, and everybody tries to capture and hold it, and everybody feels the emptiness when it's gone. But Clayton spun everyday life into happiness—all of it, even the bowl of food that might not be his favorite flavor, or the unpleasantness of shots at the vet's office—the way trees turn sunlight into food, without thinking, without any deep philosophy, but as a reflexive action, simply because without it, they can't live.

In this, he was infinitely lucky.

When Homer left us, it was the first time in Clayton's short life something had happened that he couldn't spin into happiness, and he had despaired. But now, returning home after the three days in a cold, impersonal hospital, feeling loving arms around him, feeling healthy after days of being sick, he was happy once again.

I may have understood that his happiness was only the flip side of his sadness, that it only existed *because* of that sadness—but all Clayton knew was that he was happy, now, in this moment. Happy and loved. And that was enough.

Much like Homer had taught me things about life—things so simple that I should have figured them out on my own, yet might never have without him—Clayton was teaching me something now. I learned from him that happiness sometimes leaves, but that it does come back— even if it comes in a different form than the one you've lost. Loss wasn't scorched earth. It was a clay from which good things could grow—things that were strange and different from what had come before, things it might never have even occurred to you to want, but things you couldn't bear to part with once you had them.

Even if you knew you'd only gained those things by losing others that you'd have killed and died to keep forever.

THESE ARE ALL FINE, lofty-sounding ideas. But for me—for me, personally—they form the very real substance of my everyday life.

At the time of Homer's death, his Facebook page had roughly thirteen thousand followers. Today, only two years later, that number is nearly 750,000 and counting. Having such a large audience isn't just a "cool" thing. It's a mighty thing. Shelters write to me about special-needs animals who've been with them for years, who they can't find homes for, and Homer's community gets the word out and finds them homes within days, making way for new rescues and additional lives to be saved. "Homer's Heroes" have raised hundreds of thousands of dollars to save the lives of animals in the wake of disasters both large and small across the globe. Everything from earthquakes and tsunamis to hoarding situations, or fires at shelters so tiny and volunteer-run that they don't have a single official employee. In July of this year alone, Homer's Heroes raised over forty thousand dollars to save animals in Nepal, cats being hoarded in West Virginia who stood in danger of being destroyed, and lions on a wildlife preserve in Africa. All of the money comes from small, individual donations, and one hundred percent of the funds go directly to those for whom the funds were raised.

People share their own rescue stories on Homer's page, rescues that occur in quiet, out-of-the-way places against seemingly impossible odds. Stories that inspire others to try a little harder, to save a life they might not have thought could be saved, to give a chance to an animal whose chances might otherwise have appeared exhausted.

Clayton and Fanny

The greatest gift Homer left me with when he left me for good was fresh evidence every day—every single day—of the innate goodness of most people, even when news headlines make it far too easy to conclude otherwise.

In a very literal way, Homer's passing brought life in its wake. There are countless animals alive today because of Homer's loss, and the community that grew and flourished from our shared grief—which doesn't make it "worth it," but does assure me that even in his physical absence, Homer's spirit hasn't gone anywhere.

As I write this, Fanny is doing her best to insert her head between my hands and the keyboard, and Clayton is lying in my lap, flipped onto his back with one paw reaching up in his sleep to touch my face. It's a gesture that's become everyday for us, but one that never fails to knock me out anew with all the profound trust and serenity it implies.

Clayton and I might never have found each other if we hadn't lost Homer. And as much as I know that if I could wave a magic wand and undo Homer's death, I would do so in a heartbeat—in a nanosecond—I also know that I would never trade any of the things I have in my life today because I loved Homer, and also because I lost him.

Not for worlds.

CAT BOOKS FOR CAT LOVERS!

Be sure to check out more of *New York Times* bestselling author Gwen Cooper's celebrated books for cat lovers—including tales of her real-life feline family and the world-famous Homer the Blind Wonder Cat!

Get a FREE copy of the book
Homer Returns:
More True Tales of a Blind Wonder Cat & His Fur Family
Visit www.gwencooper.com

CHECK OUT THE
HOMER'S ODYSSEY SCRAPBOOK!

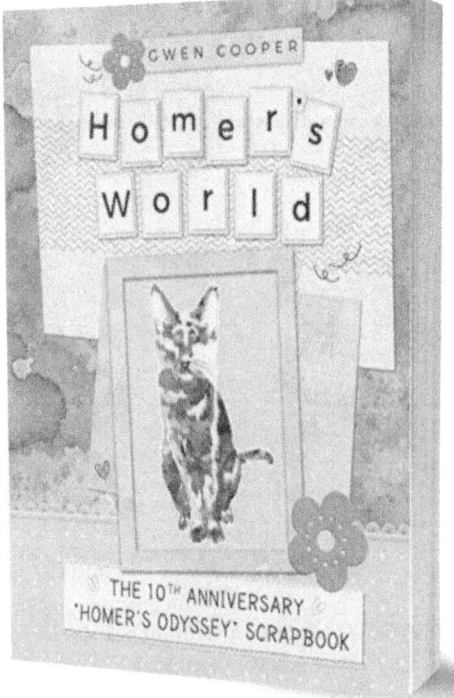

100+ OVERSIZED, full-color pages!

Hundreds of never-before-seen photos of Homer from Gwen's own family photo albums!

Pages from Gwen's first draft of *Homer's Odyssey* with her editor's handwritten notes!

New writing and stories!

GET A SNEAK PEEK AT GWEN COOPER'S NEXT CAT BOOK!

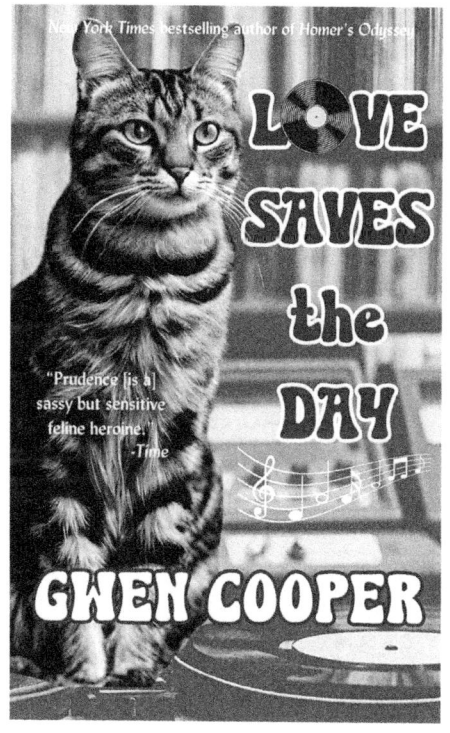

NARRATED FROM A RESCUE CAT'S POINT OF VIEW!

1

Prudence

THERE ARE TWO WAYS humans have of not telling the truth. The first used to be hard for me to understand because it doesn't come with any of the usual signs of not-truth-telling. Like the time Sarah called my white paws "socks." Look at your adorable little socks, she said. Socks are what humans wear on their feet to make them more like cats' paws. But my paws are already padded and soft, and I can't imagine any self-respecting cat tolerating something as silly as socks for very long.

So at first I thought Sarah was trying to trick me by saying something that wasn't true. Like the time she took me to the Bad Place and said, Don't worry, they're going to make you healthy and strong. I knew from the tightness in her voice when she put me into my carrier that some betrayal was coming. And it turned out I was right. They stabbed me with sharp things there and forced me to hold still while human fingers poked into every part of my body, even my mouth.

When it was all over, the lady who did it put me back into my carrier and told Sarah, Prudence has such cute white socks! She was smiling and calm when she said it, so I knew she wasn't trying to trick Sarah like Sarah had tried to trick me about going there in the first place. I thought maybe I should lick my paws or do something to show them that these were my real feet, not the fake feet humans put on before they go outside. I thought that maybe humans weren't as smart as cats and wouldn't understand such subtle distinctions unless they were pointed out.

That was when I was very young, just a kitten, really—back when I first came to live with Sarah. Now I know that humans sometimes best understand the truth of things if they come at it indirectly. Like how sometimes the best way to catch a mouse that's right in front of you is to back up a bit before you pounce.

And later at home, looking at my reflection in Sarah's mirror (once I realized it was my reflection and not some other cat who was trying to take my home away from me), I saw how the bottoms of my legs did look a bit like the socks Sarah sometimes wears.

Still, to say that they were socks and not that they looked like socks was clearly untrue.

The other way humans have of not telling the truth is when they're trying to trick each other outright. Like when Laura visits and says, I'm sorry I haven't been here in such a long time, Mom, I really wanted to come sooner...and it's obvious, by the way her face turns light pink and her shoulders tense, that what she really means is she never wants to come here. And Sarah says, Oh, of course, I understand, when you can tell by the way her voice gets higher and her eyebrows scrunch up that she doesn't understand at all.

I used to wonder where the rest of Laura's littermates were and how come they never came over to see us. But I don't think Laura has any littermates. Maybe humans have smaller litters than cats, or maybe something happened to the others. After all, I used to have littermates too.

But that was a long time ago. Before I found Sarah.

THE BAD PLACE IS a short walk from where we live in a place called Lower East Side. (Technically, it was Sarah who walked there because I was in my carrier. Still, it didn't take her very long, and cats can walk faster than humans. That's a fact.) The lady there told Sarah that I'm a polydactyl brown tabby. Sarah asked if that meant I was some kind of flying dinosaur? The lady laughed and said, no, it just means I have extra toes. I'm not sure which of my toes are supposed to be the "extra" ones, though, because I'm positive I need them all. And it's not really true to say I'm brown because parts of me are white—like my chest and my chin and the bottoms of my legs. Also, my eyes are green. And even the parts of me that are brown have darker stripes that are almost black. But I've noticed that humans aren't as precise as cats are. It's hard to believe they feel safe enough to sleep at night.

The stabbing lady also told Sarah that I was too skinny, which was to be expected because I'd been living by myself on the street. She said I'd probably fatten up quickly. I've gotten much taller and longer since then, but I'm still pretty skinny. Sarah says I'm lucky to stay that way without having to try. But the truth is I'm skinny because I never eat all the food Sarah gives me. That's because even though she feeds me every day, she never feeds me at exactly the same time. Sometimes she feeds me first thing in the morning, sometimes she feeds me when it's closer to mid-day. There have even been times when she hasn't fed me until after it's dark. That's why I always make sure to keep some food left over, in case one day Sarah forgets to feed me altogether.

And it turns out I was right to worry. Sarah hasn't been home to feed me—hasn't been home at all—in six days. The first two days I had to get by on what was left over in my food bowl. I even jumped onto the counter where my bag of dry food is kept and used my teeth and claws to make a small hole in it so I could get some food out myself. (I would normally never do that because it's bad manners. But sometimes there are things more important than manners.)

Finally, on the third day, a woman I recognized as one of our neighbors came over and opened a can of food for me. Prudence! she called. Come and eat, poor kitty, you must be so hungry.

I had been waiting under the couch for her to leave, but I came out when I heard the can open. The woman tried to stroke my head, though, so I had to go back under the couch again and twitch the muscles on my back very fast until I felt calm. I don't like to be touched by humans I don't know well. So I waited until she left before I came out to eat, even though I was starving after two days with hardly any food.

She's been back to feed me every day since then, although I still won't come out from under the couch until she's gone.

Maybe she's trying to trap me with the food. Maybe she's already trapped Sarah somewhere, and that's why Sarah hasn't been home for so long.

TO PASS THE TIME while I wait for Sarah to come back, I sit on the windowsill—the one that overlooks the fire escape Sarah says I'm never, ever, supposed to go onto—and watch what's happening on the street. This also gives me a clear view of the entrance to our building, which means I'll see Sarah as soon as she comes back.

To get to the windowsill, I jump from the floor to the coffee table, and then from the coffee table to the couch. Then I climb to the back of the couch and step right onto the windowsill. I can jump directly from the floor to the windowsill, of course (I could jump much higher than that if I had to), but this way I can check to make sure everything is safe and exactly the way I left it. If the little, everyday things don't change, it makes sense that the bigger and more important things won't change either. If I keep doing things the way I always do, Sarah will have to come back the way she always does. Probably I made a mistake of some kind a few days ago—did something in a different order than I'm supposed to—and that's what made her go away.

Sarah and I have been roommates for three years, one month, and sixteen days. I would tell you how many hours and seconds we've been together, but cats don't use hours and seconds. We know that's something humans made up. Cats have an instinct that tells us exactly when the right time for everything is. Humans never know when they're supposed to do anything, so they need things like clocks and timers to tell them. Twice a year, Sarah sets all the clocks in our apartment forward one hour or back one hour, and that just proves how made-up hours are. Because it's not like you can tell everybody to move the world one whole day back or one whole year ahead and have it be true.

You might think Sarah and I are a family because we live together, but not everybody who lives together is a family. Sometimes they're roommates. The difference is that, in a family, everybody does things together, and they do those things at the same time every day. They all eat breakfast with each other, and breakfast is always at the same time in the morning. Then they have dinner together, and that always happens at the same time, too. They take each other to school or work and then pick each other up from those places a few hours later, and both the picking-up and the dropping-off happen on a schedule. I learned all about it from the TV shows Sarah and I watch together. Even the TV shows about families always come on at the same time, every day.

(I used to think that the things on TV were really happening, right here in our apartment. Once I tried to catch a mouse that was on the TV screen. I clawed and clawed at the glass and couldn't understand why I couldn't get the mouse. And Sarah laughed and explained that TV is like a window, except it shows you things that are happening far away.)

With roommates, it's more like you have separate lives even though you live in the same place. Things happen when they happen and not at any specific time. Also, families live in houses with an upstairs and a downstairs. Roommates live in apartments. Sarah and I live in an apartment, and our schedule is always different. Sarah says this is because they always change the times she's supposed to work. She types things for a big office in a place called Midtown, and she's so good at typing that sometimes they need her to type early in the morning, and sometimes they need her to type later in the day. Sometimes they pay her a lot of extra money to type all night and not come home until early in the morning, which is when most other humans are first starting to work.

Money is what Sarah uses to get food for me and to keep our apartment. She always says you have to get it when you can get it, even if you wish you didn't have to. I know just what she means, because sometimes a cat has to chase her food when it runs by, even if she's in the middle of a really great nap. Who knows when the next time food runs by will be? That's why smart cats spend most of their time napping—to save their energy for when they suddenly need it.

But even on the days she doesn't work, Sarah doesn't do things on anything like a regular schedule. Sometimes I have to meow in my saddest voice and paw at her leg to remind her it's time to feed me. I feel bad when I have to do that, because I can tell from her face how unhappy it makes her when she forgets to do things for me. But she usually laughs a little in the way that humans do when they're trying to make something sad into something funny, and says she supposes the reason she's so forgetful is because she has an artistic temperament, even though she hasn't been an artist for a long time.

I'm not sure what a "temperament" is. Maybe it's something an artist makes. Or maybe it's something an artist uses to make something else. Whatever it is, though, I've never seen anything like that around here.

You might think from all this that I'm complaining about living with Sarah, but that's not true. Living with Sarah is actually pretty great. For one thing, Sarah is always willing to share her food with me. When she sits down to eat, she usually puts some of her food on a little plate off to the side, and I sit on the table and eat with her. Although sometimes Sarah eats things that are just plain gross. There's one kind of food, called "cookies," that Sarah especially loves even though they don't have any meat or grass or anything in them. Sarah laughs when I turn up my nose in disgust and says I don't know what I'm missing. I think Sarah's the one who doesn't know what's supposed to be eaten and what isn't.

There are two rooms in our apartment. In the room with our kitchen is also our couch and television and coffee table. This is the room people are allowed into when they come to visit us, although people hardly ever come to visit us except for Laura and, sometimes, Sarah's best friend, Anise. Anise only comes over two or three times a year because her job is going on tours in a place called Asia. Laura won't come over if she knows Anise will be here, but Sarah and I are always happy to see Anise because when Anise smiles she smiles with her whole face, and she never says anything even a little untrue. Also, as Sarah likes to say, Anise is a person who understands cats. (As much as a human can, anyway.) One time, when I'd only been living here a few months, Sarah brought home a "self cleaning" litterbox that would make a terrifying whirrrrrrr noise whenever I tried to use it. (I think it planned to keep itself clean by never letting me use it.) It scared me so much that I started going on the living room rug just to avoid it, which made Sarah very unhappy with me even though it clearly wasn't my fault. This went on for weeks until finally Anise came over and wrinkled her nose at the smell from the rug that now filled our whole apartment. Ugh, she said, doesn't Prudence have a litterbox? Then she saw the "self cleaning" monstrosity Sarah had brought home and said, Sarah, you're scaring the piss out of her with that thing. (Although really the piss was getting scared into me until I couldn't hold it anymore.) She took Sarah right out to buy me a regular litterbox, and we didn't have any problems after that.

The other room in our apartment has our bed and a dresser for Sarah's clothes and—my favorite place—our closet. There's all kinds of fun stuff for me to play with in both rooms, like old magazines that feel like the dry leaves I used to lie on sometimes when I lived outside, and framed posters on the walls that I can jump up and hit with my paw until they go in a different direction. There are shoeboxes of little paper toys that Sarah calls matchbooks, and Sarah says she has a matchbook from every club and bar and restaurant she's been to in New York since she moved here thirty-four years ago. Even though Sarah has a lot of stuff, she's careful to keep everything neat and put-away so there's plenty of room for me to run around. It's the one thing Sarah's good at being organized about.

Way in the back of our closet are a lot of clothes she never wears anymore—she wore them a long time ago, she says, back in her "going-out" days. Some of her clothes have feathers on them, so of course I thought they were birds and tried to catch them with my claws. That was the only time Sarah ever got really mad at me. But if a human doesn't want her clothes chased by a cat, then she shouldn't have clothes that look like birds.

It took me a while, but I've finally gotten the whole apartment to the point where it has a comfortable cat-smell. It's not anything a human would be able to smell, but if some other cat were to come here and try to move in with us, she would know that another cat already got here first. The back of the closet especially has a very homey and safe aroma. Sarah put some old things of hers there for me to sleep on, and it's the closest thing I have to my own private cave.

And, best of all, our apartment is filled with music. Most of it lives on round, flat, black discs that Sarah keeps in stiff cardboard holders. All the cardboard holders have pictures or drawings on them, and some of them look exactly like the posters hanging on our walls. The wall where the music lives, though, doesn't have any posters hanging on it. That's because that whole wall is nothing but music, from floor to ceiling. Sarah tells me I'm not allowed to mark any of it with my claws, which means it belongs just to her and not to both of us. Still, I get to listen to it with her. The black discs don't look like they should be able to do anything, but Sarah puts them on a special silver table that can hold two black discs at one time. Then she presses some buttons and moves some things around, and the discs sing their music. Sometimes we only listen to one or two songs, but there are times when Sarah makes the black discs sing all day. Sometimes, although not very often, Sarah sings with them. That's always my favorite.

It's because of music that I adopted Sarah in the first place. This was when I was very little and had been living outside with my littermates. We were running away from some rats one day, which are the most disgusting creatures in the whole world. They have horrible long teeth and claws, and they smell bad, and if they're not chasing you to hurt you then they're trying to steal whatever bits of food you've managed to find. Then it started to rain—a huge, terrifying thunderstorm that I was sure would drown every living thing that couldn't find a hiding place. My littermates and I, between running from the rats and then trying to hide from the rain, got separated. I ended up tucking myself under a broken cement block in a big empty lot. I was scared to be alone for the first time in my life, and I started mewing in the hopes my littermates would hear me and come find me.

Instead, Sarah found me. Of course, I didn't know she was Sarah then. I just knew she was a human—taller than most of them, with brown hair to her shoulders. She looked older than a lot of the humans who live in Lower East Side, but not really old.

Usually, I'm very good at staying hidden from humans when I don't want them to find me. Most people would walk right past my hiding places without ever seeing me. I don't think Sarah would have seen me either, except that she stopped in front of the lot and stared at it for a long time. She stared so long that the clouds went away and the sun came out, and that's when she spotted my hiding place.

I thought she was just going to walk away and leave me alone. Instead, she came closer and squatted down to hold out her hand to me. But I'd never been touched by a human before and didn't trust any of them. Plus, I couldn't understand what she was saying because I didn't understand much of human language back then.

And that's when Sarah started singing. It was the first time I'd ever heard music—almost everything I'd heard until then were ugly and scary sounds, like machines, and things shattering on the sidewalk, or humans yelling at my littermates and me when they chased us away.

Sarah's music was the most beautiful thing I'd ever heard. I'd seen beautiful things before, like the plates of perfect food that people sat to eat at outside tables in warm weather. Or the shady grass under trees in the park that humans go to, which meant my littermates and I could do nothing but hide from the humans and look with longing at how pretty the sunlight was and how cool the shade looked.

But when Sarah sang, it was the first time something was beautiful just for me. Sarah's music was my beautiful thing, and nobody was going to chase me away from it or try to take it from me.

I couldn't understand the words she was singing, but there were two words her song kept saying: Dear Prudence. She sang Dear Prudence right to me like it was my name. And it turns out Prudence was my name. I just didn't know it yet.

But Sarah knew it all along. That's how I knew I could trust her, even though she was a human. I decided then and there to adopt her, because it was clear we were supposed to be together.

MICE HARDLY EVER FIND their way into our apartment, but whenever one does I catch it and present it to Sarah, to show her that I'm willing to do things for her in exchange for her doing things for me. And I practice very hard at catching mice even when there aren't any around. I train on empty toilet paper rolls or crumpled up balls of paper, leaping on them and rehearsing my fighting techniques so that when a mouse does come in, I'm ready. If I work hard, I hope that Sarah and I can be a real family one day, instead of just roommates.

It's as I'm thinking this that I see, from my perch on the windowsill, Laura across the street. She's getting out of a car with a man I don't recognize. And I couldn't tell you how I know it. Maybe it's because Laura so rarely comes over even when Sarah is here. I get a tight feeling in my belly that spreads up to my back and makes my fur stand up higher than it usually does. My whiskers pull back flat against my cheeks, and the dark centers of my eyes must be bigger because everything suddenly looks too-bright and startling in its clarity.

Even before Laura gets to the front door of our building, every part of my body knows already that something has happened.

Heartfelt thanks and profound gratitude to the following people (and cats!), without whom I could never have completed this book.

Special thanks to Patti, Nikolaka & Koa!

- Diane Aba
- Alyson Amsterdam (and Louie & Biggie)
- Margaret Auld-Louie (and Julius & Simba)
- Jamery Sue Barry (and Colby, Sully, Misty & Georgie)
- Charles Brackney (and Shane, Chloe & Abby)
- Dorothy Brown (and Patrick, Camel & Sugar Maple)
- Jane Broyles
- Julie Burns
- Lisa Calarese (and Riley, Mordecai & Rigby)
- Deborah Foresman (and Tinkerbell)
- Paul Froiland (and Louie & Fitzy)
- Meg Galipault (and Scout, Waffles, Sisu, Dru & Huckleberry)
- Lee-Ann Gilliam
- Tracy Ginnane
- Sara Goodman (and Dennis)

- » Wanda Goodwin (and Lewie Stewart)
- » Jill Graves
- » Susan Haenicke (and Bessie & Hamilton)
- » Marianne Harding (and Charles Carlos Ambrose Harding)
- » J. Eric Hoehn
- » Susan Anne Kadlec
- » Julie Kennedy
- » Connie Keith-Kerns (and Zoey, Ari Kai & Mrf)
- » Julie Kennedy
- » Calvin & Eileen Keyser (and Ashes, Ninja & Snickers)
- » Beth Kirby
- » Ken Kistner
- » Ronald Koltnow (and Speedy)
- » Catherine Larklund
- » Louisa Lee
- » Carole Loftin (and Sadie, Biscuit & Brazil)
- » Julie Lowe (and Gracie, Cougar, Java, Raven, Meeko, & Bella)
- » Dolores Manzino (and Antigone "Tiggy")
- » Neta Mercer (and Pouncer, Felix & Snacks)
- » TJ Murphy (and Shelly, Max, Gio & Anna)
- » David Nagreski (and Chassis)
- » Matthew O'Leary (and Hank)
- » Melanie Paradise (and Idia)
- » Teresa Pesce (and TabbyCat)
- » Stephanie Peters (and Max)
- » D.H. Powell IV (and Bobby & Willow)
- » Vanessa Ramirez
- » Stephanie Reicen (and Oliver, Mickey & Helen)
- » Kathryn Rigsby
- » Felicia Roe (and Eurydice & Cassiopeia)

- » Janice Rogenski (and Buster, Misty & Alyssa)
- » Andrea Sachs (and Abby & Jimmy)
- » Kathy Schlichthernlein (and Scrappy & the Gang)
- » Zoe Shinno (and Midnite)
- » Christine Sorenson
- » Emily Stafford (and Randy & Pepper)
- » Anne Teghtmeyer
- » Lenai Waite (and Martin)
- » Allison Walls (and Podo, Rue & Dom)
- » Lola Whitehead
- » Katie Williams
- » Michele Zarichny

Gwen Cooper is the *New York Times* bestselling author of the memoirs *Homer's Odyssey: A Fearless Feline Tale, or How I Learned About Love and Life with a Blind Wonder Cat*; *Homer: The Ninth Life of a Blind Wonder Cat*; and *My Life in a Cat House: True Tales of Love, Laughter, and Living with Five Felines*, as well as the novel *Love Saves the Day*, narrated from a rescue cat's point of view. Her work has been published in more than two-dozen languages. She is a frequent speaker at shelter fundraisers and donates 10% of her royalties from *Homer's Odyssey* to organizations that serve abused, abandoned, and disabled animals.

Gwen lives in New Jersey with her husband, Laurence. She also lives with her two perfect cats—Clayton "the Tripod" and his litter-mate, Fanny—who aren't impressed with any of it.

Get a FREE copy of an all-new book about Homer and the gang!
Visit www.gwencooper.com

Printed in Great Britain
by Amazon